D1453039

THE BATTLE FOR PARADISE

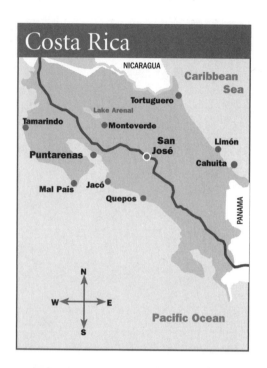

Costa Rica

NICARAGUA

Caribbean Sea

Tortuguero

Lake Arenal

Tamarindo

Monteverde

San José

Limón

Puntarenas

Cahuita

Mal País

Jacó

Quepos

PANAMA

N
W E
S

Pacific Ocean

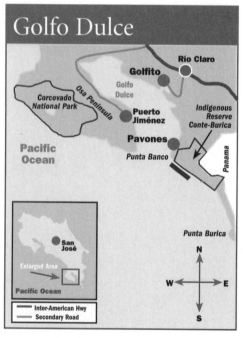

Golfo Dulce

Río Claro

Golfito

Golfo Dulce

Corcovado National Park

Osa Peninsula

Puerto Jiménez

Indigenous Reserve Conte-Burica

Pavones

Punta Banco

Panama

Pacific Ocean

Punta Burica

San José

Enlarged Area

Pacific Ocean

N
W E
S

Inter-American Hwy
Secondary Road

The Battle for Paradise

Surfing, Tuna, and One Town's Quest to Save a Wave

JEREMY EVANS

UNIVERSITY OF NEBRASKA PRESS
Lincoln and London

Library of Congress Cataloging-in-Publication
Data
Evans, Jeremy, 1977–
The battle for paradise: surfing, tuna, and one
town's quest to save a wave / Jeremy Evans.
pages   cm
Includes bibliographical references.
ISBN 978-0-8032-4689-8 (cloth: alk. paper)
ISBN 978-0-8032-8470-8 (epub)
ISBN 978-0-8032-8471-5 (mobi)
ISBN 978-0-8032-8472-2 (pdf)
1. Environmentalism—Costa Rica—Pavones
(Puntarenas)   2. Environmentalism—
Dulce, Gulf of (Costa Rica)   3. Pavones
(Puntarenas, Costa Rica)—Environmental
conditions.   4. Dulce, Gulf of (Costa Rica)—
Environmental conditions.   5. Yellowfin tuna
fisheries—Environmental aspects.   I. Title.
GE199.C8E83 2015
304.2097286'7—dc23
2015006563

Set in Minion by Westchester Book Group.

Frontispiece maps of Costa Rica and Golfo Dulce
courtesy of the *Tico Times*.

For my daughters, Olivia and Carmen

CONTENTS

ACKNOWLEDGMENTS

First, thanks to my wife, Isabelle, and my two daughters, Olivia and Carmen, for their patience. Also, thanks to my parents for listening and supporting me every step of the way. Thanks to my brother who offered his suggestions and opinions, some of which were unsolicited but all of which were worthwhile in some way. Thanks to University of Nebraska Press editor Rob Taylor whose interest in my work has given me confidence in writing better stories because I know they have a home. Thanks to Kim Giambattisto whose watchful eyes immensely improved the manuscript. Also thanks to Courtney Ochsner at University of Nebraska Press for her care and dedication to this book.

It would not have been possible to write a book that took me across international borders without the help of numerous people along the way. In Costa Rica, Carlos Manuel Rodriguez, attorney Álvaro Sagot, conservationists Peter Aspinall and Denise Echeverria, biologist Randall Arauz, Andy Bystrom, and aquaculturist Eduardo Velarde—thanks to all of you for your time and your responses to my countless emails, phone calls, and personal visits; I know this book is more accurate because of our correspondences. Thanks to *Tico Times* editor David Boddiger for allowing me to invade his office one day to scour the paper's archives, as well as for his willingness to communicate long after that day. Same goes for the *Tico Times*'s attorney, Agustin Atmetlla Cruz, who provided useful advice at no charge. And to Rodolfo, our conversation at a soda near Sabana Park was insightful.

While I am not a surfer, I was able to rely on many who were in the know in researching this book. If these people couldn't offer the information I needed, they were quick to point me in the right direction. Here are a few of them, to whom I will be forever indebted: Greg Gordon, who supplied me with invaluable data about Costa Rican surfing; Chad Nelson at Surfrider and Katie Westfall at Save the Waves; Marcus Sanders and Mike Watson at Surfline; surf writers Matt Warshaw and Allan Weisbecker; *Los Angeles Times* reporter Dan Weikel; Santa Cruz surfer Kyle Thiermann; Surfrider cofounder Glen Hening; and the *Surfer's Journal*'s Steve Pezman.

In Pavones, I am grateful to Lili, Carol, and Gerardo Mendoza, William Mata, and others who offered me a glimpse into their lives, even when they were hesitant. Thanks also to Robert Mielgo and Richard Ellis for both providing helpful information as I sought to gain a better understanding of tuna and suggesting additional contacts. In Panama, thanks to Matt Keysers for arranging my visit to the lab near Las Tablas (I promised you I'd get there one day).

Finally, thank you, Dan Fowlie for trusting me to write about your life in a way other writers have chosen not to. I'm not sure if this is what you were expecting, but it's the result of a tremendous effort to get it right. Thanks for your hospitality and willingness to allow me to connect with you, and I do hope that you get at least some of your land back one way or another and that you and childhood friend Al Nelson figure it out and drink beers as true friends again.

INTRODUCTION

It is not down in any map; true places never are.
—Herman Melville, *Moby Dick*

In a stucco garage on the dusty outskirts of Cabo San Lucas, Mexico, the world's most infamous surfer sat on a metal chair and stared at a computer screen. He was mesmerized by the images flashing onto the screen, as if he were seeing them for the first time: a yellow bulldozer clearing jungle for a cabin, white men in hats instructing brown people on how to amend soil, jeeps with fat tires swerving in the mud, and Hawaiians surfing a lonely wave. A narrator provided a running commentary that crackled through the speakers. The old man sitting on the metal chair had been that narrator, and now he took great pleasure in hearing his own voice. His head, as if stuck in a vice grip, never moved except when he nodded at something he found fascinating, the way a proud father nods in approval when his son scores a touchdown.

"Look at Buttons there, just amazing how he could work a wave," the old man said aloud but to nobody in particular.

This continued—the nostalgia and narration—for perhaps thirty minutes before the images disappeared and the computer screen turned black. The old man's beady, gray-blue eyes remained fixed on the screen, as if the video ended without his permission. This awkward pause in action became more awkward when the old man's son, a tan and brash fifty-year-old, began to speak, and the old man cut him off mid-sentence, as if he had spoken out of turn, and then pressed the play button again: the bulldozers, the surfers, the jungle, and the white and brown people reappeared, as did the narrator's voice. The old man smiled and nodded; his son rolled his eyes and said under his breath, "How many times today will he watch it?" The old man, it seemed, was convinced that the more he watched these images, the more they could ease his pain. But these never-ending strolls down memory lane only distracted him from trying to answer this question: Why did my life turn out the way it did?

The old man's name is Dan Fowlie. He's not mentioned much, if at all, in the annals of surfing. Yet, between 1950 and 1990 every surfer from Southern California to Hawaii knew Dan—or at least knew his reputation. If he is mentioned, it's usually for being the alleged mastermind of one of the country's largest drug-smuggling rings, not for attaining the surfer's ultimate dream: he procured his own wave in Costa Rica in the 1970s and never held a nine-to-five job. A tight-knit fraternity that included legends such as Rory Russell, Buttons Kaluhiokalani, and Gerry Lopez surfed Dan's wave, which remained a secret for more than a decade. And let's not mince words: it was Dan's wave.

Dan once married a beauty queen, wore animal-skin boots, chartered private jets, painted a picture for the president of Mexico, graced the cover of *Sports Illustrated*, and owned acres of beachfront property. Now he wears loafers, a flannel shirt, and jeans, the rearview mirror in his dented black truck hangs from duct tape, and he's too broke to a buy a refrigerator. To keep what few items he has cold, he drives each day into town to buy a bag of ice and places the contents in a plastic cooler. His money, possessions, and friends have all but disappeared. He receives just enough from social security and other sources to rent the stucco garage and pay for Internet service (unavailable at his house), which is critical, because, in his mind, he expects that he'll receive a life-changing email. And when that email arrives, the money will flow again like the Ganges River after a monsoon.

Having never learned how to properly type, he taps the keys of the keyboard one finger at a time. It takes him several minutes to write a three-sentence email and more than an hour to write one with multiple paragraphs. When the life-changing email doesn't arrive in his inbox, he drives his dented black truck to his crumbling brick casita north of Cabo San Lucas. It's there, on a concrete patio, that he watches the sun set over the Pacific Ocean. He stares at the horizon and trusts it will speak to him. Then nightfall arrives and the stars wink at him, as if they are teasing him with answers, but none ever come.

There are gaping holes in the casita's thatched roof, but then it doesn't rain much in Cabo. His baby palms need trimming, but he can't afford a laborer and is too old to do it himself. Inside, surfboards hang from wooden beams. One was made by Mike Hynson, a close friend of Dan's who starred in the venerable *The Endless Summer*, which is still considered the best surf film ever made. Magazines are scattered on a stained coffee table; coastal maps are pinned to walls. In the bathroom, dark green mold clings to a porcelain toilet that's missing a proper seat. There isn't toilet paper, although that doesn't matter because the toilet is strictly for urinating. It seems an injustice, if not a bit cruel, that houseguests of a man who once made $1 million a month must shit outside in the desert because there isn't proper plumbing. But this is Dan's life, and no man can blame another for how his life turned out, although this man has a solid case for doing so.

It's unclear at this moment how Dan's life will end, or whether he will be remembered for anything other than being a drug trafficker, but one thing is certain: leaning against a soiled couch cushion in his crumbling brick casita, a rectangular blue street sign with white letters reading "PAVONES DR" offers a clue about his last chance at salvation.

There is a town on the southern tip of Costa Rica, near the border with Panama, that didn't have electricity until 1995. When hampers got piled high with laundry, wrinkled hands washed clothes in buckets and hung them to dry on twine nailed to trees. A cold beer cost five times as much as a warm one. Batteries, used for household gadgets such as blenders and lamps and radios, were like gold: name your price. If someone had a generator, that person might have been voted mayor, but that was impossible because there wasn't a local government. In fact, there was no infrastructure at all: no police force, no court, no chamber of commerce, no school board. It was just a surf town that had one of the world's best waves in its front yard.

About a decade after electricity arrived, telephone land lines reached residences for the first time, crisscrossing the jungle like zip lines. Before these land lines were installed, the town's lone pay phone had a prominent place in town. Later, when some people acquired cellular phones, the pay phone remained the most reliable way to communicate with the outside world. It provided an ocean view and was bottle-tossing distance from the only bar, the Esquina del Mar, the town's first commercial operation, built in the mid-1970s by Dan Fowlie.

If several people needed to use the phone, foot races and shoving matches ensued. Oftentimes the line to use the phone stretched toward a concrete sea wall, where people sat and dangled their feet over the edge and watched the waves roll in. It was a wonderful location to wait in line, but maintaining one's position could be a diplomatic challenge. If someone needed to urinate or run an errand, he or she would ask someone else to hold the place in line, the way that people do when waiting in line for a ride at a crowded amusement park. Those requests were fine. But when people started paying others to hold their position while they went off to drink beer at the Esquina del Mar or even surf a few waves, well, not everyone liked that. Shouting matches and fist fights erupted; some locals and tourists have the scars to prove it. The pay phone remains operational, its post entrenched in maroon dirt, but its role as a communication device was further reduced when the Internet arrived in 2009. There are many places, particularly in developing countries, where technology seemingly arrived on a stagecoach, but most aren't places that surfers must visit before they die.

There are no paved roads here—just a muddy, pot-holed gravel road in, and the same muddy, pot-holed gravel road out, which makes reaching the town by vehicle difficult and sometimes makes it impossible. There's no official town square, which is rare in this part of the world, but there is an unofficial one: the soccer field. The field's soggy playing surface is a mixture of grass and mud. The field's metal goals are rusted, its white paint chipped. Nets, if present, are tattered and torn. On one side of the field is a hodgepodge of rural commercial enterprises: a market, a few open-air cafes and restaurants, some basic motels called cabinas, and a rickety two-story police station that was built only a few years ago and looks like a suburban child's fort. On the other side of the field are groves of coconut and palm trees, a playground, and a series of wooden benches and gravel paths. Beyond the field, land ends and water begins, a swift and appropriate transition since water is the ruling faction. And there is a story to tell about this surf town at the end of the road in Costa Rica—a story that's partly about an environmental battle, but really about a chameleonic town whose history can be summarized in this way: it is a peaceful place, except when it is not. Other places may be blessed and tortured, but I am less confident they have experienced a history as conflicting as this town's. As I investigated its history, I discovered that not everyone was interested in its being told, but it's a story I intend to tell.

This is a place that people don't pass through; end-of-the-road towns never are. They are sought out for any number of reasons, yet they always seem to be where nature dictates the borders humans must respect, not the other way around. Those who come to this end-of-the-road town never plan to leave. For some, it is a place to wash away sins, to bury secrets, to hide history—a place so beautiful many believe it can erase wretched pasts. Then there are others who migrated there to spend their final days surrounded by intense beauty, and I see little wrong with that. Some found life's reset button there, but others traveled an awfully long way to realize that sins and secrets are impossible to shed; they are shadows that follow their transgressors and rarely develop amnesia.

Malcontents and dreamers and fugitives—these social castaways found a home there. So maybe it's fitting that Dan Fowlie, the person who popularized the place for the reason it's known today—surfing—had the darkest of shadows following him. Surfing, after all, is nothing more than a game of chase, no different than avoiding a classmate during recess on the school playground. The more athletic and fast the classmate is, the better it feels to avoid being caught. One of the primary objectives in surfing is to prolong the chase and not get caught by the wave. Once somebody is caught, the ride ends. Perhaps that's why many surfers prefer long waves, and there isn't a longer warm-water wave in the world than this one.

People can't cheat nature, though, and can't control it on their own terms. I have yet to meet a person who hasn't felt slightly vulnerable, even inconsequential, when standing on a headland, scanning the ocean, and acknowledging its vastness; I wouldn't believe a person who felt otherwise. But if people are respectful of nature and skilled enough at surfing to handle its unpredictable temperament, they can be granted the freedom to dance with nature on its terms. This briefly explains the sport's physical attraction, but there is also a psychological one.

No matter how dark one's shadows are amidst the coconut and palm trees, no matter how tightly they latch on, shadows can't swim, and they damn sure can't surf. Riding a wave is one of the rare instances when shadows develop amnesia, which means a lot to a surfer who is trying to discard lingering emotional wounds. While the shadows return on land, surfing in this place provides a long enough mental sabbatical that it convinces those who chucked their previous life for a new one that they made the correct decision. Surfing has that effect on people, not just on those who are running from shadows but on those who want to forget the annoyances of the daily grind. This happens every day with surfers from Australia to New Jersey, but there are some waves so special, so long, that none anywhere else are worth surfing. This wave at the end of the road in Costa Rica falls into that category.

In that regard, I misspoke when I stated that water is the ruling faction. The wave is the ruling body, the omniscient being, the economic engine, the magnet. In English, the name of this town and this wave translates literally to "turkeys," hence its nickname of "Turkey Town." According to Dan Fowlie and some longtime locals, the town was named after large, undomesticated peacocks that once roamed in the area and were hunted to near extinction by its original settlers. Surfers, though, simply know this place by its Spanish name: Pavones.

Located on the Golfo Dulce (Sweet Gulf), an inland body of water shaped like a crooked index finger and one of the few tropical fjords in the world, Pavones doesn't offer much for the typical Costa Rica visitor: no high-rise hotels; no chic restaurants; no zip lines; no fleet of air-conditioned vans shuttling sun-burned tourists through rapid-fire, one-week vacation packages; and no Costa Ricans, known as Ticos, shoving worthless trinkets in your face, bless their entrepreneurial hearts. It also doesn't have many people. Perhaps only a couple of thousand live along a loose network of crumbling roads that tentacle out from the soccer field. This includes a small contingent of expatriates who escaped to a place where any additional movement is considered heading back. For all that Pavones lacks, it does have two special features, and they are fiercely protected.

When the Pacific Ocean's storm cycle aligns correctly in the austral summer, Pavones is often the first piece of land that powerful ocean swells hit on their way north from Cape Horn at the tip of South America. Churning in rhythmic and splendid chaos for thousands of miles, the gyrating ocean is uplifted by a long shelf of cobble near land, where approaching south swells produce a wave that rises, curls, glides, and then explodes onto the apron of an ash-colored, pebbly beach. White foam dissolves over the pebbles, and trickles of water retreat into the ocean or seep into the charcoal sand. Here, the oceanic forces create a surf ride that can last several minutes. At nearly one mile in length, it is considered one of the longest left-hand point breaks in the world. Here is the stuff of surfing lore, popularized in films and immortalized in stories told at night over campfires.

Oceans, though, are fickle. If the winds shift to a different direction, Pavones is flat and tranquil as a swimming pool. Surfboards lean against tree trunks, and surfers are grumpy. For days, even weeks, while waiting for the next swell to arrive, surfers exist in a state of inertia, swaying in hammocks and sipping Imperial beers under groves of coconut and palm trees, which hover over the beach. The perfect swell doesn't happen often, but when it does, globetrotting surfers and the fortunate ones who happen to already be in Pavones spring into action.

Like surfers, fishermen view the ocean as a way of life. Unlike fickle ocean swells, fish swim beneath the cerulean Golfo Dulce whether it's choppy or placid. For anglers, trolling the surrounding waters puts food on the table, a roof over their heads, and clothes on their backs. Fishing has provided life's staples for decades, well before a German pirate first board-surfed Pavones in 1973. (The German pirate was later found dead in a ship off the coast of Panama, according to Dan Fowlie.) Most mornings, as the rising sun remains tucked behind emerald-tinted hills to the east, the only noise that cuts through the pounding surf is the buzz of boat engines swerving into the Golfo Dulce.

While many locals welcomed the growing surf presence of foreigners, fishermen have been able to maintain their old ways. Elsewhere in Costa

Rica, anglers have watched coastlines carved up for resorts and vacation homes marketed to foreigners. This widespread knifing has displaced Tico fishermen and created an underlying resentment of the haves by the have-nots. But down there, on the southern tip of Costa Rica, a few miles from the Panama border, that development shit don't fly.

Pavones has developed an automatic skepticism toward outsiders, and the acquired attribute has served it well. After all, the very reason people consider such a place paradise is the very reason money follows. Paradises found often become paradises lost. Regrettably, humans have a well-documented history of altering landscapes, whether intentionally or unintentionally. Pavones has remained largely immune to the unfortunate realities—what some label progress—that have reshaped much of Costa Rica's Pacific coast, although it's certainly not from a lack of interest.

Costa Rica was the first country in Central America to produce bananas for export. Even as early as the late 1800s, there were 350 banana farms spread over 4,000 acres, and large-scale production occurred by the twentieth century. In 1899, the U.S.-based United Fruit Company was established there, turning Costa Rica into one of the original banana republics. Initially the company's headquarters were on the Caribbean coast, but then, in 1838, they moved to Golfito, twenty-five miles north of Pavones. (If the road is passable and the bridges are intact, a bus ride between the towns takes between two and three hours.) By 1955, the company employed several thousand mostly local people, some of whom eventually moved south and mingled with the first Costa Ricans to settle in an area that became known as "Rio Claro de Pavones," or what today is called "Pavones." Bananas remained the country's largest export behind coffee, and 95 percent of the country's banana exports were being shipped from Golfito in the 1980s. But in 1985, the company ceased operations following a series of labor strikes. Organized labor groups demanded increased pay and threatened legal action if United Fruit didn't raise wages and improve working conditions, so the company closed its doors. The action left many jobless and acutely aware that the benefits of foreign investment continue only as long as the company maintains an acceptable balance of maximum profits and minimal hassle. When United Fruit closed, uncertainty returned to the jungle, which prompted mounds of tangled fishing nets and piles of rusted anchors to be pulled from storage and tossed into the sea. Down the road in Pavones, where few residents worked at United Fruit, another industry was emerging.

It was also around the 1980s when Pavones was discovered by North Americans who had a much different objective. Real estate parcels with ocean views and within walking distance to a world-class surf break became hot commodities. Nortes, slang for "Norteamericanos," snatched many of the parcels. Some came with legitimate titles, others illegitimate ones. Land disputes developed between Ticos and Nortes and led to the "Squatter Wars" of the late 1980s and 1990s, when there were shootouts, machete ambushes, dog poisonings, and murders. Most of these disputes were over Dan Fowlie's land; at the time, he was in prison and unable to defend his property, which many felt was acquired as a result of his drug enterprise. Meanwhile, the rest of Costa Rica was benefitting from its reputation as the "Switzerland of the Americas," a safe haven surrounded by unstable Central American governments, but Pavones continued to be considered a dangerous place. When organized bands of squatters fatally shot an American in 1997, the U.S. State Department issued a travel warning advising its citizens to avoid the region.

Surfers rejoiced since they figured the travel warning would reduce crowds and they could have the surf Eden that Dan had created back in 1974 to themselves. But then the postcard images of the tropical setting and empty beaches convinced two million tourists to visit Costa Rica each year never did draw many visitors to Pavones. It's remote, unrefined, and too much of what Costa Rica used to be instead of what it has become. And if they do make it that far south, even the archetypal intrepid travelers with *Lonely Planet* guidebooks tucked into their backpacks complain there isn't anything to do besides surf, fish, and sit on the beach.

Declaring that relations between Ticos and Nortes became completely harmonious would be misleading, but the Squatter Wars did end by the beginning of the twenty-first century. Peace returned to the jungle since the disputed land was allocated to everyone's satisfaction. Well, everyone's except Dan's. He vowed to return one day and reclaim his land by whatever means necessary. Locals, in time, accepted that foreign investment, even on a limited scale, would boost and diversify the town's economy and attract both hardcore surfers, who stayed for months and years, and traveling surfers, who stayed for days and weeks. So locals became more welcoming of this new migration of Nortes. While some of these outsiders were looking to profit off Ticos's land, others were looking for a place to kick back and surf. Either way, Pavones became a less volatile environment and encouraged small-scale tourism, which remains the area's chief industry. Restaurants and cabinas were built around the soccer field to augment the sport-fishing and surf-related businesses that were established. Pavones is rarely accused of being anything other than a dumpy, mismanaged town, yet it remains a classic surf paradise: a remote jungle enclave built around a muddy soccer field, with trees the tallest thing anywhere, and nowhere being farther or more difficult to reach from San José, the capital.

By 2005, however, Pavones's reputation as a surf paradise was being threatened as Granjas Atuneras (or "Tuna Farms," in English), a multinational company with investors from several Latin America countries, announced plans to install the world's first yellowfin tuna fish farm near the mouth of the Golfo Dulce. The company's scheme was to capture juvenile yellowfin tuna at sea and bring them to circular cages where they would be fattened and sold to markets in Asia and North America. The location of the cages would be directly south from the cobblestone point that creates one of the world's great waves.

If the farm was installed, the Golfo Dulce would suffer from the massive quantities of tuna excrement that would flow into the gulf and be deposited along the shores of its beachfront hamlets. In Pavones, it could damage the fishing industry not just because Granjas Atuneras wasn't committed to employing locals but because the existing species fishermen catch would gravitate to the bait used to feed the juvenile tuna in the farm's cages where fishermen wouldn't be permitted to fish. Most convincing to the town's residents, however, was that the deteriorating water quality could jeopardize the one thing that keeps the town afloat—surfing.

"Without that wave, we can all pack up our things and leave," said one restaurant owner. "All of our lives are tied to that wave. If nobody comes here to surf, then there is no money for anybody. There is no Pavones without that wave."

The town's mood further soured when it was discovered that the government didn't properly notify residents of the project, a violation of Costa Rican law. If a San José–based environmental group that protects sea turtles hadn't stalled the project in the court system, the cages might have been installed in a matter of months and without any input from locals. For a country that both benefits from tourism, 20 percent of which is surfing-related, and markets itself as an environmental steward, this was odd behavior. Tuna farms are considered by many experts to be environmentally catastrophic and have severe long-term effects on water quality. In addition, scientists have been unable reproduce yellowfin tuna in captivity, which in turn means that a tuna farm like the one proposed by Granjas Atuneras isn't designed to increase the yellowfin tuna population. In fact, studies suggest that the farm would actually reduce the overall population of the species. Moreover, the farm itself would remain viable for only several years before it became become unsanitary and unprofitable. Then, the cages would be yanked out of the water, leaving the community to clean up the mess. This information was available in 2005, but the government approved the project with only a cursory glance at the research and followed with a cloak-and-dagger announcement. The fast-track approval process had the stench of a Third World business transaction, where palms are greased, pockets are stuffed, and a few celebratory cigars are puffed after the final handshakes.

Proponents of the fish farm argue that Pavones is a pawn in a global game of oceanic chess. They argue that fish farming is a sustainable way to satisfy the world's increasing demand for seafood and sushi. One-third of the world's 6.8 billion people rely on fish as part of their daily diet, but relying on fish to survive is one thing; eating tuna for pleasure is another. Solely confined to Japan until the 1960s, sushi's appeal is now global. In the United States the number of sushi restaurants has quintupled since the mid-1990s, increasing from under two thousand in 1995 to more than ten thousand by 2013.

In this sushi craze, yellowfin tuna is a necessary component, satiating the desire of consumers and their discriminating palates. Known as "ahi," yellowfin isn't as fat or fleshy as the bluefin, therefore it isn't as expensive, but when the bluefin becomes extinct, attention is expected to turn toward other species like the yellowfin. This sushi craze is obvious in Japan, where 80 percent of the world's bluefin tuna is consumed. In 2012, a single bluefin tuna sold for $1.76 million at a Tokyo fish market. Yellowfin doesn't command such prices, but it is a delicacy, it is desired, and its cost is expected to increase. Studies indicate that more than three quarters of the world's bluefin tuna population has disappeared since 1970; overfishing has placed the species on the verge of extinction. If bluefin tuna disappears from oceans, experts contend that commercial fishermen will turn their attention to other species of tuna, like yellowfin. Unless consumer eating habits change, an increased production of yellowfin tuna will be necessary to supply the world's growing appetite for seafood and sushi.

With tuna being a $5 billion-a-year industry, Granjas Atuneras pegged Pavones as a prime location to mine the ocean for a chunk of that money, although it underestimated the wave of opposition it would encounter. The subsequent environmental battle eventually reached the country's highest court before a decision was made. For the first time in the town's history, gringos and Ticos buried their long-held hatchets, swept their differences under the rug, and, with the help of the international surf community, developed a collective goal: save Pavones.

For me, why Pavones was worth saving and whether it could defeat Granjas Atuneras seemed to make for a good story. It was a classic David versus Goliath battle pitting a ragtag group of surfers and fishermen against a multinational company with government support and deep-pocketed investors. And so as a journalist without any experience in writing about surfing and aquaculture I found myself in Pavones, at the end of the road in Costa Rica, reporting on people who had found paradise and a company that was indifferent to whether paradise was lost.

That I ended up as the person reporting on Pavones may seem preposterous, even blasphemous, to some surfers. In their judgment, my authoring this book might be considered a fraudulent act. Admittedly, I have little in the way of credentials from a surfer's perspective. While I've caught waves in my life, even some in Pavones, I live at six thousand feet above sea level in the Sierra Nevada, and nobody would ever accuse me of being a serious surfer. Nor do I have an extensive background in aquaculture. A whale-watching field trip in middle school is about all. Then, too, my favorite dish is seafood, and I enjoy eating sushi. Still, I am a writer, and my previous book is about hedonism in the mountains and how ski towns in the United States have become symbols of greed. So I was captivated by Pavones's fight with Granjas Atuneras, as well as with the surfers who routinely engage in environmental battles around the world in attempts to save waves. It's that spark, that curiosity, that conviction that there is a compelling story to tell that sprung me into action, like the surfers in Pavones.

As a journalist, by definition, I should be nothing more than a voyeur. It's not nearly as fun watching from the sidelines as others enjoy the pleasures of being on the field, but it ensures that the tenets of the profession remain intact. Somewhere along the line, some journalists have come to view themselves as active participants and the only ones worthy of writing on a certain subject. Nowhere is this more evident than those who write about outdoor sports or what marketing gurus have cleverly dubbed "action sports" or "extreme sports." Skiers write about skiing; snowboarders write about snowboarding; climbers write about climbing; surfers write about surfing; and so on. What if only politicians wrote about politics or only professional football players wrote about the National Football League? Talk about myopic. Somehow, outdoor sports journalism has gotten a pass in this regard, and those who digest the results of this type of reporting rarely seem to mind. Not that the insider approach has anything to do with the subject's complexities; writing about the intricacies on Capitol Hill or dissecting an NFL playbook is infinitely more difficult than describing someone skiing or surfing.

There's a prevailing belief that only an outdoor journalist's participation in the activity qualifies him or her to produce accurate and genuine reporting on the subject. Since some outstanding journalism has indeed been produced by those most familiar with the sports they are covering, a reactionary conclusion has developed to the effect that a journalist who isn't a participant produces less accurate, less genuine reporting. This, I decided, is complete nonsense, despite my having benefitted from being such a journalist. When I wrote about ski bums, the reporting came naturally. I skied growing up and switched to snowboarding after college. I had a passion for mountains and snowboarding and climbing and easily related to my subjects. But I came away unsatisfied with the final manuscript, to the point where I nearly vomited when I read my book in its bound form. I didn't realize why until I heard about a surf town at the end of the road in Costa Rica protesting a fish farm.

In my previous book, I was a ski bum writing about ski bums. I was a resident of ski towns for almost a decade, and I was someone who didn't have sex with his girlfriend on powder days—at least not until after the chair lifts stopped operating. As a journalist, I was no longer a voyeur, but a participant, and one who had built-in prejudices, prior knowledge, and hubris—the most dangerous trio of characteristics for a reporter to possess. The result is that journalism tends to be compromised, and while the final product is trumpeted as objective, it's actually an affected journalist's version of objectivity. Plus, when journalists are also participants, rather than voyeurs who strictly observe and report on other people's lives, they tend to operate as know-it-alls, and the problem with know-it-alls is they learn very little new information since know-it-alls believe they don't have anything to learn. Journalists should accept they are merely observers in someone's more interesting world. When they are finished observing, interviewing, and taking notes, they should synthesize that information and act as nothing more than a conduit to the public. That way the reporting comes from the most accurate source, one's senses, and not the source that some journalists have convinced themselves to be more accurate, one's head.

At least this is how I justified stepping out of my comfort zone to write about surfing and aquaculture. What wasn't out of my comfort zone—and this is why I became captivated by this story—is my fascination with those who engage in alternative lifestyles in remote and undeveloped places, whether a surf town in the jungle or a ski town in the mountains. My interest was further piqued when I learned of Pavones's history: the German pirate who first surfed Pavones and was found dead off the coast of Panama; the Squatter Wars; Pavones's reliance on surf tourism to subsist in the twenty-first century. But most of all, I was curious about Dan Fowlie, the one-time alleged kingpin of the West Coast's largest marijuana trafficking operation who bought the entire Pavones coastline in the 1970s and created an exclusive boys' club that included surfing's biggest stars.

Ultimately, though, I was curious if David or Goliath would win in today's world, one that seems to be shrinking yet remains fraught with greed and corruption. This has always been the case, it seems, but the game changes when the demand for earth's precious resources is no longer met because of a dwindling supply. Either way, I set out to the southern tip of Costa Rica to see if a wave—and Dan Fowlie—could be saved.

THE BATTLE FOR PARADISE

1   A Fish Story

He always thought of the sea as la mar which is what people call her in Spanish when they love her. Sometimes those who love her say bad things of her but they are always said as though she were a woman. Some of the younger fishermen, those who used buoys as floats for their lines and had motorboats, bought when the shark livers had brought much money, spoke of her as el mar which is masculine. They spoke of her as a contestant or a place or even an enemy. But the old man always thought of her as feminine and as something that gave or withheld great favours, and if she did wild or wicked things it was because she could not help them.

—Ernest Hemingway, *The Old Man and the Sea*

The morning started off like most for William Mata, which is to say an alarm clock wasn't required. The macaws squawked, the monkeys howled, the insects buzzed, and very few could sleep through such a jungle cacophony. The noise nudged him forward with the day's proceedings. His bulging forearms lifted his body upward from a mattress spread on the tile floor. He put on a faded blue T-shirt, slipped on a pair of black shorts, tiptoed around others who were sleeping, stepped out onto his porch, and sighed. The sun hadn't fully risen behind the hills to the east. What sunlight there was flitted between clouds and trees and cast columns of shade and gold across the verdant landscape. He walked along the village's gravel roads to the fish house, a white building with a tin roof and a mural on one wall. Across the way, on the other side of the main road, was a bus stop with a surfboard nailed to wooden beams.

When he arrived that morning, William sifted through an assortment of fishing gear: rusted anchors, metal hooks, poles, extra line. He poured gasoline into plastic buckets and tossed ice into a cooler. He would be away three days on this trip. It can be lonely at sea on a twenty-foot fiberglass boat. During storms, sleep is impossible. If the weather cooperates, the gentle rocking of the boat makes his eyelids heavy, and William sleeps like a baby cradled in a mother's arms. Sometimes he returns with so many fish that they spill from storage containers. He must gather them, hose them clean, squeeze them into the containers, and sit on the lids until they snap shut. Then he waits. Soon, a truck belching exhaust rumbles toward the edge of town. When it stops at the fish house, a man steps out of the truck, and William sells most of his catch to this man, who reenters the truck before it rumbles back down the road, headed for markets in San José. Other times, the containers are empty and the lids fly away in fierce wind gusts, and then his family eats rice and beans.

After selling his fish, William could restock his boat and return to the water, determined to spend however many days necessary to catch fish, but three days is generally the limit. As president of the fishermen's association, he feels responsible for determining a proper balance between what man needs and what nature can provide. Under his governance, the rules prohibit anybody from fishing more than three consecutive days and discourage fishermen from overfishing a certain location. If an area produces a larger than normal yield, William suggests that people fish somewhere else to allow that area to reproduce and repopulate. Of the two dozen men who are association members, no more than half are permitted to fish at one time. William keeps track of everyone's schedule in a flimsy spiral notebook. Such a quota, he believes, ensures a livelihood for future generations.

"We are lucky to be here and live in such a beautiful place. We are also lucky that nature gives back to us," says William. "It's not important to catch as many fish as we can sell. It's more important to catch enough fish for us to live in such a wonderful place and to allow our children and grandchildren to live in such a beautiful place. If they wish to fish when they are older, fish will be there for them. This is our responsibility to the environment, to our kids."

Today, it is his turn, and he continues gathering gear at the fish house, which is tucked into the northern corner of the bay where Pavones's famous wave ends. The air was still that morning, perfectly still. The sky was significantly bluer when dappled with puffed white cumulus clouds. A breeze later that afternoon would be welcomed when William's skin sizzled, but at that moment it was neither available nor was it desired. As so often is the case during the rainy season, the dull, stagnant morning air would become pungent and choked with humidity by afternoon when the wind arrived and leaves rustled. By evening, leaves would be slapping against the trees, and a metallic sky would erupt, spraying sheets of rain across the soccer field. There would be no gentle rocking and soft lullaby for William on this night. The temperamental rain would turn sideways and douse him, rendering his boat's plastic cover as useless as a wool jacket in the Sahara Desert.

The weather often mirrors the behavioral pattern of the town, for Pavones is rarely in a rush and only gradually acclimatizes to the day. The sun must slide completely over the hills before shop doors are unlocked, property gates are swung open, and porches are swept clean. Activity increases as the day continues: kids ride bikes; the indigenous Guaymí people prepare tables to sell handicrafts; trucks barrel over pitiful roads and test even more pitiful bridges; families gather for picnics on the banks of the Rio Claro, which flows into the Golfo Dulce and deposits cobble into the gulf. But this doesn't apply to those who ride the wave. If there is a nice swell, and there was on this day, surfers are early risers, their heads bobbing above the water, necks snapped southward to scan the horizon for sets of incoming waves.

With the wind absent, the water was glassy and shiny and smooth like a freshly washed dinner plate. As William organized his gear, fish poked above the palette of buttery royal. A school of them poked through the surface and paraded above the water with their heads erect and bodies twisted before disappearing into the abyss. Surfers straddled their glory sticks and waited near the river-mouth break and the cantina break, named for where the wave breaks next to the Esquina del Mar cantina. Most of them don't live in Pavones and have been waiting in their offices and their homes, dreaming of being right there, waiting for the ocean to uplift them and provide the tug they've been chasing since catching their first wave.

If this was a big swell, the river-mouth and cantina breaks would connect and form one of the world's longest waves. If there was the combination of a big swell, no wind, and glassy water, Pavones would turn into "one of the best waves in the world," as Robert August, costar of *The Endless Summer* with Dan's friend Mike Hynson, once told me. On big-swell days there are more spectators—photographers, shop owners, girls in bikinis, kids pointing at their fathers—gaping from the beach or standing on the sea wall than surfers in the water, which is saying something because there can be one hundred surfers in the water on big-swell days. But on this day, the waves weren't epic. They were sizable and consistent, and there was little to complain about. Surfers were content to straddle their boards and study the horizon. Such contentment had begun earlier when some in the lineup had surfed under a full moon, its glow flashing a faint reflection of hollow white that blinked over inky water.

As the pink dawn unfolded into morning, surfers couldn't hear the macaws squawk and monkeys howl and insects buzz because sets of incoming waves disrupted a calm ocean. If they could have, the sounds would have been their cue that William was walking along a rutted road to the fish house. They couldn't have known such information, and so they couldn't have known that a conversation on the fish house's concrete platform several years earlier precipitated the beginning of an environmental battle that threatened the very wave they were surfing.

There are some mornings, though they are rare indeed, when nothing squawks or howls or buzzes, and there are no waves; there is only silence. All William hears is the crunch of earth beneath his sandals, a child coughing from an unlit bedroom, a woman singing in her open-air kitchen. These singular acts never last long—that's what makes them special—and he waits in anticipation for the next time his commute offers such melodies. Every morning, he exits his lime-green house and carefully descends concrete steps and walks onto an uneven dirt road. The road is too narrow for vehicles wider than pickup trucks, although that is rarely an issue because motorcycles, dirt bikes, four wheelers, bicycles and one's legs are the most popular methods of transportation.

He sometimes rides his bike to the fish house; it's a shiny purple contraption with minimal gears and unreliable brakes.

William's existence in the lime-green house is cramped. Between the front door and the concrete steps is a porch with plastic chairs and flower pots hanging from an eave. The porch is bisected by columns that match the home's exterior. Far removed from the town's commercial center, the rowdy house is surrounded by a tangle of jungle. Though there are only three bedrooms, as many as eight people live there. This number accounts for all but four of William's family members, who live in Pavones. There sometimes aren't enough proper beds for everyone, so mattresses are strewn on the floor to provide additional resting spots. Male and female, young and old, cousin and uncle—they sleep there, their voices over morning coffee carrying over the property's untrimmed flora. The bushes lining the street are several feet thick, perhaps twice that in height, and partially mask gray metal electricity towers. Yellow and red flowers poke out of the bushes and lean over the street. As impenetrable as the vegetation seems, it cannot mute the voices.

William never complains of the noise or limited space. He also doesn't consider fishing an escape from reality or an opportunity to exhale. He adores his family and loves that they live with him there, for he knows no other way. His living situation is markedly better compared to the one he had growing up in Guanacaste, a region in northern Costa Rica, which is the country's tourism gem. The coastal section of Guanacaste is rife with all the benefits and consequences of a tourist-driven economy. Although increased employment has raised the standard of living for locals, it can't cloak the ills of a changing landscape: gated vacation homes, towering hotels and condominium complexes, overpriced cafes, and drunken gringos accosting prostitutes. This cultural shift forced many Ticos, including some of William's extended family, to live far outside of town, where there are no gringos, even though they wanted to live near the center.

His father abandoned his family at a young age and left his mother to raise William and his siblings. There wasn't electricity or running water in their house. Candles were burned at night, and water was collected in buckets during the day. Life was challenging for his mother, who was uneducated and struggled to provide life's necessities. William remembers the sweet taste of sugar on his lips after drinking his first Coca-Cola. It is easy to remember such a thing because soda was a luxury. A luxury should be an occasional, decadent moment, for if it becomes common and easy to forget, it is no longer a luxury but an expectation. He didn't blame his family's poverty on a lack of education because, well, he didn't think he was living in poverty. Major differences in socioeconomic classes usually aren't apparent until one is introduced to other classes and the comparisons begin. Moreover, working on a farm doesn't require an advanced education, and William considered high school an advanced education.

More than he understood arithmetic and grammar, he understood that time spent inside of the classroom meant less time spent outside the classroom to earn money for his family. His mother didn't encourage him to remain in school, so he dropped out after the third grade. He is an example of how, just because Costa Rica offers free, universal education to every child in the country—a noble act indeed—it doesn't necessarily mean every child utilizes its good-hearted investment. In 1869 Costa Rica's president, Jesús Jiménez, supported legislation to increase the number of schools and create schools for girls, which were nonexistent at the time. By 1927 illiteracy in the population fell from nearly 70 percent to less than 25 percent. By 2000 Costa Rica enjoyed a literacy rate of 95 percent, the highest in Latin America. William, though, falls into the 5 percent of the population who can't read or write.

He grew up in Guanacaste in the 1960s and 1970s, when it was mostly a rural farming region, before the tourism boom. This was a time when three-quarters of the country's poor lived in rural areas and two-thirds of them were landless. The landless part of this equation changed once families from Guanacaste migrated in the late 1970s to Rio Claro de Pavones, where landless Ticos had an opportunity to attain land under Costa Rican homesteading laws. These laws allow citizens to settle on any unused land and eventually gain ownership as long as they improve the land and make it usable, which usually means cultivating crops or managing livestock. Designed to encourage poor farmers to gain ownership of unused land, the homesteading laws also seek to prevent the country from suffering the same wealth gap as its neighbors, such as Mexico,

El Salvador, and Guatemala, where the vast majority of land is owned by a few families who are absentee landowners.

Unlike other countries that allow homesteading, where property possession can take years if not decades to achieve, Costa Rica's Agriculture Development Institute (IDA) allows citizens to start gaining possession rights in as little as three months and to file for appropriation after a year. Although there was specifically designated IDA land available for homesteading, any piece of land in Costa Rica that is unoccupied may be homesteaded or "squatted on." If landowners don't remove squatters within the first three months, evicting them can be an expensive, exhaustive process. If the IDA declares the land in conflict, it's often sold or handed over to the squatters anyway. And if it's a dispute between a Tico and a gringo, the IDA almost always sides with the Tico—a situation that precipitated widespread violence in Pavones when Dan Fowlie, who owned nearly four thousand acres, was in prison. After he left, squatters and others engaged in a large land-grab of his land while he was unable to defend it. In Pavones, this good-hearted attempt to provide impoverished farmers land became the culprit for murderous land disputes in the 1980s and 1990s, when the IDA ignored the bloodshed spreading in paradise. Yet development had begun rather peacefully before William arrived.

The first Tico families settled in the early 1960s in the canton of Pavones, which is flanked on the east by the border with Panama, on the west by the Golfo Dulce, and ends at the land sliver of Punta Burica, Costa Rica's southernmost point, which pokes into the Pacific. Before the Ticos arrived, only the indigenous Guaymí populated the area; they generally lived on a reservation in the mountains stretching toward Punta Burica. The Tico families immediately began chopping down the rain forest to grow crops and graze cattle. Once his family and friends left Guanacaste, William wasn't far behind. The prospect of obtaining land by working hard was an appetizing prospect because, as a child, William prioritized work over school. Manual labor was more valuable in his mind than learning to read and write. The way he saw it, he never earned money by doing a math problem or writing a sentence. Despite his third-grade education, he amassed a mental vault of figures and conservationist theories that marine biology students in America's colleges are often unable to grasp, let alone formulate.

"It's actually amazing that he can teach me things and is repeating things that I had to spend thousands of dollars to learn," said a Stanford graduate student who hired William for boat trips as part of her marine research for her master's degree.

This library of information did not betray William when it mattered most.

Several years earlier, in 2004, a man named Eduardo Velarde arranged a meeting to speak with the town's fishermen on the concrete platform of the fish house. William wasn't president of the association at the time; that title belonged to Walter Mendoza, whose family was one of the original non-Guaymí families to settle in Pavones. Everyone congregated on the platform and fanned out from Velarde in roughly a pie formation. Velarde introduced himself as the owner of a fish-farm company and began proposing a project that would be a win-win for everyone. With light skin and a deep voice that blended well with his advanced rhetoric, Velarde was a smooth talker. He was charming, perhaps too charming.

"He told us there would be more jobs, we'd make more money, he'd provide us with more modern fishing equipment, even pave our roads and build a processing plant that would allow us to sell more fish," said William later on.

As the other fishermen nodded in approval, giddy at the thought of making more money for their families, William furrowed his brow. His friends in Guanacaste told him stories about outsiders with big ideas. In an attempt to connect with locals, representatives of development companies spoke to his friends about jobs and increased quality of life. All they had to do was support a proposed hotel project or golf course or condo complex. William felt this light-skinned Velarde was cut from the same cloth as the foreign developers in Guanacaste, whose rehearsed sales pitches never mentioned a project's long-term effects.

Velarde provided written information so the fishermen could familiarize themselves with his project: four circular cages to start, ten at maximum; they would be placed about fifteen kilometers south of Pavones toward Punta Burica and filled with yellowfin tuna, a species William and the other fishermen already fished. The illiterate William didn't understand the fancy words in the pamphlet, and neither did the other fishermen who were also illiterate. None of this seemed to bother Walter Mendoza, the charismatic president of the fishermen's association at the time. With a coiffed head of thick hair, silvery in only the smallest of sections, not quite chubby but full-figured and handsome, the animated Walter had made up his mind. It was as if Velarde had already gotten to Walter earlier, delivered this speech, and convinced him the project was a great idea.

William didn't know it at the time, but he and others would uncover Walter's true source of adulation for Velarde; for the time being they just had to sift through this tidal wave of information. William struggled to comprehend what the slick-talking Velarde was telling them about the benefits of a fish farm and the cutting-edge science behind the project. William knew fishing, he knew how fish behave and how they reproduce, and so he knew what Velarde was telling him was bullshit.

"When I talked about the project, I talked about it being tuna and eventually other species," Velarde told me several years later. "I am an aquaculture preacher man and a good one. I love my profession with a passion, which makes it a laudable adventure, not a profession."

As William recounted that initial exchange in 2004 from the same concrete platform years later, he pointed to the Golfo Dulce, the sun glinting off its turquoise water. A surfer walking along the beach rubbed his thigh muscles after a long ride. William was still concerned about the gulf's future. He was concerned about the surfer in front of him and the other surfers who would visit after him, but mostly he was concerned about his town, which was supported by the surfers.

The source of his consternation went back to that day in 2004 when Velarde showed up uninvited and vowed to improve everyone's life.

In a nostalgic moment, with the waves still arriving as if on cue, William reminisced about how a yacht scooted on the horizon after his arrival in the late 1970s, how its lights winked at him, how it was driven by Danny Fowlie, the drug trafficker who became the town patriarch. He remains a mythical figure, so much so that some surfers who arrive in Pavones don't believe Danny was real, but he is. Danny provided everyone jobs; he built roads, schools, and churches; he reforested the jungle; he taught everyone how to live off the land; and then he disappeared one day. They were halcyon days when Danny ran the show, William reminded me, and he remains one of the few outsiders that original locals trust. Eduardo Velarde, meanwhile, didn't stand a chance.

Big promises from outsiders who never stick around are common-place in Pavones, and they often leave messes in their wake. Velarde was no different, William thought. Even Danny abandoned Pavones. Still, William knew that if Danny were around, he would have promptly ush-ered Velarde out of town and they would never have seen the man again. To make Velarde and the tuna farms disappear, though, William had to trust untrustworthy outsiders—more slick-talking city folk who were not all that different from Velarde.

As he left for his three-day fishing stint that day, William rolled his fiberglass boat on logs over sand and into the water. As the boat entered the water, William's balled calves sprung him into the boat, and he said to me as he turned on the engine that he never quite understood why exactly Eduardo Velarde entered his life. Down the road from the fish house in a neighboring village, another man wondered the same thing and eventually uncovered Velarde's true intentions. Nobody in Pavones knew then that the country's forgotten town would become mired in an environmental battle that would reach Costa Rica's Supreme Court in a case of surf environmentalism that would have been inconceivable only decades ago.

2   Killer Dana

That was a real sad loss for the surfing world. But all the boat owners were happy, and the people in Dana Point who saw their property values skyrocket were, too. Progress sets the pace.
—Corky Carroll, *Orange County Register* surf columnist

There is some debate about the specific event that spawned surf environmentalism, but most surf historians accept that the first real opposition force targeting public officials arose in Dana Point, California, where renegade surfer Ron Drummond attempted to save a beloved wave. On August 29, 1966, the U.S. Army Corps of Engineers dropped a ten-ton boulder into the Pacific Ocean and instructed a group of surfers that they were no longer welcome. Drummond, the group's shaggy-haired leader, had attempted to stop the act before he received those instructions. In the days and weeks leading up to the boulder dropping, he voiced his concerns to the Dana Point town council. When he was ignored, he contacted state officials and argued that the building of a marina would not only ruin the biggest wave outside of Hawaii but would damage the ocean. Cute story and all, the officials concluded, but his pleas fell on deaf ears.

Under a rocky bluff that is part of a headland jutting into the ocean, the first boulder was dropped into the water. The government declared all marine activities were prohibited from that day forward because Dana Point was building a new marina. The boulders were dropped to create jetties, man-made piles of concrete or rock intended to protect structures threatened by unruly waterways, but they can also affect waves as they interrupt currents and shift sand bottoms.

Currents and sand bottoms are not only key factors in creating a wave but also influence a wave's speed and shape. In some cases, jetties actually improve wave quality for surfers, but that didn't happen in Dana Point. Constructed to create a navigation channel between rough, open-ocean chop and the soon-to-be calmer waters of the town's new marina, the jetties eroded sand on the sea bottom and affected currents, and over a period of several years, the wave known as Killer Dana was systematically destroyed.

To officials, the loss of a wave and any possible damage to the ocean were unimportant in comparison with the benefits of a new marina. For them, the construction of Dana Point Harbor was progress. As early as 1964, there had been rumors that the town's chamber of commerce was seeking financial assistance to build a harbor and energize the local economy. (The popular view in those days—and oftentimes today despite studies that suggest otherwise—is that surfers are uneducated bozos on the fringe of society and that surfing doesn't benefit the economy.) By 1965, the government had committed $100 million toward the marina project, and the announcement resulted in a three-day celebration. When the first of many boulders was dropped in 1966, spectators stood on the shore and clapped, marveling at the sight and excited for the future economic boost. Killer Dana's surfers were also there that day, powerless to stop what they considered to be nothing more than aquatic rape. They were saddened and stunned as the boulders were dropped into the cove, which had been the setting for some of their greatest surfing moments and was, to some, their second home. For others, it was their only home.

In the 1960s, Killer Dana was the most serious wave in California and the biggest in the country outside of Hawaii. It broke at the cove and received its name because it lifted out of deep water and broke onto rocks along the beach. Legend has it that Killer Dana crushed unsuspecting passersby, a few of whom died from the impact. From a surfing perspective, it was a big right-hand point break, capable of reaching heights in excess of twenty feet, the threshold for recreational surfers even today, let alone for surfers in the 1960s. In 1939, it was said to have produced the largest wave ever ridden on the West Coast, although this was before the discovery of even more colossal waves later in the century such as

Maverick's and Todos Santos. Killer Dana attracted a tight group consisting of perhaps two dozen surfers who were regulars there in the 1950s and 1960s. (Even Dan Fowlie surfed there on occasion.) Their surfboards were often left unattended but were always waiting for them when they returned. Now their surf spot was being destroyed for V-neck-sweater, khaki-wearing jackals who wanted a nice place to park their yachts next to the other jackals' yachts. That was bad enough, but the surfers' larger concern was really centered on the future of California's waves. Their wave was finished, they were certain of that. But if Killer Dana could be destroyed, then any wave could be placed on the chopping block and guillotined by developers or officials.

"It was like a sudden death that you couldn't talk about," surfer Chris Ahrens told Greg Heller of Surfline.com, one of the world's most visited surf-related websites. "I couldn't even look at it for probably ten years, just the most painful thing you can imagine. It was a whole world, a whole history erased. If they can do that, they can do anything."

When the U.S. Army Corps of Engineers told the surfers they could no longer surf there, Drummond engaged in a final act of defiance by paddling out and catching a wave. It was a weak right-hander that day, but it was a special moment nonetheless because he and a few others were the last to surf that cove in Dana Point in Orange County, the birthplace of the surfing industry on the American mainland.

In 1954, Hobie Alter opened the country's first retail surf shop in Dana Point and built his Hobie Surfboard Company factory there. *Surfer* magazine is also based in Dana Point; its offices are tucked in a rugged stretch of coastal hills about halfway between Los Angeles and San Diego. The *Surfer's Journal* is in San Clemente, the next town south; and a few miles north of Dana Point is Huntington Beach, which has been nicknamed "Surf City." Despite this being a self-proclaimed title made by the city tourism officials, there is some truth to it. Huntington Beach hosts numerous professional surfing events each year and is now the corporate headquarters for Quiksilver, a publicly traded company that is synonymous with surfing. It's impossible to spend much time near the pier in Huntington Beach and not be slightly overwhelmed by all the advertisements in store windows and billboards promoting products made by Quiksilver and other leading companies such as Billabong, Rip Curl, and O'Neill. The Surf Industry Manufacturers Association estimates that, in the United State alone, surfing is an $8 billion industry and that worldwide, surfing is a $15 billion industry. While Quiksilver, Billabong, Rip Curl, and O'Neill possess the majority of the market share of the surf industry, Quiksilver remains the most profitable. By 2005, economists reported that its assets were valued at more than $2 billion, the most in the surfing business. It's a testament to how far surfing has come, if not a poignant reminder, that a few miles south of Quiksilver's headquarters is where one of the state's best waves was ruined despite pleas from outraged surfers. Dana Point officials, to their defense, made a decision at a time when surfing wasn't big business. On the other hand, Drummond wasn't as concerned about the wave as he was about water quality, so their wrongdoing can't be completely ignored. But when officials essentially told Drummond and his buddies to stick their surfboards up their asses, they never considered this: What would happen if the surfers were right?

In Dana Point, most visitors have no idea that a world-class wave existed near the shops and restaurants and tourist traps that now surround the marina. These days, there are 2,500 boat slips that are spread over 212 acres and display some impressive watercraft in organized rows. The only reference to the wave in town is the Killer Dana surf shop. Despite Drummond and his buddies' objections, the marina's construction pro-ceeded relatively smoothly in 1966, and there were no violent protests or further acts of defiance. Once that initial ten-ton boulder was dropped, more boulders were deposited over the next few years to create breakwater jetties. Water between the jetties was pumped out, and marine life was transplanted. When construction was finished, water flowed naturally in from the ocean again, and sea life returned. On July 31, 1971, almost five years after Drummond had surfed Killer Dana for the last time, Dana Point Harbor opened. Forty-five years later, Drummond's fears, the ones local and state officials ignored in 1966, had come true: the wave had vanished and the ocean was filthy.

In November of 2011 Congressman John Campbell, who represents California's Forty-Eighth district, which includes Dana Point, stated that when the U.S. Army Corps of Engineers constructed the breakwater jetties, they altered ocean currents in the harbor and at the beach at nearby Doheny State Park. He concluded that the harbor restricts water circulation, increases bacteria counts, and diminishes water quality. Although its waves don't compare to Killer Dana, Doheny State Park remains a popular surfing beach despite its being consistently ranked the most polluted beach in California and among the dirtiest in the country. A leading reason for its unflattering status is that the jetty that extends from the harbor obstructs ocean currents that would naturally flow along the shoreline and cleanse the water. As a result, the water in and around the harbor has become stagnant, attracting bacteria and other contaminants. (Water contamination at Doheny State Park exceeds public health standards at least a quarter of the year.) Drummond wasn't a biologist, but perhaps the environmental degradation from the harbor could have been avoided had city officials listened to Drummond's pioneering display of surf activism instead of brushing him off as a low-life malcontent. After all, who spends more time in the ocean than surfers?

"A lot of us point to Killer Dana as being a real catalyst for surfers," said Chad Nelsen, environmental director for the Surfrider Foundation, which was started in 1984 and has since become the world's most influential group of surf activists. "It caused everybody to say, 'Wow, if we don't start taking an active role in protecting the coast, nobody else is.' Boaters and fishermen spend a lot of time on or around the water, but they really don't get wet. Surfers tend to feel the impact more than others because they are actually in the water. They are immersed in the ocean more than any other user group. They really are the canaries in the coal mine for the ocean."

On the one hand, the first instance of surf activism could be described as an unorganized crusade that failed miserably. On the other hand, Drummond's efforts are considered a success on a philosophical level. He obviously wasn't equipped with the right tools to change the actions of government officials. He had neither the money to hire environmental attorneys who knew how to play the game nor the political clout to create a forum where policymakers would learn about the marina's potential environmental consequences. There simply wasn't a blueprint for this sort of thing in the 1960s. Still, the gauntlet had been dropped.

Surfers were no longer going to stand on the shore and allow non-surfers to destroy the ocean or dictate what happens to waves—at least not without a fight. After Killer Dana was destroyed, surfers started acquiring the proper tools, which resulted in a louder, more influential megaphone. In a way, it was all Gidget's fault.

Although Hawaii is generally considered the birthplace of surfing in the United States, Malibu is where mainstream surf culture and surf activism started. Located about one hundred miles north of Dana Point, Malibu is separated from the greater Los Angeles area by the shrub-covered Santa Monica Mountains, which rise several thousand feet above the Pacific Ocean. The range bisects the Pacific Coast Highway south of Malibu, establishing an artificial barrier between the hurriedness of Los Angeles and the laid-back beach lifestyle associated with Malibu. Malibu's surf history dates back to the 1920s, when the town was remote compared to what it is now, which, in geographic terms at least, is essentially an extension of Los Angeles. But it was in the 1950s when Malibu became synonymous with the spawning of surf culture.

Of all the stories from that time, the most influential in popular culture involved a privileged blonde-haired teenager from an upscale neighborhood descending to the beach in search of adventure. Her name was Kathy Kohner, and in 1956 she began hanging around in Malibu, where she fell in love with surfing and the surf lifestyle. She befriended locals who gave her the name of "Gidget," a combination of the words "Girl" and "Midget." Her adventures at Surfrider Beach were documented in the novel entitled *Gidget*, which was penned by her father, a screenwriter. Columbia Pictures bought the film rights and turned the book into a movie in 1959; it was a blockbuster hit. Seemingly overnight, Americans became infatuated with this cute girl who spent her days on a surf board and hung out with a group of hunky men on the beach.

The general storyline seems tired and rather cliché by current cinematic standards, but the combination of sun, skin, and sex was completely new to the country in the late 1950s. In those days, women were expected to be homemakers whose life goals were limited to getting married and having children. In fact, if a girl wasn't married by the time she graduated from high school, she was a social pariah. So the glamorization of a girl transitioning into adulthood by fraternizing with men on the beach was rather risqué. Gidget's exploits, sampling several guys who had no intention of marrying her, not to mention the glorification of a beach bum lifestyle that encouraged play over work, made some Americans uncomfortable and challenged previously accepted social norms. Yet America—and the world—fell in love with Gidget and surfing.

In 1957, before either the novel or movie was released, there were an estimated five thousand surfers worldwide. By 1963, once Gidget had become known around the globe, there were more than two million. While many of these already lived in Southern California, others flocked there each year to surf at Surfrider Beach. Currently there are an estimated twenty-two million surfers worldwide. Back in the 1950s and 1960s, Hawaii could offer bigger and, in most cases, better waves, but Surfrider Beach had the world's most famous wave and famous surfer. Gidget shouldn't receive complete credit for Malibu's popularity, though. It had inherent qualities of its own, including what was reputed to be the perfect wave. As the esteemed surf author Matt Warshaw once wrote, "An impressive if somewhat temperamental wave so far, here it wraps itself into the cove (better known as 'First Point') and becomes the faultless Malibu wave of legend—the curl unspooling for two hundred yards along a crest line so precise and well-tapered that it looks surveyed."

In 1950, Malibu surfers recalled no more than a dozen surfers in the water at a time. When the novel *Gidget* was published in 1957, there would be as many as one hundred, and by the 1960s, after the movie was released, Malibu was considered the state's first overcrowded wave. (Nowadays surfers call it a zoo.) Once the crowds came, the shoreline around the Surfrider Beach was developed, creating a much different surf experience than in previous years. Surfers started exploring the surrounding coastline for other waves. This exploratory process was good for expanding the sport—and it led to the lifestyle of Dan Fowlie and other surfers who traveled internationally in search of secret waves once California's best surf spots became overcrowded. But while surfers lamented the crowds, they were largely ignoring what was happening to the water quality at Malibu, where the Malibu Creek flows from the Santa Monica Mountains and deposits its contents into the Malibu Lagoon along the shoreline.

In 1965 a sewage plant was installed along Malibu Creek near its lower watershed to service a population of about three thousand. At the time of the plant's installation, nobody gave much consideration to Southern California being the country's fastest growing region; nor did anyone think that more than one hundred thousand people would eventually live near the creek's lower and upper watersheds. But the fact is that what drains into the upper watershed flows into the lower watershed and, ultimately, into the ocean. Starting in the 1960s, sewage started draining into Malibu Creek, and, over the next few decades, additional runoff from parking lots and golf courses drained into the creek. Like Doheny State Park, Malibu is now considered among the dirtiest beaches in California. In 2011 *Outside* magazine wrote: "By any scientific measure, the lagoon's water is about as clean as a septic tank's."

Long before the magazine commented on Malibu Lagoon's lack of cleanliness, the combination of sewage, pesticides, and other contaminants had created a mess. In 1983, an attempt was made to dredge the lagoon and clean the polluted water. The dredging project failed, and it also disrupted Malibu Creek and damaged the wave in the process. Local surfer Glenn Hening had seen enough. Killer Dana might have been the site of the first instance of surf activism, but Malibu's Surfrider Beach became the womb for what became the Surfrider Foundation.

Started in 1984 by Hening and Tom Pratte, Surfrider has since become the world's most influential surf activist group, one that has developed the political muscle and financial strength to effect real change and convince surfers that a wave can be saved. The group also changed the perception of surfers as grungy Ron Drummond types who contribute nothing to society to one of law-abiding, educated, and productive members of society whose financial impact on local economies is substantial.

By 2008, when Surfrider stopped a toll road project between Los Angeles and San Diego that would pass through San Onofre State Park, home to the famed Trestles surf break, it had saved numerous waves nationwide.

It also had beach cleanup programs that weren't directly surf-related, and had matured into a group that had to be listened to when any coastal project was launched. Trestles, though, was the group's barometer.

"If we can't do a good job of saving Trestles, which is in not just our backyard, but in the surf industry's backyard, that doesn't say a lot about us," said Matt McClain, Surfrider's director of marketing and communication at the time. "There's a real line in the sand."

Trestles remains the largest and most publicized case in the history of surf activism, and an indication of how far surf activism had come since Drummond's antics. In an eight to two vote, the California Coastal Commission decided the $875 million dollar road project would threaten wildlife, camping areas, and the famed surfing beach of Trestles.

Trestles is actually a series of breaks that flow over cobblestone reef with sand deposited from nearby San Mateo Creek, creating a perfect combination as it drains into the Pacific. The toll road, environmentalists argued, would cut across the watershed, and the concrete for the road would limit sediment flow and weaken Trestles, considered the last of California's great waves not bruised by development. The world's most decorated pro surfer, Kelly Slater, encouraged a revolution if the California Coastal Commission approved the project.

"Just stand up and voice opinions and join with Surfrider to help stop what's happening," Slater told the *New York Times* before the commission's decision. "Lobbying the right government and state park officials until they are completely inundated will inevitably have an effect. If that doesn't work, take it to the streets."

The denial of a toll road slicing through San Onofre State Park in northern San Diego County, the largest stretch of nonurban developed land between San Diego and Los Angeles, was the biggest decision in the commission's thirty-six-year history. A crowd of 3,500 people awaited the decision at the Del Mar Fairgrounds. Companies such as Billabong, Vans, and Reef transported hundreds of toll road opponents to the fairgrounds; Surfrider even received a $30,000 donation to fight the cause from the rock band Pearl Jam, whose lead singer, Eddie Vedder, is a former competitive surfer.

The situation reached such a heightened level of scrutiny that the Sierra Club, the most powerful environmental group in the American West, joined forces with Surfrider. In 2008, one would be hard pressed to drive the streets of Southern California's beach communities and not see a "Save Trestles" bumper sticker or T-shirt. In February of 2008, the commission's voting down of the toll road prompted an eruption of cheers in the surf community.

One notable surf activist, Serge Dedina, told the *New York Times*, "I'm calling this the Woodstock of surfing and environmentalism." Dedina went on to write in his book *Wild Sea*: "The biggest lesson is that surfers cannot fight coastal battles on their own. While the Surfrider Foundation did a brilliant job of mobilizing the masses and creating the coolest marketing campaign in the history of the environmental movement, the Save Trestles coalition included the best and brightest of the California's environmental community. To save other endangered waves, we have to build equally strong teams that include birdwatchers, biologists, and lawyers. . . . Being a real surfer means defending your spot against development and ruination—whatever the cost."

After the victory alternative engineering studies to those used by Surfrider found that less than 1 percent of the watershed from San Mateo Creek would have been affected by the toll road construction, prompting some to characterize Surfrider as just another conservationist, anti-development group masquerading as surfers. Lisa Telles, spokesperson for the Transportation Corridor Agencies that wanted to push the project through, told the *New York Times* that "there's a fear that it [the project] will change the way the surfing community utilizes Trestles, but there's no data. There's nothing besides emotion that will back up that argument." Even the mayor of San Clemente, Jim Dahl, a surfer, supported Telles's view. The decision also left the surf community somewhat divided. While most surfers rejoiced at the outcome, some believed that Surfrider was using any possible environment argument to stop a project that organization itself didn't want and that there wasn't a true environmental threat. Some wondered if surf activism had gone too far. Here are two of the more pointed responses from *Surfer* magazine's online forum about the announcement of the toll road being shot down:

This is an anti-development movement masquerading as a "Save a surf break" movement. A corporate campaign at its finest.

The issue I am bringing up is . . . the marketing of this movement. It is marketed that this toll road will negatively impact the surfing experience at Trestles, and that surfers should oppose it for this reason. Well guess what? The issues about its impact on the surf experience at Trestles have been DRAMATICALLY overstated and EXAGGER-ATED. It's still a dumb plan, but not because Trestles is any danger. "Save Mateo campgrounds" doesn't have the same ring to it. . . . The marketing is systematically trying to milk money out of surfers who are too lazy to look into the issues deeply enough to map out the toll road route and positions of the watersheds.

Surfrider said the naysayers were applying a short-term impact argument to a long-term issue.

"There are a couple of responses to claims that we are antidevelopment," said Chad Nelson, Surfrider's environmental director. "We're antidevelopment if something is going to have an impact on the coast. We're not antidevelopment for everything. There are ways to develop the coastal zone without having giant urban sprawl, water quality problems, and completely destroying the functions of our watersheds. It kind of goes back to the slow motion disasters. The toll road is not going to bury Trestles in a few years or maybe even a few decades. But in a hundred years of messing with an ancient river mouth, if you mess with those processes, there's no question over time that the quality of that wave is going to decline and the quality of the watershed is going to be diminished. I think that is the debate with these surf arguments. It's all about short term versus long term. We think long term."

Waves, it turns out, are hard to gauge and easy to alter. In Pavones and everywhere else, waves are created and influenced by a variety of factors, including tide levels, wind conditions, and shoreline structures if present. According to the article "Surfers as Coastal Protection Stake-holders" published in *American Shore and Beach* in 2011,

Coastal engineers and managers don't intentionally design shore protection or navigation projects to be detrimental to existing surfing resources. Comparably many coastal erosion control and navigation projects have also inadvertently created excellent surf spots, such as Sebastian Inlet, Florida, Manasquan Inlet, New Jersey, Oceanside Harbor, California, among others. Yet many projects adversely affect surfing. . . . Ideally, project designers should first seek to avoid impacts and thus preserve existing surf spots during the feasibility and design phases of a project. . . . Surfable waves are typically found on beaches where seabed slope and offshore bathymetry [water depth measures] combine with wave height, period and direction to form the necessary platform needed to transform shoaling waves into peeling breakers. . . . In addition, a sloping bottom along the length of a sandbar is typically needed to ensure adequate length of ride for the surfer, as opposed to an abrupt change in seabed slope which can cause the wave to close out (collapse on itself). All of these conditions combine to generate breakers adequate for surfing.

Surfers, though, are an odd bunch. Even when corporations actually take steps to improve the environment, surfers will protest if it means their surf break is altered. In 1997, Mobile Oil Corporation had planned to remove a pair of sixty-year old piers smothered with barnacles at a beach in Ventura County, California, before they met resistance from surfers. Surfers felt the piers created perfect conditions for peeling waves and sand and that these would disappear with the removal of the piers. The waves were a natural resource worth preserving, they argued, yet Mobil wanted to spend $5 million to remove the piers and fulfill the lease agreement that was drafted in the 1920s to remove the piers once oil production stopped in the area. While surfers petitioned the State Lands Commission to keep the piers, they were ultimately removed, and measures were taken in subsequent years to artificially restore the surf spot and bring back some of the qualities of the wave there.

In the case of Pavones, the tuna farm project would do nothing to affect the wave's characteristics—its height, period, and direction—or the tide levels or wind conditions. When an environmental group based in Costa Rica decided to expand its argument against the farm to say that the project threatened the legendary wave, the position was specious but influential nonetheless. This clout, which arose from Drummond's dropping of the gauntlet in the 1960s, grew and became stronger with Surfrider's Trestles victory, which demonstrated the maturation and influence of surf activism in the forty years since the destruction of Killer Dana. However, it should also be emphasized that it did take four decades for surfers to be heard in the United States, which has among the strictest, most onerous environmental regulations in the world. Foreign surf breaks are at greater risk because developing countries don't have the coastal stewardship of the United States.

"Surfrider is really domestically focused," Nelson said.

The United States clearly has the some of the strongest environmental laws and that helps us in the democratic process. For example, we've been able to help with the Clean Water Act and have influence with the California Coastal Commission to help shape our coastal communities. The challenges are greater in foreign countries. Even here in the United States where we've made some strides, surfers don't get enough respect. There are challenging, negative stereotypes that are untrue but persist. In developing countries, they are even more prominent. Surfers are treated as a marginal group and not an economic contribution to tourism. We are not valued at the level we probably should be, so that can make it hard for surfers elsewhere to make a strong case and be listened to. I don't know for sure, but my guess is that's what happened in Pavones and Costa Rica.

3 Paper Chase

There are some who frankly and boldly advocate the eradication of the last remnants of wilderness and the complete subjugation of nature to the requirements of—not man—but industry. This is a courageous view, admirable in its simplicity and power, and with the weight of all modern history behind it. It is also quite insane.

—Edward Abbey, *Desert Solitaire*

One day in August of 2005, Peter Aspinall sat in a chair and read the most recent available issue of *La Nación*, Costa Rica's largest daily newspaper. The issue was several days old, a common occurrence in Pavones. Based in the capital of San José, *La Nación* doesn't circulate in Pavones, and likely never will. Many San José residents haven't heard of Pavones, and even ones who have can't locate it on a map. Set in a verdant mountain valley, San José is a chaotic blend of cracked sidewalks, vehicle-choked roads, and buildings that need a good scrubbing. Despite its blemishes, San José and the surrounding valley have the highest concentration of educated residents in the country, and the most important politicians and businessmen live there. It's very rare that anything that happens in Costa Rica doesn't first start, at some level, in San José.

Since roughly two-thirds of Costa Rica's population of 4.7 million people live in San José or in the central valley and highlands, the country's most influential print publications are also headquartered there. Moreover, these publications' advertising base doesn't extend far beyond the mountains and volcanoes guarding the central valley. So, not surprisingly, these papers shape their coverage around the interests of those who live in the vicinity of San José. Official distribution is confined as well. Outside of San José, finding any leading newspaper, let alone the most recent issue, is a challenge. As a result, rural Ticos often don't read newspapers and prefer television or radio for their news coverage. Indeed, there are many rural Ticos who ignore all forms of media because the San José-centric outlets ignore them. Whether justifiable or not, they suffer from media apathy.

If there is a newspaper to be found near Pavones, most likely it will be in Golfito, a port town located on the Golfo Dulce, or in Paso Canoas on the Pan-American Highway at the border with Panama. Both towns are about two hours from Pavones, and reaching them requires driving over crumbling asphalt and gravel roads. Unreliable road maintenance often lengthens the drive since pot holes and collapsed bridges are common obstacles. In short, nobody makes a special trip to buy a newspaper. If a Pavones resident is conducting business in Golfito or is shopping for duty-free products at the border and comes across a stack of papers, it's a nice gesture to bring a few copies back to Pavones. If they are available in town, they can be found on the counter near the register at the Super Río Claro, the largest of town's three markets. The cashiers use the newspaper sheets to wrap grocery products, and nobody seems disappointed if one can't be purchased. While acquiring any newspaper in Pavones requires a combination of luck and timing, there is one publication that is impossible to obtain, and it's the publication that Peter Aspinall should have been reading that day instead of *La Nación*.

La Gaceta is almost unheard of outside the central valley, and isn't found at gas stations or sold by street vendors. *La Gaceta* is published once a week and is the official publication for the Costa Rica government. It is read by lawyers, politicians, journalists, and businessmen, essentially the only people who are affected by such content and who probably wouldn't fall asleep reading it. According to Costa Rican law, whatever the government approves must be officially announced to the public, and a listing in *La Gaceta* serves as that announcement. If it's an important government decision, one of the national newspapers will write a story, and the public will thereby be notified in clearer terms; a story in a newspaper is also considered by the government to be an official announcement. But since Pavones residents didn't have access to *La Gaceta* in 2005, and they can only rarely procure any newspaper in a timely manner, they were unaware of what was published in *La Gaceta* and later was mentioned in a financial newspaper. Pavones wasn't intentionally kept in the dark by these publications—its isolation is a geographical reality—but government officials who were aware of the town's frontier-like existence and knew about Eduardo Velarde's tuna farm project and his 2004 meeting with William Mata and other fishermen didn't notify Pavones residents, even when given the chance. Not only do Pavones residents suffer from media apathy, but they also mistrust the government. A 2006 survey by the University of Costa Rica, the country's most respected higher education institution, found that eight in ten Ticos believe their country is "corrupt" or "very corrupt."

"We have an enormous amount of corruption in Costa Rica," said Peter Aspinall. "It can be entertaining if not a bit sad to read what goes on in my country. But our people have almost become numb to the corruption, to how money can make good people do bad things, things that hurt our country."

Peter grew up on a farm in the highlands outside Alajuela, a suburb outside San José where the airport is located, and, unlike William Mata, was educated at the finest schools. He has a soft voice and blue-gray eyes. His light skin is freckled, and his hair is thinning though he still looks much younger than his fifty-nine years. He represents a demographic that is unique in Latin America, which is dominated by the mestizo, a mixture of indigenous and European blood. In Costa Rica, there are more direct descendants of Europe and only 1 percent of the population is indigenous, the lowest percentage in Latin America. It's quite common to see many residents of light complexion walking San José's dirty streets, although this is less prevalent outside the central valley.

Peter's mother and father came from wealth. His grandparents moved from the United Kingdom in the late 1800s to work on the country's burgeoning railway system, which paved the way for Costa Rica to emerge as the region's economic powerhouse. They also became original investors in Instituto Costarricense de Electridad (ICE), the country's largest electrical company. These ventures generated returns that made the Aspinalls large landowners and one of the more influential families in the country. His parents enjoyed the perks of financial comfort: his mother was a pilot who owned her own plane; his father was a revolutionary figure during the country's civil war in 1948 and helped draft the country's constitution in 1949. Peter learned at an early age that reading newspapers is a critical element of the education process. As a member of the Aspinall family, being informed wasn't a luxury, it was a civic duty. This mindset was passed down through the generations and was absorbed by Peter.

Fluent in English and without a hint of an accent—and this occurred before he attended the University of Florida and received a bachelor's degree in Horticulture—Peter is also an avid reader of the *Tico Times*, an English-language weekly newspaper also based in San José. It, too, circulates in a similar fashion as the others. But on that day in August 2005, he read *La Nación*, which is also read by all the important politicians and businessmen. *La Nación's* first issue was published in 1946 and it quickly gained a reputation of representing the business elite. If there was a story about something that would impact the people of Costa Rica, it would appear in *La Nación*. Unfortunately that was neither the publication nor the issue that would shape the next few years of Peter's life, as well as William Mata's and Dan Fowlie's, and eventually threaten Pavones.

High above the ocean, the crashing waves still audible in the afternoon breeze, Peter sat in the metal chair and thumbed through the pages of *La Nación*, a glass of juice within arm's reach on the glass table placed beside him. There were the usual stories about vehicle accidents, murders, and the popular soccer club Saprissa, but nothing stole his attention from such a wonderful afternoon. Although the stories were unimpressive, they were a welcome break from gardening, particularly for his sore hands. Peter plants about six hundred trees each year on his eight-hundred-acre ranch in the hills above the oceanfront hamlet of Punta Banco, where a mud and gravel coastal road that originates in Pavones ends at a pepper-speckled beach.

In the 1970s, Peter traveled throughout Asia and South America, collecting seeds from various tropical locations. By the end of the decade he had accumulated more than one hundred species of tropical fruits, brought them to Costa Rica, and tilled them into the soil at his ranch in Punta Banco, which he purchased after graduating from college. Over the years, the seeds spread and created an arborist's dream. (The Aspinall ranch also has three hundred species of birds and an assortment of mammals, including monkeys and sloths.) His conservation and social efforts are equally impressive: he was in involved in the reintroduction of the scarlet macaw to the region, the creation of a sea turtle nest protection and education area, the development of a native tree restoration program, the construction of a school and health center, and the building of a suspension bridge for the indigenous Guaymí. Guaymí land begins where Peter's ranch ends and extends into Panama, and Indians are free to cross the border as they please.

With the newspaper in his grasp, Peter's hands were a mess, a sloppy mix of soil and condensation from his perspiring glass. The pages were bleeding ink at an impressive rate and the deteriorating quality of the newspaper prematurely ended his reading session. He tossed the paper aside and was about to continue planting a tree when his phone rang. On the line was Randall Arauz, the founder of Pretoma, an environmental group that protects sea turtles and created a nesting site in Punto Banco, one that Peter helped manage.

If Peter had had access to the June 28, 2005, issue of *La Gaceta*, he would have seen in small-type font that the Costa Rica government's environmental branch had accepted a viability study for a yellowfin tuna farm at the mouth of Golfo Dulce. If he had had access to August 14 issue of *El Financiero*, a weekly financial newspaper under the umbrella of *La Nación*–owned newspapers, he would have read in greater detail that the farm would include ten floating cages, each about 50 meters in diameter, or roughly the width of Pavones's soccer field, and that these would be located almost within sight of Peter's ranch. The *El Financiero* article also stated that the project had the support of the president, Abel Pacheco, the municipality of Golfito, and the community of Pavones. Peter, of course, didn't have access to those articles, but Randall provided the details over the phone.

This was all so strange, Peter thought. Costa Rica's environmental minister, Carlos Manuel Rodriguez, had visited his ranch in June and gone on a nature walk with Peter's wife. At the time, Carlos's office knew of the proposed project because a few days later it officially announced its approval in the June 28 issue of *La Gaceta*. In fact, Peter's wife recalls that she and Carlos talked about everything except a tuna farm during their two-hour jungle walk. At one point, she remembers that Carlos stopped and admired the view of where the Pacific Ocean flows into the gulf, roughly the location of the proposed tuna farm site. Peter surmised after hanging up the phone with Randall that perhaps Carlos was admiring the view for a different reason.

Peter returned to his chair, tilted his head slightly while musing over the confusing chain of events, took a sip of juice, and wiped his moistened brow with his forearm. His light blue-gray eyes stared at the confluence of these two great bodies of water and then moved beyond the water to the forested ridges of the Osa Peninsula on the other side of the gulf. The view hadn't changed since the 1970s, when he and his wife moved here and introduced tropical fruits from the rest of the world and fused them with Costa Rica's finest offerings. His conversation with Randall at Pretoma made it seem that not only would the view change but that the ocean was already in some ways a much different place than it was in the 1970s. This was one of the remotest locations on earth, far away from cities and industrial centers and all the trappings of society. Why this place? Peter asked himself.

Before he became too nostalgic, Peter needed information. He knew that Carlos's signature was on the environmental permit issued to the tuna farm company, Granjas Atuneras, because no aquaculture project in Costa Rica could be approved without it. (What Peter didn't know is that Granjas Atuneras was the first to request a marine license in Costa Rica and that the country's fisheries and aquaculture laws were recently rewritten to include such a license.) But it was the questions he didn't have answers for that bothered him most: What was Granjas Atuneras? How many jobs was the project going to create? How exactly did the community show support for the project, as stated in *El Financiero*, when nobody had heard anything about it? Had all the required permits (environmental, fishing, and water) been issued? Did the government realize that the Golfo Dulce would be threatened from algae bloom and other bacteria? Did it realize that a tuna farm would pollute the local waters with tuna feces and that the water quality would deteriorate? Did it realize that Pavones subsists on surfing and that surfing in tuna shit isn't appealing? Did it realize Pavones's economy could collapse without surfing or fishing? The answers to these questions were not in Granjas Atuneras's environmental impact statement, a document that nobody outside the company except a select few government officials had seen yet, but that would change. None of the answers to those questions appeared in *La Gaceta* or *El Financiero*, not that Peter really expected that they would.

Journalists have been killed in Costa Rica for not minding their own business. In 2001, a radio journalist named Parmenio Medina was gunned down outside his suburban San José home after he reported alleged fiscal improprieties at a local Catholic radio station. It took six years for the killers to be brought to justice in a courtroom, ending with murder convictions of two men. Before Medina's murder, the Committee to Protect Journalists reported that more than half of the journalists at *La Nación* said they received some kind of threat in their careers. This is not to suggest that Costa Rica is as dangerous as Iran or Syria for journalists, but the Committee to Protect Journalists (CPJ) report did state that journalists are careful, even reluctant, to investigate certain stories in Costa Rica because the country has punitive press laws that have left journalists vulnerable to criminal charges for defamation.

Three journalists received prison terms in the 2000s for reporting on rather routine topics such as embezzlement. In 2004, the Inter-American Court of Human Rights stated that Costa Rica needed to amend its outdated criminal defamation laws because they were incompatible with international human rights standards. (By 2009, the Costa Rican Supreme Court ruled to eliminate prison terms for criminal defamation, but the outdated law was still a concern in 2005 when the tuna farm project was revealed.) In fact, both *La Nación* and the *Tico Times* continue to retain lawyers to review controversial stories. The lawyers are concerned only with the risk of a defamation lawsuit, not with the accuracy of the story or whether it meets journalistic standards. If the risk is too high, even if the sources quoted in the story are credible, editors don't publish these stories because they aren't worth the hassle of a lawsuit. Although the threat of criminal defamation lawsuits diminished with the Supreme Court's ruling in 2009, the laws remain liberal and editors continue to run controversial stories through lawyers. Even though the threat to journalists has diminished, physical retaliation remains a reality.

Realizing the country's journalists probably wouldn't investigate this situation to the point of uncovering transgressions by the government and the company Granjas Atuneras, Peter ignored the tree he had intended to plant that afternoon and made his first phone call to Carlos Manuel Rodriguez. While many questions were swirling through his mind, the one he was most fixated on was the most puzzling of all: Why was the government's official announcement in an obscure and seldom-read paper when the official who signed the environmental permit was a recent guest at his home and never said a word about the project? It would take years for that question to be answered to Peter's satisfaction. At any rate, it was awfully convenient that it took at least four days for this news to reach Pavones.

According to the laws governing the environmental branch of Costa Rica's government, a citizen can appeal a new project as long as it is filed within three days of the project's official announcement. If an appeal is filed, the complaint is heard and action can be taken if a review board believes there is merit to the citizen's complaint. It's actually a pretty effective way to allow concerns to be heard from citizens who typically don't have much of a voice; some projects have been stopped as a result of this process. But if no appeal has been filed in the three-day window, the opportunity to file a complaint is gone, and the project moves forward because the government interprets the absence of dissent as acceptance.

On June 28, 2005, it was announced in *La Gaceta* that the Secretaría Técnica Nacional Ambiental (SETENA), under the direction of environment minister Carlos Manuel Rodriguez, had approved the tuna farm project in the Golfo Dulce, citing the environmental impact statement as the basis for its decision. The government considered June 28 the official announcement date for the project. That meant that June 29 was the first day a formal appeal could be filed, and July 1 was the last. Carlos had gone on a walk with Peter's wife at the end of June, in the week leading up to the *La Gaceta* article, yet he made no mention about the world's first yellowfin tuna farm or the country's first marine aquaculture project coming to her neighborhood—notable events indeed. By the time Peter learned of the project in the middle of August, it was far too late to file an official appeal. This fight, Peter concluded, would have to be fought in a different arena.

He called Carlos Manuel Rodriguez, who, Peter joked later on, still had mud caked on his shoes from the nature walk he'd taken with Peter's wife in June. The phone rang a few times, Carlos picked up, and Peter demanded to know why he didn't tell his wife about the tuna farm project. Peter recalled that Carlos told him that he didn't know about the project when he visited the ranch and that when he did find out, there was pressure from above (the only person above him is the president of the country) to accept the environmental impact statement.

"That is not true, there was no pressure from above," Carlos said to me. "That is not how things work in Costa Rica. We are a country of laws. This project wasn't illegal because aquaculture projects are allowed under law. It's not my job to determine what projects should happen or should not happen. My job is to allow those projects that are allowed by law. That's what I did, even though personally I sympathized with the opposition."

Many years later Peter chuckled at that response from Carlos, who was an avid surfer and one of the first Ticos to have ever surfed Pavones.

"He could have done more . . . he was the one person, as the environmental minister, who could have stopped it," Peter said. "He just didn't know about [the environmental impact of] tuna farms. None of us did."

During their conversation in 2005, Carlos asked Peter why he didn't contact him sooner if he was against the project. Peter reminded Carlos he couldn't get *La Gaceta* or *El Financiero* in Pavones and that online access to either publication was impossible because Pavones didn't have the Internet.

"He said he didn't know that, it was rather unfortunate, but that there was nothing more that he could do," Peter remembered.

Then the phone went dead.

"I've been a conservationist my entire life," said Peter. "I moved here because this was the last undeveloped part of the Southern Zone. It's where my wife and I moved to enjoy nature and preserve the thing this country is famous for, which is the environment. I wasn't going to let one of the most damaging things to any environment happen in my own backyard, where I could see the ocean being destroyed in front of my own eyes every day. I told my wife 'We need to be the ones to fight this because nobody is going to help us.' And my wife agreed with me."

4   Geckos and Iguanas

For most of history, man has had to fight nature to survive; in this century he is beginning to realize that, in order to survive, he must protect it.

—Jacques Cousteau

I didn't know it at the time, but my connection to this story and Pavones started in 2008 on a warm July afternoon in the Costa Rican beach town of Dominical. Large cumulus clouds hovered on the horizon of the Pacific Ocean. Within hours an inky sky exploded into a crackling grid of lightning. I was staying at a dirtbag hotel along a rugged section of the central coast, which serves as an unofficial demarcation line between two versions of coastal Costa Rica. To the north are Jaco and Tamarindo, swanky beach towns with designer clothing stores, Pilates and yoga studios, dance clubs, and sushi bistros. (Tamarindo is the tourist hub of Guanacaste, where William Mata was born.) Many of the houses there have bright red-tiled roofs, turquoise swimming pools, and manicured lawns. They would fit perfectly in, say, any middle-class neighborhood in California or Florida.

As one travels south from Dominical along a coastal highway, the jungle tightens its grip. The trees are taller, the leaves greener, the tree trunks thicker. Even on cloudless afternoons the sun's rays aren't strong enough to penetrate the forest canopy; it's so dark that drivers often turn on their vehicle's headlights. Distances between towns also seem greater. Homes are unpolished, with fading exteriors and peeling paint instead of freshly painted siding, rusted tin roofs instead of bright red tiles, and arrow-shaped metal antennas instead of dinner-plate-sized satellite dishes.

Hammocks are frayed instead of tightly woven, sidewalks busted instead of smooth, and yards overgrown with clusters of weeds instead of showcasing neatly organized rows of flowering bushes. Children's T-shirts are tattered and blemished, the lettering cracked instead of smoothly pressed. Perhaps these differences are more subtle than I have described, but my eyes convinced me otherwise.

My dirtbag hotel in Dominical cost five dollars per night and had an ocean view. My room consisted of four wooden walls, one square window, two single beds with wrinkled white sheets, a sputtering ceiling fan, and an unreliable light source. The entry was a wooden door with a lock that never locked. The splintering wood created an assortment of vertical slits that allowed strips of light to enter the room. Caramel-colored geckos crawled on the room's darkly stained wooden walls; I never quite determined their port of entry. The square window had a mesh flap and chicken wire that was designed to deter insects. It also had a shutter with a latch in case the torn wire didn't quite do the trick, which it never did.

The ocean view was the dirtbag hotel's most redeeming quality for Terry, a surfer from Gold Coast, Australia. Terry had been staying at the hotel for nearly two months. After the first week, he became indefinitely stationed in Dominical, so he negotiated a price of three dollars per night with the owner. Each morning, Terry looked out his window to assess surf conditions. He could have opened the door and looked roughly one hundred yards to the breaking waves, but he considered that an unnecessary step. It was amusing to Terry that he could evaluate a swell from the comfort of his bed, simply by sitting up and looking west. (In Gold Coast, a room with this type of view would cost several hundred dollars per night.) It was a silly ritual because there wasn't a single morning that he didn't crawl out of bed, tuck his surfboard under his armpit, and stroll to the pebbly beach for a surf session. Even if he woke up next to a naked girl, he'd slip on his board shorts and swing the door open, allowing her flesh to be cooled by the breeze. And if she was waiting for him when he got back, well, there are certainly worse ways to end a surf session.

Between sessions one afternoon, Terry and I drank Imperial beer on a wooden table that was located on the hotel's untrimmed lawn. We swapped stories about our different, yet parallel, lifestyles. He asked me what it was like living in the mountains and snowboarding, and I asked him what it was like living near the ocean and surfing. When we finished our beers, we tossed our bottles onto the grass. By late afternoon, the large cumulus clouds on the horizon had moved inland and a growing collection of bottles was strewn across the lawn. Iguanas scurried on the hotel's tin rooftop and scaled rusted drain pipes. Oftentimes the iguanas crept close to our feet, which were sunk in tall blades of grass. For me, this was rather unnerving. For Terry, it had become a common sight and not worthy of further discussion. What was worthy of discussion was Pavones, a town to the south that had become the focal point of his and his shaggy-haired friend's 3,500-mile journey.

Six months earlier, Terry and his friend purchased a brown minivan in Los Angeles with the intention of driving it to Pavones. At that point, they would sell the van, use the money to fly back to Australia, and continue on with their lives working in an occupation that was "to be determined." There wasn't a surf break they missed since leaving Southern California: Mexico's Baja Peninsula and Puerto Escondido, El Salvador's La Libertad, Nicaragua's Playa Yankee, Costa Rica's Nicoya Peninsula—they hit them all. They hadn't stayed longer than a few weeks at any one spot until reaching Dominical, and now there was only one spot left for them to surf: Pavones.

"If the swell is just right, I've been told that you can ride that wave for several minutes," Terry told me as he took a swig of Imperial, his smile widening. "It's the classic surf paradise. Surfers camp in tents and pick fruit from trees. At least that's what I've heard."

Popularized by Allan Weisbecker's *In Search of Captain Zero*, which commences in Pavones, the Southern California–to–Central America road trip has become less impressive to hardcore traveling surfers, though not any less adventuresome. The closest either Terry or his friend had been to Pavones was when Terry's friend surfed Cabo Matapalo on the Osa Peninsula, a notable break across the Golfo Dulce from Pavones. His friend felt it was a magical setting with a noticeably different texture from the rest of the country, even Dominical. He glowed when describing monkeys howling in the trees, macaws coloring the sky, rough surf, and jungle spilling onto empty beaches. Any time spent in the wilder southern reaches of Costa Rica, they both agreed, would be the perfect ending to their trip.

My role emerged once I offered to share gas costs if they could drive me as far as Golfito. From there, they could continue to Pavones, and I could take a ferry to Puerto Jiménez, a gateway to Corcovado National Park, where I was planning to spend several days backpacking that summer. Terry accepted my offer and assured me they would leave the next morning because computer forecast models called for a sizable south swell to hit Pavones within a few days. The next morning, however, became the next morning, and the next morning became the next morning, and so on. Regrettably, I never traveled south with Terry and his friend because the original forecast was incorrect. For them, it would have been anticlimactic to drive all that way to end their once-in-a-lifetime surf trip by staring at a flat ocean.

Before we parted ways, Terry learned I was a journalist who was writing a book on ski bums. The connections between surf and ski cultures were numerous, yet I had failed to make those connections in my book about ski bums, as a reviewer in the *Wall Street Journal* correctly pointed out. Terry told me that Pavones was the rebellious cousin to other surf towns in Costa Rica, towns that he felt had perhaps sold their soul—piece by piece—to developers. He certainly made Pavones seem like a surf stronghold and a haven for surf bums just like him, people who went for a south swell and never left, abandoning their former lives for a new one. Of course, he had never been to Pavones and was relying on secondhand information. It's entirely possible that alcohol was influencing his rapturous description and that all he was saying was pure conjecture. When I brought up this possibility, he scowled and remained adamant that Pavones really was as wonderful as he described it. Part of his fascination, he admitted, was that this might be his last chance to surf Pavones.

Since leaving Baja, he had heard a rumor floating around coastal surf towns that Pavones was in danger. He wasn't sure of the reason, but our conversation was in July of 2008, long after Eduardo Velarde had met with the fishermen in town and the official announcement about the tuna farm had been published in *La Gaceta*. Though I can't say with total confidence, I suspect that the tuna farm was the culprit in the rumors

Terry and his friend had heard on their trip. He had also expressed some safety concerns about a surfer-turned-drug-dealer who had recently been released from prison and was causing security issues, and I later learned he was speaking of Dan Fowlie.

After we finished the last of our Imperials, I lay in my dirtbag hotel room's bed that night, dreaming of Pavones and convinced that it sounded like a place worth visiting one day. But when the lightning stopped flashing and the thunder subsided, I fell asleep in my creaky bed and didn't think about Pavones for a long time.

Then one day, while sipping tea in front of the computer at home in South Lake Tahoe, California, and planning another trip down south, I investigated the rumor. Just like many writers flirting with possible story ideas, I conducted a routine Google search and perused the Internet. Sure enough, search results confirmed that the rumor had merit and much more had transpired. Now, I had no idea if Terry even made it to the end of the road or whether I would find him in Pavones all these years later. But I did know that while we sipped beers in Dominical that Pavones was crying for help, and had a very good reason to be shedding tears.

After learning about the tuna farm project from the environmental group Pretoma, Peter Aspinall's first phone call was to environment minister Carlos Manuel Rodriguez to question his department's issuance of the permit. His next phone call, to Álvaro Sagot, Costa Rica's most powerful environmental attorney, was an even more important one. Pavones may have missed the three-day window to file an appeal following what the government considered official announcements in *La Gaceta* and *El Financerio*, but Sagot assured Peter that there were other courses of action that could be taken.

At first blush, Sagot doesn't seem like much. His office isn't in a shiny, glass-encased office building in a posh San José suburb but rather in a drab, gray building a few blocks from a park in the modest central valley town of Palmares. The lobby has a color scheme and furniture arrangement that would make an interior designer projectile vomit: faded green tile, two orange chairs, an orange couch, and a warped wooden bookcase with dusty, coffee-stained magazines and torn Yellow Pages on its shelves.

Once you're inside his U-shaped office, Sagot doesn't exactly strike fear. Of lighter complexion, he is balding, has silver-rimmed glasses perched on a well-defined nose, wears a collared shirt without a tie, and possesses a weak handshake. But what he lacks in appearance he makes up for in substance.

Sagot entered national headlines for his role in fighting Las Crucitas, an open-pit gold mine near Costa Rica's border with Nicaragua. About the same time that Costa Rica's Secretaría Técnica Nacional Ambiental (SETENA) issued an environmental viability permit for the tuna farms near Pavones, it also issued one for Las Crucitas. During his 2002–2006 presidential term, Abel Pacheco had announced that the country wouldn't be an enclave for oil exploration or open-pit mining. A month after his inauguration, in June of 2002, he signed a decree banning open-pit mining and oil exploration. As is the case in other countries, in Costa Rica, when there is a change in presidencies, incoming presidents must handle previous administrations' decisions.

In 1998, an economist and entrepreneur was president, and he summarily encouraged the brokering of numerous concessions, including one that SETENA issued to Houston-based Harken Energy for offshore drilling exploration in the Caribbean. A formal appeal was filed in the three-day window, and the project's environmental impact statement was reviewed by the environment minister. Over the next few years, during the appeals process, there was political posturing and a public relations campaign; there were protests and a media onslaught that illustrated a point that the government couldn't ignore: How could Costa Rica, where more than two million tourists visit each year and where tourism is the third-largest economic engine behind agriculture and coffee exports, allow such a project when the majority of tourists ventured to Costa Rica on account of its eco-conscious reputation? The bickering delayed a decision for so long that it spilled into Pacheco's term. By February of 2002, several months before Pacheco took office, SETENA, citing various concerns with the environmental impact statement, reversed its 1998 decision and declared that the project was no longer environmentally viable. Naturally, Harken Energy appealed. Pacheco's administration, which was on record as being against offshore drilling and mining, handled the appeal. His environmental minister was Carlos Manuel Rodriguez, who hiked with Peter's wife in 2005, days before the official announcement of the tuna farm project.

In the offshore drilling case, Rodriguez reviewed the environmental impact assessment, upheld SETENA's decision to stop the project, and rejected Harken Energy's appeal, effectively canceling the 1998 concession. It took nearly four years and two presidents from when the concession was granted to reach a final decision, mostly because of the glacial pace of the appeal process. Of course, in Latin America, this isn't entirely surprising. Tomorrow is always the busiest day in Costa Rica because things always get done "mañana."

Cultural idiosyncrasies notwithstanding, a puzzling governmental protocol was also to blame. Only when a formal appeal is filed is the environmental minister obligated to review an environmental impact statement. Offshore drilling is allowable under Costa Rican law, and since Harken Energy had followed the law and received a concession to explore a 1.2-million-acre area in the Caribbean, it was allowed to drill there until SETENA delivered a decision following the appeals process. It was foolish for Harken to continue drilling knowing the new president was publicly against offshore drilling, and now his environmental wing was deciding the company's fate. Having invested millions in the exploration process, Harken predictably entered litigation with Costa Rica in 2003 after Rodriguez officially canceled the project. Harken sued Costa Rica in an international court and sought $57 billion in a judgment over lost revenue, a figure that included current costs and future profits. (Harken eventually dropped the lawsuit because it felt it could not win.)

Yet because there was a formal appeal regarding the drilling concession issued by the previous administration, and because it was passed onto the Pacheco administration, Rodriguez was obligated to review the environmental impact statement (EIS), and he quickly discovered gaping holes in logic and outright negligence.

After initial conversations with Velarde, the man spearheading Granjas Atuneras's tuna farm project, Carlos Manuel Rodriguez suspected there were similar holes in his company's EIS. But since aquaculture is allowable under Costa Rica law, since Granjas Atuneras complied with the law every step of the way, and since there was no formal appeal to stop the project, Rodriguez did not pursue the matter further. If there is no appeal filed against a project, the environment minister signs off on it unless the project violates Costa Rican law.

"The environmental impact assessment study is totally autonomous under the ministry, and I don't have a say there," Rodriguez said. "The only competence that I had [for the tuna farm project initially] as a minster was when they issued an administrative resolution and somebody appeals it, that goes to me, the minister, and I solve it. With the tuna farm, there wasn't a formal appeal, so it wasn't my responsibility to review the environmental impact statement. I can't say no because of a personal decision. In the case of the tuna farms, there was no appeal, and that is why I never got involved, never had to review the environmental impact assessment. I never saw it, SETENA saw it, and the minister is not responsible. I have zero influence unless there is an appeal."

Upon hearing his explanation, Peter Aspinall balked at such obfuscation, particularly when he recalled Rodriguez telling him "there was pressure from above."

"He's a politician. He could have stopped it," Peter said.

Despite Pacheco's decree in 2002 that banned offshore drilling and open-pit mining, SETENA issued a mining concession during his term, in 2005, to Industrias Infinito, a subsidiary of a Canadian mining company, for a gold mine in an area of the country called Las Crucitas. Again, unlike in the case of the tuna farms, a formal appeal was submitted by an environmental group within the three-day window, and Sagot was hired to lead the opposition. Rodriguez was scheduled to handle the appeal and review the environmental impact assessment. But Pacheco was on his way out of office, and just as the Harken offshore drilling project had been passed on to him by the previous president, Pacheco would leave the Las Crucitas situation for the next administration to handle. For a president who was sympathetic to environmental causes, Pacheco's decision turned out to have been unwise because the next president, Óscar Arias, was probusiness and prodevelopment; some even considered him anti-environment.

Not long after the mining concession was granted, the mining company got to work. According to the *Tico Times*, Industrias Infinito cleared hundreds of acres of rain forest, with the result that thousands of trees were destroyed, including a nationally protected almond tree. In addition, the clearing threatened the endangered green macaw, whose domestic population hovered at a mere 250. Moreover, the company also assumed control of acres that were used by local farmers for growing crops and keeping livestock. These concerns weren't properly addressed in the EIS; those related to the trees and birds became a focus for the critical arguments made by Sagot and the environmental group he represented. After years of encouraging citizens to protest and massaging various media outlets to spread the message of a community's suffering, as well as the plight of the green macaw and the almond tree, Sagot got his day in court.

Although SETENA approved a modified EIS in 2008, and later that year Óscar Arias issued a presidential decree ignoring Pacheco's ban on open-pit gold mines and declaring the Las Crucitas mine project to be in the "national interest," Sagot took this case all the way to the country's Supreme Court, where, eventually, the tuna farm case would also be heard.

In 2008, the Supreme Court ruled to halt all activity at the mine. Then two years later, it ruled the concession was invalid because the environmental studies that led to the concession were incomplete. The court ordered a criminal investigation of Arias's decision to ignore Pacheco's 2002 decree against open-pit mining and sign off on a project backed by incomplete environmental studies. Several years after the government granted the concession for the mine, it ordered the company to pay for environmental damages, and Sagot promised to "squeeze them for every last penny," according to the *Tico Times*.

Sagot pounced on the mining company's blatant disregard for protected tree and bird species in the EIS. He encouraged the tuna farm opposition to use similar tactics as those used against the mining and offshore drilling projects, but the timing and methods would have to be modified. Regardless of having missed the three-day window to file a formal appeal, Sagot convinced Peter Aspinall that he could circumnavigate the appeals process and SETENA altogether and, by whatever means necessary, take the case to the Supreme Court.

"I put Peter in touch with Álvaro Sagot because he's always been a great fighter and great for tough cases," said Denise Echeverria, director of the Vida Marina Foundation, an environmental group with which Sagot had worked previously. "I considered him very serious and very committed. I think he was great for this kind of fight, because he really believed in the town's cause."

With Sagot already in national headlines over the Las Crucitas case, Granjas Atuneras had a serious problem on its hands. It didn't have the political muscle or financial backing of a North American mining or energy company. It didn't even have a lawyer, and it was going to need one for what Sagot had planned. Still, its head, Eduardo Velarde, was confident. Although SETENA issues whatever environmental permits it wants regardless of how faulty an EIS is presented, Velarde figured it only possesses the authority to revoke permits later if an appeal is filed in the three-day window. SETENA hadn't received an appeal, and it was that fundamental fact that led Velarde to believe his project wouldn't be caught in a quagmire.

"I had been in Costa Rica long enough to know that all the non-government organizations [NGOs] would be after me. That's why I was very careful in my environmental studies," Velarde said. "But this Álvaro Sagot, he is a mean son of a bitch and went against the law. He is very famous here and very powerful. He only takes high profile cases. But I swear to God, he doesn't play clean. He dirties his hand to get things done. If you have an argument and you beat me with better arguments, well shit, great, but this guy doesn't play this way. I had read about him before getting involved with him and he is no angel, but I didn't think it would be a problem. I had the community behind me and science behind me."

Velarde migrated to Costa Rica from Peru in 1989, when the Shining Path terrorist organization was ravaging the South American country. Shining Path had killed over twenty thousand people by that time, and gringos were a main target. Born in Lima, Velarde looks like a gringo and felt he was in danger if he stayed in Peru. His skin is pale, he has blue-gray eyes, and he assured me that his usual attire of blue jeans and a short-sleeved collared shirt hasn't changed much over the decades. It didn't take me long to figure out he enjoys playing the martyr role, but he had legitimate gripes when it came to staying in Peru.

"Even though I had nothing to do with this shit, I was the enemy in Peru because I look like a fucking gringo, so I had to migrate," Velarde said. "I was growing shrimp in Tumbes in the north of Peru, sending them to Lima, and my business went down the drain . . . and my life was going down the drain in Peru because of the Shining Path revolution."

Velarde was in his mid-thirties when he moved to Costa Rica, seeking political asylum and a fresh start. He didn't choose Costa Rica on a whim, however. In the mid-1970s, he majored in agriculture at the University of Arizona. After graduating in 1979, he worked for a few years in Galveston, Texas, where he learned how to artificially reproduce shrimp in a controlled setting. He returned to Peru in the early 1980s and applied what he learned in Galveston in his start-up shrimp reproduction business. He gravitated toward aquaculture because he wanted to follow in the footsteps of his childhood hero, Jacques Cousteau, the famous French oceanographer and conservationist. He was well on his way until his Peru business went bust. He wanted to stay in aquaculture but needed a new home that was safe and where he could resurrect his business. He enjoyed his time in the United States but, when deciding where to seek political asylum, he wasn't sure he could live there.

"I had lived in the States for eight years but everything is too boxed in, too many rules," Velarde said. "You buy a four-wheel drive car and you can't drive it anywhere you want, you can only use it here and here, can't always go way out in the wilderness. There were too many rules. I'm not saying it's bad, it's just different."

Costa Rica, meanwhile, was gaining a reputation as a peaceful utopia, immune to the violence and political instability surrounding it in countries like El Salvador and Nicaragua. During his ~~during his~~ first presidential term from 1986 to 1990, probusiness Óscar Arias was awarded the Nobel Peace Prize in 1987 for his role in ending civil wars in neighboring countries. Costa Rica seemed a nice alternative.

"When Óscar Arias won the Nobel Peace Prize, that inspired me because I wanted my kids to live in a place like that," said Velarde. "It was not like

Peru, violent and unstable. Costa Rica was like between Peru, which was too wild, and the United States, which had too many rules. It was in the middle. And when I got here, it was *pura vida* [pure life]."

Granted political asylum, Velarde flew to San José's international airport jobless, yet he was committed to being a shrimper. There were two major shrimp farms in the country in 1989: one was owned by a shrimp-boat captain and was doing well; the other was Canadian-owned and struggling. Velarde saw an opportunity. The Canadian-owned farm was in Chomes, near the Pacific coast, and he drove there. The first person he met was the farm's biologist, a Tico, who confided that the Canadian owner was making a mess of the company, showing up only occasionally and that when he did show up, he was more interested in partying than running a business. Velarde contacted the company's lawyer, another Tico, and wanted to know when the Canadian was coming to town. The Tico lawyer was tight-lipped, but Velarde knew money has a way of changing people's behavior. He offered a *propina* (or tip) to the lawyer, who told him what day the Canadian owner would be arriving and the hotel where he would be staying.

Velarde booked a room at the hotel for that same night. Walking down to the bar that evening, he noticed two Canadians sharing cocktails. As he approached the men, who were brothers and already drunk, he figured out who was the boss. Then he said, in perfect, unaccented English, "Hello, my name is Eduardo Velarde, and I am your new general manager." The two looked at each other, not sure exactly how to respond, and Velarde continued with his sales pitch. "Your shrimp farm has these problems," and then rattled them off in rapid-fire fashion. "If you want to start making money, hire me and I can correct the problems." The Canadian boss seemed receptive, but he was drunk, and Velarde was sober. He told Velarde that he would go to his room and drink a barrel of coffee and that he wanted Velarde to drink a barrel of beer.

"He figured that way I'm coming up and he's coming down, and we could meet in the middle," Velarde said. "Forty-five minutes later, he comes down. He contracted me that night, and we both got blasted until two-thirty in the morning. I got a taxi home, and I had a job. That was my way of getting my first job here."

It was his first job but certainly not his last. Over the next decade, with the help of Daniel Benetti, a professor and director of aquaculture at the University of Miami, Velarde went on to become one of the leading aquaculturists in Latin America. He reproduced shrimp and processed anchovies in Peru, and then was the first to spawn snapper in Ecuador. In 2002, a marine park focused on conservation and research of marine species opened in Puntarenas, a steamy, impoverished port town west of San José. It was there that he began reproducing shrimp and red snapper from eggs, becoming the first to spawn snapper in Costa Rica. One day, the park director asked Velarde to give a tour to a Spanish guy. At first he balked, citing his other duties, but he sensed a serious tone in his boss' voice when he said, "Please, Ed, take care of this guy."

They strolled through the park together, Velarde explaining his life story and what he did with the snapper and shrimp. The Spaniard was impressed with his technical knowledge, as well as his passion for aquaculture, and then asked: "What do you think about tuna?" Velarde didn't know much other than that bluefin tuna was nearly extinct in Europe, that farming tuna was impossible at that moment because it couldn't be grown from an egg, and that, anyway, he wasn't sold on the idea of farming tuna because it would do nothing to repopulate the species. He ended by saying he didn't think it was worth focusing on tuna.

"I am interested in farming it from an egg, and I am interested in you doing that for me," the Spaniard said. "I own three tuna clippers and sell tuna to Sardimar, the largest tuna company in Costa Rica. I can invest in this project if you are interested. Would like you like to go to lunch?"

"Lunch time," Velarde told him.

By the time they finished lunch that afternoon, they were business partners. He didn't know it at the time, but Velarde's partner, Manuel de Iglesia, was one of richest tuna clipper owners operating in that part of the world. De Iglesia was also connected with Spain's Fuentes family, owners of Europe's most lucrative bluefin tuna business—and a reason why bluefin was nearly extinct in the Mediterranean Sea, which was about the only thing Velarde knew about tuna when the two strangers met earlier that day. Now, the two had formulated a plan to bring the world's first yellowfin tuna farm to Costa Rica, and both men stood to become very rich.

"I've been doing shrimp and snapper for like the past twenty years, so maybe it's time for a change."

De Iglesia had the investors. All Velarde had to do was find the perfect location for the farm.

5   The Pavones Bus

The traveler sees what he sees. The tourist sees what he has come to see.
—G. K. Chesterton

Technology is divine but relying on technology is a fool's choice, and I was once a great fool. After investigating the rumor about Pavones being in trouble and convinced it sounded like an interesting story, I made plans for another trip to Costa Rica. Before I got to Pavones, my iPhone was stolen from a hotel room in Golfito, a gritty port town that has seen better days. I hadn't handwritten a single note from Tamarindo to Golfito; instead, I'd recorded audio interviews and typed notes, which I stored on my phone. The theft seemed a monumental disaster at the time, and my ensuing tirade at the hotel's owner reflected my feelings about the seriousness of the situation. If I wasn't convinced that the owner's children had used the hotel's set of keys to enter my room when I went to buy fruit, I might have believed my outburst could have resulted in some empathy from the owner. In reality, the owner didn't care about me or my iPhone and wanted me off the premises. Knowing this, I sat on the bed in my room for hours like a petulant child until the police arrived and questioned hotel staff about the theft.

Nothing came of the police's official interrogation, as I knew it would before any questions were asked. For starters, neither of the two officers had a pen, and this was just one of many things that suggested a complete lack of professionalism. Nevertheless, the chubby officer asked to borrow one of my pens so he could take notes on a wadded piece of material. It closely resembled a napkin, likely leftover from his morning's breakfast.

If I had to guess, taking notes about my stolen phone was probably the least important thing he did that day. When I was finished answering their questions, and both officers were finished interrogating the hotel's three-member staff, which consisted of the parents of the children who stole my phone and the grandmother of the children who stole my phone, the officers had figured it out: someone used a plastic card to open my room door.

Everyone but me in the open-air lobby nodded their heads in approval at such stellar detective work. When I reminded the audience that my money belt, which contained a passport and three hundred dollars in cash, went unmolested despite being in plain view, everyone shrugged their shoulders in utter bewilderment. Not quite ready to give up on what I thought was a key bit of information, I asked the chubby officer why a thief capable of breaking into a hotel room with a plastic card would ignore such valuable items and instead rummage through a zipped pocket at the bottom of my backpack for unknown contents. He didn't answer and neither did anyone else. So I asked a final question: How, in the few minutes I was away buying fruit, could a thief go unnoticed to the hotel's owners? I reminded them that the thief would have had to walk directly in front of the owners to reach my room, work his or her magic with the plastic card, and then walk directly past the owners again, all the while not being noticed and then disappearing into the humid morning air like a fart in the wind. I added that in the twelve hours I had stayed there, I had always seen at least two adult members of the hotel's three-person staff lounging on a couch in the lobby and watching Spanish-language soap operas on a television bolted to the crumbling wall. (Because I could hear the drama of the soap operas unfold in my room, I added that they listened to them at a ridiculously high volume.)

When I am flustered, my Spanish worsens, so to compensate I emphasized these critical points with a theatrical performance that involved facial expressions and hand gestures. Everyone chuckled at my gesticulations. Their grins implied that they had heard enough and that a gringo stupid enough to leave an iPhone and a money belt in a hotel room in a gritty port town deserves whatever fate comes his way. Such reasoning may not have been a solid defense in an American courtroom but this wasn't

America; this was way down in Costa Rica's Southern Zone, where there is a different set of rules, and I was a long way from home. Therefore, it was a convincing argument under the circumstances, and I had no smart-ass rebuttal this time around. I later learned from a Pavones hotel owner that in Costa Rica, there must be at least two witnesses to a claim of theft or a judge can't legally prosecute the criminals. While such a law increases the likelihood of vigilante justice, I didn't know about it. The interrogation ended, and it was clear that I was overstaying my welcome. The chubby officer who took notes with my pen said, "I am sorry. You can leave now."

I left the premises and found myself on the cracked sidewalks paralleling Golfito's decaying main street. I walked at a brisk pace and skirted past men who leaned against wooden shacks. They stared at me, and I couldn't blame them. There isn't much to do in Golfito, where unemployment is high and the midday humidity slows everyone to a halt. If one walks too fast in the tropics, the quantity of sweat that emerges from one's body in a short amount of time is rather alarming. A gringo walking madly and cursing and leaking buckets of sweat is a cheap form of entertainment. I wasn't gone from the El Tucán hotel for more than a minute when I looked back and noticed the officers leaving. The chubby officer tossed a crumpled wad of paper into the nearest puddle, and there was no reason to think it wasn't his notes. Then I saw him tuck my pen into his shirt pocket before opening the car door and driving away in the other direction.

By the time I had reached the bus stop, the volcanic anger over my stolen iPhone subsided, likely leaving with the sweat running down my skin. I must have done something in my past, this I can be sure of, but I couldn't be sure why such a transgression afflicted me there, surrounded by jungle and humidity and predators who were after my perceived wealth. I may have seemed a prince to them, a peasant to others, but those kids at the hotel wore rags and had no proper footwear, so surely I possessed something of value to them in my rucksack. There are many good and honest people, but to recognize those qualities suggests one must know there are people who are bad and dishonest, for there is no other way. Perhaps the kids who stole my phone did me a favor. The trappings of technology are a crutch and have weakened me. I should have never brought the phone;

instead, I should have done things the old-fashioned way, with a pen and paper. Now, though, I had only paper since the chubby police officer stole my pen and tucked it into his pocket. It's the reader who will be cheated at the loss of my precise notes and audio recordings, but feeling cheated means a person must have had expectations of certain results, and that is his or her fault, not mine.

It's amazing, and at times frightening, what one thinks of while waiting for a bus that might not ever come. It's not ordinary thoughts, for this was no ordinary bus stop. I had traveled south along almost the entire length of Costa Rica's Pacific coast, but now I had to travel farther, to the farthest point south in the country, where there is nowhere else to go. The bus stop was located outside a market across from a hospital with a rusted tin roof. The roof adjacent to the market was also rusted tin. It took about fifteen minutes to walk from the hotel to the bus stop, and along the way I began to wonder if the jungle had become too difficult an opponent for Golfito, an adversary that never relented and enjoyed tightening the noose.

Plants and trees swallowed entire homes; the weight of the flora punished structures and tilted them sideways. Walls were cracking and crumbling; fences were toppled over. The smell of rotting fish filled the moistened air. Men's faces were sad; most didn't bother to tie their shoelaces, and their shirts were soaked with sweat. Streets were fissured, buildings tired and sagging. Boats had ripped masts; in the harbor engines leaked fluid, displaying a sheen of colors on the water. With nearly two hundred inches of rain falling in Golfito each year, this must be the cumulative effect of erecting a town in one of the wettest spots on earth. Or maybe it's the result of a town's neglect, of its surrendering to the conditions. Either way, I didn't want to return to Golfito anytime soon. Yet I learned that would be impossible because things that happen in Pavones usually happen first in Golfito, the region's corrupt, bureaucratic hub.

I stood under the rusted tin roof, lifting one leg against a wall, and drank a Coca-Cola. I had purchased two ballpoint pens in the market and safely tucked one away in my backpack. It was 9:30 a.m., and the bus was scheduled to leave for Pavones at 10:00 a.m. Bus transportation and punctuality are often mutually exclusive in Costa Rica. The hands of time are as different as the contour lines of one's palms, yet it's those palms that drive the busses and make the only schedule that truly matters. It's an unruly system since departure times usually become mere suggestions, but there is something charming about that, as long as you don't have to be anywhere at a certain time. Now, it should be noted the bus was parked outside the market when I arrived; it was empty and locked and wouldn't leave until later. In the meantime, there I was, leaning against a rotting wooden wall, drinking my Coca-Cola, fanning myself with a notebook, and trying to mentally prepare for what has been considered one of the more adventuresome trips in Central America: the one aboard the Pavones bus.

While I waited for the bus in Golfito, Gerardo Mendoza shouted through a megaphone in Pavones. Gerardo is tall for a Tico, nearly six feet with raven-black hair and oversized walnut eyes. He has a soft, soothing voice, almost feminine, which causes males to trust him and females to adore him. As he stood on a chair and directed traffic, the ocean was placid, barely a weak curl to be seen. There was a light wind and thin, wispy clouds smearing a cobalt sky. It was an ideal day to hold the town's inaugural cultural festival, which attracted groups from every region of Costa Rica. Local cuisine unique to each region was on display, and by all accounts it was a rousing success, a mixture of Ticos and gringos congregating and sampling food and discussing the big swell that was predicted to slam into Pavones the next morning. When the swell arrived, Gerardo would be surfing. But on this day, his index finger was never far from the megaphone's trigger, ready to provide directions at high volume, as seems to be the preference in Latin America. When he spoke, everyone stopped and listened. When he spoke, you could hear a sleeping baby snore. When someone else spoke, you couldn't hear the baby crying next to you because nobody listened to that person. Respect: others wanted it; Gerardo had it.

"Gerardo wants to be president one day, and he'll probably be president," a local hotel owner told me later that night. "The kid is sharp, always organizing stuff, and ambitious as all hell. He's always asking people to donate money for some group or some event. Even if it's my last dollar, he makes me believe it's worth giving to him. It helps he speaks English, he's been to college, been to the United States. There aren't many guys like him around here, and you won't be able to write a book about Pavones without talking to him. His family is one of the original families in Pavones and his father was close with Danny Fowlie, the guy who discovered Pavones before anybody here knew what a surfboard was."

In time I would learn a lot about Danny Fowlie—maybe too much for my own good—but at the moment the most puzzling thing to me was Gerardo's unwavering commitment to Pavones. Most ambitious, educated, and well-traveled men who grew up in rural Costa Rica move to San José or the central valley, vowing to never return. There are limited job opportunities in rural Costa Rica, where poverty and unemployment rates are two to three times the national average. For as long as the government has been documenting its social progress on a national scale, the southern zone, where Pavones is located, has historically ranked among the country's poorest, with nearly 35 percent of its people living below the poverty line (those earning less than forty-five dollars per month). In San José and the central valley, which has a slightly higher monthly salary average for its poverty rates since they have been adjusted for an urban area's higher cost of living, only 15 percent live below the poverty line (of sixty-eight dollars per month). Even back in the 1930s, author Chester Lloyd Jones noticed the glaring differences between the central valley and the coastal and lowland regions. In his *Costa Rica and Civilization in the Caribbean*, Jones wrote:

> They are regions in which hot climate, trying rainfall conditions, malaria, a low standard of life and in some small areas a large percentage of almost nomadic indigenous population make the campaign to "banish" illiteracy difficult. Least well favored is the Pacific province of Puntarenas in which all the cantons have a greater average of illiteracy than the average for the republic—the highest being almost 74 percent. On the coasts and in the lowlands, the tropical climate and inaccessibility of all but a small part of the land have kept the population low in number and low in standard of life. Outside the chief towns, life on the cattle farms of Guanacaste and Puntarenas still has the primitive characteristics which always go with the existence on far frontiers.

Families live almost unto themselves. Their houses are of the roughest adobe or bahareque (erecting uprights by horizontal narrow boards, strips of bamboo, or cane). Occasional mule trails are found in the greater part of this area but there is no attempt by the public authorities to maintain any routes of communication. The real Costa Rica, that part of the republic in which the greatest advance has been made in establishing a modern civilization, lies in the restricted highlands of the central plateau.

Before the explosion of tourism in the 1980s in the coastal and lowland regions, rural Costa Ricans made their living farming. It's a way of life that requires not a college education but the physical ability to engage in back-breaking labor and a willingness to work long, difficult hours outside in the heat, humidity, and rain. It nearly always involves wearing knee-high rubber boots to, yes, keep one's feet dry but more importantly to protect oneself from venomous snakes, of which Costa Rica has more than a dozen, including the infamous fer-de-lance. Pavones is a prime habitat for the fer-de-lance, known as the terciopelo in Spanish. When it bites, it usually injects about one hundred milligrams of venom, twice the amount needed for a bite to be fatal to a human. In all, Costa Rica has more than 120 snakes, and it also has an assortment of spiders and scorpions. The fear of interacting with any of these should be enough to deter most from dropping out and working in the fields. Even more disturbing than the threat of reptiles and insects is the implication of Costa Rica's widely boasted 95 percent literacy rate. Being able to read doesn't mean that you're highly educated; it just means you have the basis to become educated.

Many teenagers start dropping out in middle school. Of those who enroll in kindergarten in Pavones, it's not unusual to see more than half of those kids not graduate from high school. And here is another unfortunate reality of Costa Rica, one that links education with poverty: the wealthiest 20 percent of Costa Ricans average 12.1 years of school; the poorest 20 percent, which includes many people in Pavones, average 5.2 years of school. As disappointing as those figures are, it doesn't take much money to live in the rural areas of the southern zone. A life consisting of a home with a dirt or concrete floor, four walls, a tin roof, a few chickens running around in the yard, and a menu that includes an endless supply of rice and beans costs less than one hundred dollars per month, which is above the poverty line in Pavones.

"I think there are several Costa Ricas," Román Macaya, an executive for a pesticide company and now ambassador to the United States, once told the *Tico Times*. "I think there is a developed Costa Rica, with segments of society in which people have very good jobs, high incomes, big houses, two cars and all the amenities that you would expect in the upper class of developed countries. Then there's a poor Costa Rica, which is suffering quite a bit. You go into a poor residential area and you find every single problem there is. . . . I wouldn't even say those areas are developing. They have stagnated in a general despair."

A high school diploma might make somebody a few more dollars per month in Pavones but they can eat and live without the extra, so is school really necessary? This is an argument Gerardo hears repeatedly from those who dropped out of school. Gerardo doesn't necessarily disagree with them, because if they want nothing more out of life, they can live that way. And, sadly, he knows that they will likely always live that way. It doesn't take algebra to push a pale-skinned tourist from Iowa into a wave during a surf lesson; it doesn't take grammar to maneuver a fishing boat; it doesn't take economics to gut an eighty-pound yellowfin tuna at the fish house; proficiency in world history doesn't make one a better dishwasher.

"For those who go to college, which many do, they often attend college on weekends at the border and that requires them to pay for food and hotel every weekend," Peter Aspinall said. "That can get expensive for families here. Even when they stay with it, they are usually learning a specific trade, such as taking classes to be an accountant or a medical assistant or an educator. But those types of jobs aren't available here, so those certifications don't do our students any good (unless they plan on moving elsewhere)."

Gerardo was never interested in pushing pale-skinned tourists into waves or gutting fish his entire life. He took his ability to read and continued on the path toward being educated. He enrolled in college and became a teacher. He learned to speak English. For a country that attracts millions of tourists from English-speaking nations, many of whom barely know how to say hello and good-bye in Spanish, this is a critical requirement to thrive in a tourist town. Shortly after he began teaching children in his spare time, he started a restaurant and was voted town president.

"I am interested in making Pavones a better place," Gerardo told me. "I do not want to live in San José where there is traffic and pollution and lots of people. I want to live in Pavones where it is beautiful. My family is here, and life is more relaxed."

Many believe Gerardo is still destined for San José or the central valley, if not to be the president then something else that Pavones can't offer. But all Gerardo cared about the day I arrived was the cultural festival and the incoming swell. He was in his element that morning, walking to every hotel and restaurant, and riding his bike to every residence. There wasn't a door he didn't knock on or a fence he didn't shout over. When he was certain that he had contacted everyone within a several-mile radius of the soccer field, he walked back to a grassy area near a chain-link fence, stood on a chair, and grabbed a megaphone.

He wore flip flops, a tank top, and khaki shorts. On one side of the chair was a playground with a tan-colored slide and on the other side was a stand of palms. Behind him, children played in the muddy Río Claro and coconuts rested on top of fallen palm leaves. The trees provided much-needed shade for the festival's workers, mostly women who wore colorful dresses and prepared food under thatched roofs.

Several hundred people ate food, drank, conversed, and danced into the early afternoon hours, when the wispy clouds became bloated and turned silver and promised rain, and the wind intensified and shook the trees. By the time I arrived from Golfito, there was no food left. Every region had sold out its allotment, but people were drinking and dancing, and nobody objected. One Tica offered me *chancho*, which I knew from my numerous travels in Latin America can often mean the less pleasant part of a pig's anatomy. I declined her offer and searched for a place to stay. With an army-green backpack on my shoulders, not much larger than the one I wore in school to haul textbooks, I strolled along the other road connected to the soccer field and stumbled upon Carol's Cabinas, a collection of ten basic rooms catering to surfers and travelers. This is where

Gerardo would be smoking cigarettes and sipping canned beer later that night. He didn't talk to me when I arrived that afternoon, and he didn't talk to me later that night either, but other people did.

"Good place to stay, man," said a blond-haired gringo as he walked past and noticed me assessing Carol's. "When you get settled, come on down to the festival. There hasn't been this much action in months. You have perfect timing. Ocean's been flat for weeks. Big swell coming. Party today. Surf tomorrow. It doesn't get much better than this."

I told him I wasn't in Pavones to surf.

"Then you're in the wrong place or you must have taken a wrong turn somewhere," he said as he shook his head and walked away.

Although he was correct in assuming I wasn't a serious enough surfer to be here waiting for the impending swell, I was as lucky as any serious surfer in that I arrived in time to secure a bed. By the end of the night, every available bed, all three hundred of them, was accounted for by surfers. "No Vacancy" signs hung from hotels. At Carol's, rain pounded the tin roofs throughout the evening. Taxis and rental cars with surfboards strapped to the roofs skidded into the gravel driveway before someone from the vehicle jumped out of the car and sprinted to find Carol. When they received the bad news, they sprinted back to their cars, slammed the door shut, and peeled out of the driveway, hoping there would be a room at the next place.

When the swell ended after a few days and the ocean was flat again, all but a few of those surfers were gone. The ones who didn't leave had nowhere to go, no schedule to follow, no home or job to return to, and so they hung around for the next swell. "Vacancy" signs appeared again at the hotels, and Carol smoked cigarettes and drank rum and wondered when the next infusion of income would arrive. On the first morning of the big swell, the waves were booming, already audible from the hammock outside my door by sunrise. I walked down to the beach and sat on a bench and understood why Gerardo never wanted to leave this place: there wasn't another wave he wanted to surf.

"This is a hit-or-miss wave, feast or famine," said a surfer and actor from California who attended college in Hawaii. "Even in Hawaii, which has the best waves in the world, people know about this wave. When it's on, everybody wants to be here and will do whatever it takes to get here. When it's not, nobody wants to be here and everybody takes the next bus out of here. Must suck for business owners."

The Pavones bus might come with a badge of honor that means something to travelers who have been to the end of the road in Costa Rica, but the vehicle itself is nothing special. It's a former American school bus that was discarded for safety reasons. I had seen busses like this in Nicaragua. Nicaraguans usually didn't bother to repaint the sides of a bus, so while "Sarasota School District" might be printed in black letters on the side of one, there weren't any schoolchildren from Florida on it. Here, instead of the traditional yellow, this old school bus had been painted tan and had yellow and red lines along its sides. There was a blue sign at the top of the driver's window with "Pavones-Golfito" stitched in white letters. The tires were smooth like the inside of a coconut, surely not capable of gaining traction on anything but asphalt, but there they were. The bus' lug nuts and axles were caked with mud. Like most buildings in San José, they needed a good scrubbing, but what would be the point? The bus would stay clean only until the next trip, which was now just a few minutes away.

The driver made a rock star appearance, flashing smiles, waving to familiar faces, and getting numerous pats on the shoulder as he walked up the three rubber steps leading to his leather seat. In many places, passengers would be furious that the driver arrived an hour late, but here he was shaking hands and being welcomed like the pope in Vatican City. The bus driver in these parts is an esteemed member of the community, a superhero who links everyone in the rolling hill country between Golfito and Pavones. After the United Fruit Company ceased banana operations, it eventually used its landholdings to establish less labor-intensive African palm plantations, which produce cooking oil and soap. If someone isn't involved in surf tourism in Pavones, these plantations provide what few jobs are available.

The driver had seasoned dark hair that was fighting off aggressive strands of gray and a receding hairline that seemed to suggest he was in his fifties. He wore black-rimmed glasses, had a graying if not a chalky beard, and had a bald spot on the crown of his head. He was handsome and stately and would have had little problem masquerading as a philosophy professor at Berkeley. He'd been the bus driver for this route for as long as anyone could remember, and was the first person courageous enough to travel the route in the 1980s when vehicles had to be transported over the Río Coto river crossing on sketchy wooden barges, a practice that continued until a permanent bridge was installed about a decade ago. Now, he fired up the engine, and the tailpipe belched plumes of exhaust. Nurses in white uniforms scurried across the road from the hospital, not wanting to rely on the next bus. One was in fact scheduled to leave in six hours, but in the rainy season, which it was at the time, nobody was sure if that bus would arrive.

Despite the importance of making sure one gets on the bus, everyone was relatively well behaved. Some people were motivated by the misguided thrill of obtaining a desirable seat on an American school bus and started forming a line on the curb outside the bus' glass door at 9 a.m. And that is where they stayed for the next two hours, careful not to lose their position and gently nudging anyone with the audacity to challenge it. The number of passengers waiting in line swelled in time; most of them were women in soggy T-shirts holding babies with matted black hair and dried mucus stuck to their faces. I didn't want to spend a second longer in Golfito than absolutely necessary, so I finished the last of my Coca-Cola, swung my leg off the wall, and began to make my move.

New arrivals jostled and angled for position at the end of the line, mothers using their babies as shields to keep me from slithering in front of them. The line had extended toward the market's entrance. I established my position in line and worked to keep it from the tardiest of passengers, typically men whose chests met by my backpack if they got too close. Just like in grade school, it was one-at-a-time up the rubber stairs. Once on board, I handed the driver the required fare in coins and noticed an available window seat toward the back. Other passengers were getting settled, blocking the aisle and cramming what items they could in the space under the seats. Not wanting to lose my window seat, I maneuvered around these people and steadied myself by sliding my hands along steel bars mounted to the ceiling. I sat on the brown seat and snapped my head back on the lighter brown, almost clay-colored, head rest. I grabbed the knobs on the window and yanked them down to welcome what breeze there was to cool my perspiring forehead. The driver shouted at the last passengers on board that we were leaving and everyone took their seats. Once the engine came alive, the driver checked his mirrors and then adjusted his black-rimmed glasses. He grabbed the steering wheel with both hands, spun it sharply, and the bus veered onto the main street, passing El Tucán hotel on its way out of town.

6   Red Road

The World is a book, and those who do not travel read only a page.
—St. Augustine

There weren't any other gringos on the bus, which was fine. A few miles outside Golfito we steered right at a junction, and gravel replaced pavement. We passed shacks and roadside fruit stands. Passengers exited the bus, and new ones boarded at seemingly every road that bisected the highway. The landscape was an agricultural mosaic: valleys that had been razed; African palm-oil farms splattered against naked hillsides; valleys and hills crisscrossed by red-dirt roads and rivers. Where there were official bus stops, each had a ceiling that provided shelter from the rain. Plastic bottles and candy wrappers littered the stops. Nobody could blame someone for passing the time with a cold drink and chucking its container onto the dirt: one could wait hours before a bus ever arrived in these parts.

Most of the homes were square and small, some painted pink or blue or green, no larger than six hundred square feet. Some homes were tidier than others and had yards with flowering gardens; others were busting apart at the seams and had yards overgrown with weeds. There were stands of banana trees with blue bags wrapped around the sprouting fruit to protect them from insects. Where the earth hadn't been cultivated, the jungle closed in and became thicker, but since many of the rolling hills had been wiped clean of their vegetation, it reminded me of the wine country of northern California after a wet winter. Overall it was a pleasant drive, and I began to wonder why so many travelers believe it should come with a badge of honor.

At Conte, pavement reemerged, and we reached a T-intersection where the driver turned right and came to an abrupt stop. Another bus was parked in front of us, this one having started near the border town of Paso Canoas; those continuing on to Pavones were instructed by our driver to switch to the other bus. Most adults, many with children had exited the bus and disappeared into the sweltering heat. On the new school bus were mostly school children wearing uniforms: powder-blue polo shirts with navy slacks for the boys and navy skirts for the girls. Having taken a bus from the Panama border to Conte, three gringos boarded the bus, including two with surfboards in large silver bags. I sat across from a Dutch woman who wasn't a surfer and was excited about the prospect of reaching Pavones and surviving the ride.

We gringos were clustered in the middle of the bus, with the school children sandwiching us in front and back. It was afternoon, and the children were headed home to Pavones or other villages along the road. They elected to pass the time by playing games like shoot the gringo in the back of a head with a squirt gun. For some reason, I was their lone target, but never put up much resistance, instead laughing with them as they laughed at me. But when they ran out of water, they played another game that involved blowing on my hair until I violently shook my head as if a bee were buzzing at my follicles. These games went on for quite some time before the children eventually lost interest, allowing me to focus on the surroundings.

From Conte it's roughly eleven miles to Pavones, although it takes an hour to cover that distance. While the drive from Golfito to Conte was relatively smooth and punctuated with bucolic scenery, this final leg was curvy, mountainous, and the first step toward a referral to a chiropractor. The road tilted unevenly in places, and basketball-size boulders and bucket-deep potholes contributed to the worsening conditions. The road cut through bulges of mountain where landslides had washed away entire stretches of road, the red earth turning into a labyrinth of tire tracks from what seemed to be the sturdiest of vehicles. As we ascended higher, white crosses occasionally dotted the shoulder, memorializing the road's victims. After climbing nearly one thousand feet, our sputtering bus crested a forested hill and provided our first unobstructed view of the Golfo Dulce since Golfito at a bend known as Cuervito.

"Holy shit, look at that," one of the gringos said.

Far below was Playa Zancudo, a perfectly crescent-shaped beach that shone white with sand and glinted from the sun. The beach, though, disappeared as we started a steep descent that included a series of hair-pin turns. The bus' brakes turned mushy and finally got a rest when we reached flatter ground at another T-intersection. Pavones was still five miles to the south along another stretch of jaw-breaking road, this one dancing with the coastline the entire way. My spine and joints were tingling by the time we'd crested the hill and now were numb. I was certain the bus' suspension had been deposited outside of Conte, yet the bus pushed on, turning left at the intersection and immediately suffering from a rocking motion that caused intermittent shaking, similar to a ride at the county fair. The school children were not concerned; some were reading magazines.

The ceiling of trees lowered, and the jungle closed in tighter still, its low-hanging canopy scratching the bus' roof. The sun shimmered off the Golfo Dulce's surface, and speckles of silver glittered above the deep blue hue. I could see land on the other side of the gulf that ended at the rocky outcrop of Cabo Matapalo, the surf spot that Terry's friend had visited during their stint in Dominical. The longer we stayed on this road, the closer Matapalo became, and the more it felt the road would end at any moment. It didn't seem like the bus was capable of making it much farther without endangering everyone on board. It pressed on, though, crossing several streams that tumbled out of the verdant forest and flowed under flimsy bridges, some of which were planks of wood just long enough to graze both banks. Car tires and other automobile parts were strewn along the river's banks, suggesting that these bridges had previously failed. (On my second trip to Pavones, one of the bridges had collapsed and vehicles were unable to cross the makeshift bridge; the driver parked the bus on one side of the bridge, and then we boarded another school bus that was parked on the other side.) Within a few minutes, we crossed a final bridge and the tires' outer rubber curled over the edge of the bridge's planks. We stopped at a piece of drift wood resting on two tree stumps that formed a bench.

"Pavones," the bus driver shouted.

With that, he turned off the engine, and everyone exited. I stepped off the rubber steps, and my body acted strangely on solid ground. My knees were radish-red from all the rubbing and slamming against the seat in front of me. My lower body had been flexed since Conte to avoid excessive shifting during the ride, and my buttocks and legs were cramping. The Dutch woman set her backpack down and lit a cigarette. After her first toke, she exhaled and said with pride, "I can't believe I made it to Pavones." The phrase conveyed accomplishment, but neither of us was quite sure where the town was exactly.

The stop itself was nondescript. There were ramshackle boats marooned on a gray-sand beach and a series of volcanic rocks rising above the water's edge. Piles of driftwood were scattered on the beach. The school children and other Ticos disappeared, and the only passengers left were us gringos. The two surfers slung their bags over their shoulders and walked down the road, which the bus driver could no longer navigate. I followed the narrowing road and soon found myself at a soccer field. I heard a voice when we exited the bus that got louder and louder as we neared the field, and then I noticed a tall Tico standing on a chair and delivering directions through a megaphone. Gerardo.

When I declined to eat *chancho* and got settled at Carol's, I walked down to the beach and sat on a log. There was only one person in the ocean, and he was standing on a surfboard and propelling himself with a paddle, an activity known as stand-up paddle boarding. The water was lake-like, placid. It was hard to believe that the ocean would become so rough in a day's time that surfboards would be broken and people would be injured. There was a group of swimmers at a small bend in the charcoal-colored beach where the Rio Claro flows into the gulf. Crabs scurried in all directions and curled into their shells at the slightest movement near them. Busted coconut shells were scattered among hulking pieces of wood. A few other people were on the beach, either sitting on logs or chucking rocks into the water and watching them skip. To my right was a blue tent pitched under the last stand of palms before the water's edge. A Tico with dreadlocks was camped there, and I learned he was the town's prominent drug dealer. He surfed and liked to play ping-pong at the Esquina del Mar, also known as the cantina, built by Danny Fowlie, the self-proclaimed King of Pavones who was now resurfacing in the town's affairs after a lengthy prison sentence.

To supplement his income, the drug dealer with dreadlocks used a machete to cut fruit and sold coconuts and bananas. He once worked for Carol's Cabinas but was fired after he stole a camera from a guest. When he surfed, he made sure someone watched his belongings, all of which quite easily fit into his tent. He slept with his surfboard along his side and fortified his teepee-shaped shelter with a palm-covered ceiling, which allowed the rain to slide off and away from his tent. When the first sprinkles came down before sunset, he sprinted out of his tent, his dreadlocks bouncing off his shoulders, attempting to save his sleeping bag, which he had left drying on a piece of wood. He brought it back inside the tent before the rain began in earnest, which it had by the time I walked back to Carol's.

A soccer game was underway, and the field's chalk lines were faint and uneven. After the festival had ended, tables were folded up and placed in truck beds and hauled away. Whoever wasn't on the beach was leaning against the chain-link fence surrounding the field and watching teenagers play soccer. Nearly everyone watching the game was in shorts and bare-chested if they were male, or in a bikini top and shorts if they were female. Everyone was talking about the incoming swell, either because they wanted to surf or because they wanted to make money off others surfing. I wouldn't say that I saw anybody "working" that day in the traditional sense of needing to be at a certain place at a certain time. If I entered a market, someone would follow me inside and tap the buttons on the cash register. If I ordered a hamburger at a restaurant, somebody would follow me inside and take my order and collect my money. When the transactions were finished, the people returned to the soccer field and conversed with others or swayed in hammocks and took a nap. And this was the busy season. In the slow season, like December, when the south swells are nonexistent, or at best an unexpected surprise, most businesses around the soccer field are boarded up and never open. If there are no surfers, there is no business. After all, locals aren't paying six dollars for a plate of chicken, rice, and beans.

My room at Carol's had two single beds and a purple hammock on the patio. I shared the room with a surfer from San Diego. It was a spartan room, its most noticeable luxury being the ceiling fans and mosquito nets above each of the beds. As the rain intensified that night, I lay in the hammock and listened to someone playing Bob Marley songs on an acoustic guitar; it was loud enough to slice through the pitter-patter of the rain. When the rain ended, I spent the evening drinking canned beers at La Manta, a two-story thatched roof bar and restaurant, with my room-mate and his friend, an aspiring actor from California. They had been surfing in Costa Rica for several weeks, when they heard about a sizable swell headed for Pavones. They boarded the first bus heading south. It was a several-day journey, which included a ferry ride and an overnight stop in Dominical. We got to know each other fairly well during the rain storm at Carol's, and they weren't amused when, after having recounted my days in Dominical and Terry's incorrect forecasts, I mentioned the possibility of a flat ocean.

"This isn't like at a ski resort on a powder day and then a few days after when there's still packed powder," the aspiring actor said. "There is one wave, and everyone wants it. It's all or nothing here. The computer models have called for it, and people are coming, and they will continue to come all night. It's going to be crowded. I like the pace and how different it is from the rest of Costa Rica, but I'm not coming here—and nobody is coming here—if the wave isn't here."

That may be, but surfers do often get skunked. Since Pavones faces south instead of west like most surf spots along the Pacific coast, and since it's tucked inside the mouth of Golfo Dulce, it's protected from usual incoming ocean swell patterns. Its bathymetry, which is to say the depths and shapes of underwater terrain, presents a revealing picture. (A bathymetric map basically paints a picture of the land under the water.) At Pavones, the sixty-foot contour topographical line approaches unusually close to the coast, starting at Punta Banco near Peter Aspinall's place and extending offshore to Pavones. This depth, along with the natural bend of the coastline, is why a swell from the south creates long, peeling waves that creep north along the shelf, according to Mike Watson of Surfline .com. Southwest swells also bring waves, but the waves really burst alive when swells come from due south, which was the current trajectory of this particular incoming swell.

Pavones is actually a series of points: south-southwest beyond the river mouth, the river mouth itself, and the cantina break, named after Danny Fowlie's Esquina del Mar beach bar. All three points face south, with the cantina serving as the end section since it's the northernmost point. While southwest swells can send surfers through the progression of breaks, including past the cantina, they often wrap in stronger and result in the closing out of the various sections. When swells come from due south, which tends to happen during the austral winter, one of the best surf experiences on the planet develops: all the points link together because the wave doesn't close out, creating rides of nearly a mile. In these conditions, surfers end their ride near the fiberglass boats at the fish house. Since swimming back to the river-mouth break from the fish house would take too long—not to mention accelerate the tiring of one's upper body—surfers walk along the beach back to the river mouth where they swim out to the southernmost point to catch the next wave.

The three of us sat at a wooden table at La Manta and watched surf movies on a large projector screen. My roommate's friend, the actor, was of average height with bushy black hair and fair skin, a rarity for an experienced surfer. My roommate was tall for a surfer—he was six foot seven, and a former college basketball player. He constantly picked at a gash on his foot, which he suffered during a previous surfing accident. Every table was occupied by tanned, muscular men and the women they were chasing, or maybe vice versa. Everyone was swapping surf stories, and I was out of my element. While I could relate to the chatter because it was similar to the conversations my friends and I held during winters in Lake Tahoe, I was simply ill-equipped to share surf stories, at least those that anybody at my table would be interested in hearing. My roommate said he worked "long enough at my jobs to earn enough money before I quit them to go surfing," while the actor worked at a hotel when he wasn't auditioning for parts in films or commercials or surfing at Rincon or Malibu.

As the movie played, geckos crawled over the screen, but everyone stayed focused on the footage. The energy intensified and the chatter volume increased when an amateur video filmed in Pavones flashed on the screen. There was obviously a big swell on April 9, 2007. The waves were the quality that everyone was hoping for in the morning, glassy and clean, and all agreed they would happy even if the waves were half that size. The walls of the waves were slow to collapse, and measured about twelve feet in height, or what is known as "double overhead." Surfers danced along the face, touching the rim before darting down for a few seconds, going back onto the lip, and repeating the process. It was a conveyor belt of waves, a reliable machine that pumped out wave after wave, each seemingly bigger than the previous one. I knew that the waves were increasing in size because, as they continued, I could no longer see the lower part of Cabo Matapalo, the rocky outcrop on the other side of the gulf. Jaws dropped and people hollered at the screen. One guy got so excited he bought a round of beers for our table. Fortunately, the beers arrived right before the screen suddenly went black and geckos were no longer visible. The video was over, and it was time to leave.

We walked in the dark along a muddy road to Carol's, careful not to step on any of the croaking frogs or startle a fer-de-lance. The surfers' pace was slow, and it made me think I might need to operate at a slower pace, not necessarily physically but in terms of my expectations with Gerardo. One American who lived in San José told me that Ticos from rural parts of the country can appear almost rude in their reluctance to open themselves up to foreigners and that they often consider people from San José foreigners. He assured me it's nothing personal. When we arrived at Carol's, three guys were seated in rickety plastic chairs, and I flopped into a nearby hammock, leaned back, and looked at the stars. I heard a soft voice coming from the direction of the chairs. I popped up and noticed the raven-black hair and the walnut-sized eyes, and recognized the voice from earlier that day at the cultural festival. It was Gerardo, and everyone was sarcastically calling him "the town mayor"; by the following summer he officially earned that title.

I wasn't aware that Carol had mentioned my desire to speak with him, something that only caused him to maintain his distance from me. As I pondered my next move from the safety of the hammock, Gerardo mostly listened to the others and rarely spoke. He interjected only if someone said something incorrect. The guys were locals, and they talked about development issues, increased drug use at the cantina, real estate scams, and the lack of girls in town. I suppose these topics aren't all that different from what three guys would talk about over beers in, say, Fargo, North Dakota.

To gain Gerardo's attention, I struck up a conversation with a guy who was walking to the hotel's community kitchen to fetch beers. His name was Freddy. He had paler skin than Gerardo and a thin mustache above a narrow mouth. Freddy and I talked about the time he was almost bitten by a shark after a friend's surfboard fin gashed his shin; about how as a kid there were no cars and the road from Conte was always closed and he would walk upwards of four miles from his home in Pilón, surfboard tucked under his arm, to surf Pavones; about how he learned to surf from his older brother and how these were his best memories; lastly, about the future of his town. When I mentioned the tuna farms, his face grew stern, he stated that nobody wanted them and that they are "*muy malo, amigo*"—very bad, my friend. He continued: "Let us be, leave us alone; we only want nature and surf. We feel it's important to protect these things." Freddy said if I wanted to know more about the tuna farms that I should talk to his friend Gerardo, who was sitting over there in a plastic chair, since he was the leader of the town in its movement against the farms.

I felt slightly guilty because I already knew that Gerardo was the symbolic leader of the town's opposition, and only broached the subject because I thought Freddy might convince Gerardo to speak with me. Freddy and I talked about many of the environmental concerns the tuna farms presented, including the ones that Peter Aspinall had considered in 2005. We spoke in Spanish, which I hoped would gain Gerardo's attention and respect. But after a few minutes of our high-pitched blabbering I noticed that he was leaving, and I promptly asked Freddy to introduce us. He waved him over. Gerardo was shy and almost apologetic that he had refused to speak with me earlier that day. He was now wearing a green short-sleeve polo shirt and khaki shorts. He said that he was busy with his new business, a restaurant overlooking the wave, and that he wasn't sure he could talk to me while I was here, even though I told him that I would be here indefinitely.

"I don't like to talk about myself," he said. "You should talk with Peter Aspinall. He knows more than I do."

I interpreted his response as a polite warning that he didn't trust me and to leave him alone. We shook hands, and he walked toward his bike, which was leaning against a tree, and then he pedaled away into the dark, dipping into a few puddles along the way. I took his spot in the circle of conversation. Freddy made excuses for his actions, saying that his friend had to be at work early in the morning and that he would talk with me eventually. Another guy in the circle, someone who had been present when Carol told Gerardo that a journalist at her place wanted to speak with him, was sympathetic to Gerardo.

"He doesn't trust you. A lot of Ticos don't trust until you've been here a while and they have looked at your face for a long time. It's a cultural thing. Once that happens, then they will talk. He also doesn't know your motives. For all he knows you could be working for the tuna farm company. You can see why he's skeptical."

Gerardo had reason to be skeptical: I later learned that the Granjas Atuneras had sent associates to Pavones to penetrate the town's power structure. I kept asking myself: What exactly went on down here? After Gerardo left, I sheepishly began discussing the brutal road conditions between here and Conte, as if everyone else didn't travel on the same road to get here. I was shocked at the poor quality of the road, but Carol reminded me that "Danny built that road. He built all the roads, the cantina, the church . . . he built everything in Pavones. You can't tell the story of Pavones without telling the story of Danny. Maybe you should focus on that first and worry about Gerardo later."

Developing my relationship with Gerardo would have to wait, I decided, and ultimately it never happened. For now it was necessary to find out why this place was once called "Danny Land." While rather frustrating at the time, this sequence of events made sense in the end, for I first needed to understand Pavones's role in surfing history before I could understand why its citizens would fight to protect its wave. Every wave, every surf town has a story, to be certain, but not many are like this one.

7 Danny Land

Surfing, alone among sports, generates laughter at its very suggestion, and this is because it turns not a skill into an art, but an inexplicable and useless urge into a vital way of life.
—Matt Warshaw, surf writer

Somewhere over Nicaragua, if Danny Fowlie's memory is correct, the pilot dipped the plane's left wing toward the Caribbean, then its right wing toward the Pacific, and began an initial descent into San José. Cumulus clouds mushroomed on the horizon and billowed from emerald-smeared mountains like geysers. Chocolate-colored rivers snaked through the jungle below, their surfaces a flickering palette, either dark from the shadows of trees or golden from the sun's rays. The pilot slalomed through the clouds with dart-like precision, handling the craft so efficiently that the ice cubes in everyone's drinks didn't clink. As the clouds thinned, the pilot steadied the plane over two large lakes, leveled its wings one final time, and aimed its silver-tipped nose due south toward Costa Rica's central valley.

The year was 1974, and the plane's passengers were Danny, his son (Dan Junior, also known as "Pequeño"—"Little One"), and his son's two friends. They wore khaki pants, plaid collared shirts, colored socks, and had slightly scuffed shoes. Everybody's hair was a shade of blonde, feathered, matted to their heads, and long enough in spots to drape over their ears. Danny was dressed like a variety of people that day: a doctor on his way to a clinic; a businessman on his way to a meeting; a drug dealer on his way to Colombia; a lawyer on his way to a trial. He was none of those things, at least not that day. On that day, he was a dad taking his son and his friends on a surf trip, abandoning the crowded beaches of Southern California in search of a secret wave in a remote jungle.

Everyone pressed their noses against the windows facing west, fixated on what seemed to be an endless stretch of peeling waves crashing into rocky bluffs along the contour of Nicaragua's Pacific coast. There was untouched surf down there, they were sure of that, but the wave they were chasing was still farther south, beyond the horizon. They were giddy at the thought of their own private wave; they could not see the gun-toting rebels hiding in the jungle expanse below, nor did they know that a civil war taking place. The war continued until 1979, when those gun-toting rebels marched toward Managua, the capital, assassinated key government officials, and seized control of the country. Danny wasn't immune to violence, but seated in the plane, he didn't care about Nicaragua or its rebels or its civil war. He wanted to buy a present for his children in the form a secluded paradise that included an undiscovered wave and acres of open land.

He figured it would be the ultimate playground for Gus and Dan Junior, his two sons, and Michelle, his daughter. All three had their specific interests: Michelle rode horses, Dan Junior surfed, and Gus rode motorcycles. The whole point of this reconnaissance mission was to seek an alternative to his family's life back in Orange County, a place to exhale and a place for Danny to bury his secrets and avoid what his future held: a thirty-year prison sentence for his role in the largest marijuana-trafficking ring in the western United States. The veracity of the charge was never actually revealed, in Danny's estimation, during court proceedings in the late 1980s and early 1990s, but in 1974, he was considered a surfer, a waterman, and a successful businessman.

Sitting in the airplane that day, at the age of forty-one, Danny looked like a stereotypical surfer: muscular, shaggy haired, laid back. But upon closer inspection, he wasn't a stereotypical surfer. For starters, most surfers don't charter planes to Central America. Secondly, most surfers don't travel with suitcases full of cash because they plan to buy a surf Eden in a foreign country. Despite his appearance, Danny Fowlie was not a stereotypical surfer. In fact, he never quite fit into any of society's accepted roles for an adult. He lived on the periphery and associated with others who lived on the edges. He was on this particular reconnaissance mission because he was acting on a tip from Kenny Easton, a kid from Pacific Beach in San Diego, where Danny himself had spent his formative childhood years. Instead of getting involved in typical stick-and-ball sports, Danny gravitated toward surfing and fishing, two activities that are typical of any beach town. He spent countless hours underneath Crystal Pier catching fish and at marinas gutting fish and washing boats; he gleaned and absorbed whatever information he could about people who earned a living off the ocean.

Born in 1933 in Minnesota, Danny came from a privileged background. His father, Dan Senior, was the owner of the Executive Transport Corporation, a company based in Dallas, Texas, which converted aircraft into executive planes and sold them to corporations. According to Danny, his father's company was the first to sell Douglas DC-3s to Braniff Airlines, which was also based in Dallas and operated from 1930 to 1982. The Douglas DC-3, a fixed-wing propeller plane that increased speed and capabilities of passenger jets, improved U.S. air transport in the 1930s and 1940s. His father's various transactions for Executive Transport made him a multimillionaire, and the dollars trickled down to his children. In 1941, Danny was eight when his family moved from Minneapolis to Pacific Beach, known as "PB" to locals. Danny was a teenager when his father died in 1949, and he inherited a sizeable chunk of his father's fortune. Heeding the advice of the family financial advisor, Danny put some of the money in offshore bank accounts and invested the rest in real estate. At sixteen, he bought a land parcel in La Jolla, north of Pacific Beach and near Windansea. This was a surf break frequented by legends like Pat Curren, who eventually moved to Hawaii to become one of the pioneers of big-wave riding. Danny fraternized with the Windansea crew, which accounted for most of the several dozen surfers on the California coast in the late 1940s and 1950s. Danny wasn't the most gifted surfer, but as was the case during his adult years, his friends were. Curren may have been the highest-profile member of the crew, but it was a lesser-known Windansea surfer named

Al Nelson who eventually accompanied Curren to Pavones and became etched in the annals of the town's sordid history.

Danny's house was just a few blocks from the ocean, and most mornings before school he dove and fished for lobster and abalone. Danny attended La Jolla High School and many of the school's classrooms overlooked Windansea. Danny sat by the window and daydreamed of being out there surfing instead of sitting inside a stuffy classroom pretending to care about English, which was never his best subject.

Danny was an entrepreneur, even as a child. Prior to enrolling in high school, he captured small animals such as skunk and rabbits in nearby canyons and sold furs to department stores that needed pelt for clothing products. He learned the skill after spending a summer with loggers near Minnesota's border with Canada. He also sold abalone and other fish he caught to restaurants in La Jolla. As a senior in high school, he sold tickets to extravagant parties held in his backyard. An admission ticket included steak, salad, beer, and the opportunity to watch the premier of amateur surf movies, which had been filmed at local surf breaks and as far away as Hawaii. His yard filled up so quickly that his parties were standing-room-only affairs. He then decided to raise ticket prices in an effort to maintain profits and enhance the experience for his guests with smaller crowds. But people came anyway and gladly paid the higher admission price.

With money and friends, Danny was well-liked, and people usually forged relationships with him because of what his money and social network could do for them. Although they may have been rather inconsequential at the time, these realities would betray him later and play a key role in the critical phase of his adult life. In 1950, after high school, he moved to Hawaii to surf and dive with a buddy from La Jolla. While in Hawaii, he constructed surf boards of light balsa wood. He purchased the wood at a lumberyard in Southern California and had it sent to Hawaii that summer knowing that he would be spending the winter of 1951 on Honolulu's Waikiki Beach. In 1952 he served in the Korean War, going back and forth between tours in Korea and rest and relaxation periods on bases in Hawaii. During one R&R stay in 1954, when the war's fiercest battles had ended, he went surfing at Makaha, the birthplace of big-wave surfing.

Makaha wasn't huge that day, but a photographer snapped a shot of Danny surfing and the photo landed on the October cover of *Sports Illustrated* that year. With the Korean War over, Danny returned to California and subdivided the La Jolla property he had purchased as a teenager. Under the guidance of Pat Curren's father, a La Jolla developer, he profited from the deal and focused his business interests on his abalone diving operation.

By the late 1950s, he had married a beauty queen and fathered three children with her: Dan Junior, Gus, and Michelle. The marriage didn't last long, and he divorced in the early 1960s when his abalone business was thriving; it was the first of three failed marriages for Danny. One of his employees in his abalone business was Kenny Easton, who got into a fight with his grandfather one night in their PB home. Kenny's grandfather was a drunk and the two exchanged words, then punches. After one particularly fierce blow from Kenny, his grandfather fell back, hit his head, and died. Kenny was charged with manslaughter and was sentenced to a jail term. Kenny was the prototypical beach rat: a surfer, schemer, diver, fisherman, and all-around hell-raiser. Despite having worked a litany of odd jobs, he was flat broke when he punched his grandfather and didn't have much in life, including an attorney.

As a PB guy, Danny had a soft spot for the kid. And as his boss, Danny claims he was able to reduce his sentence in large part because of an impassionate plea he made to the judge on Kenny's behalf. Danny argued that Kenny's grandfather had been a real son-of-a-bitch and that Kenny hadn't meant to kill him; it was just an accident stemming from an act of self-defense. The judge was persuaded, according to Danny, and Kenny was soon back working for him as an abalone diver. When pressed for details on how that exchange really went down, Danny's memory fails him. His memory doesn't fail him, though, when it comes to Kenny's role in the gringo discovery of Pavones.

During one abalone diving season in the mid-1960s, Kenny spun yarns about an endless left-hand point break in the southwest corner of Costa Rica, pure and untouched, like the girls they dreamed about in PB. In 1963, during one of his many beach-rat jobs outside the country, he stumbled upon the wave while working in the Golfo Dulce. He was harvesting copra, the dried, fleshy part of a coconut shell that's used for extracting coconut oil. He worked for a company based out of Golfito. The company sent him searching for copra toward Punta Banco, where Peter Aspinall arrived the following decade and hired Danny to clear trees and help him build a private air strip.

With no roads going in that direction, Kenny and his crew loaded mules and horses onto a series of canoes and boats and paddled through rivers splintering off the Golfo Dulce. As they moved down the shore toward Punta Banco, he noticed a point break near a river mouth: endless sets of waves, seemingly on a conveyor belt, coming in one after another. They were consistently overhead, measuring anywhere from six to eight feet in height. Kenny told Danny he was never able to surf the wave on a board because in 1963, no one was surfing there and no equipment was available.

Kenny did manage to body surf on several occasions though, and his stories emphasized that the wave was so long that he would run out of breath from exhaustion and bail on the wave before it quit on him. The wave took him so far from his origin point that the fastest way to catch the next wave was not to swim in the water but to swim to shore and walk several minutes back up the pebbly beach and then reenter the water. Truth be told, Kenny Easton was the first gringo to ride the waves of Pavones, albeit as a body surfer. Kenny's description of the smoothness and length of the wave, his noting that it broke left, which would benefit Danny's goofy-footed son, Dan Junior, and that it was untapped and ripe convinced Danny that he wanted to own that wave if he ever got around to flying to Costa Rica.

"Goofy foot" is the name for the stance in which one's right foot is placed forward on the board; "regular foot" is when one's left foot is there. Goofy-footers tend to prefer left-hand point breaks because they can use their stronger side to carve more aggressively into the wave as it breaks. Regular-footers tend to prefer right-hand point breaks for the same reasons. Regardless of which foot is forward, if you surfed, this wave sounded irresistible.

"I told Kenny this sounds perfect. Show me this wave on a map, and I'll go find it one day," said Danny.

Although Kenny's description of the wave was indeed influential, Danny wasn't quite prepared to seek it out in the mid-1960s. In addition to his abalone business, he started Leather Gypsy, Inc., a handbag company that grossed millions of dollars from national accounts with Sears and JC Penney, an interesting coincidence considering those were the companies he sold animal furs to as a child. Leather Gypsy, which he later sold for $3 million, became the financial springboard for the next phase of his life, the phase he and his supporters prefer to remember him by: as the principal landowner in Pavones from the mid-1970s to mid-1980s, a decade when he employed every local, planted thousands of trees, and constructed roads, a soccer field, a medical clinic, a cantina, a church, and a school. (All of these things are still in use except for the cantina, which arsonists burned to its concrete foundation in 2011.) United States officials, though, argued that Leather Gypsy became the financial springboard for the phase of his life that his detractors prefer to remember him by: as the purported leader of a drug-smuggling ring that distributed 53,000 pounds of marijuana, the majority of which was trafficked during his reign in Pavones.

One side believes the two phases are separate; the other side believes the two phases are intertwined. As for me, I believe Danny wanted to take his son and his friends surfing in 1974.

Kenny pointed to where the wave was on a map, and Danny put his finger on the spot to verify its location. So when his silver-tipped plane landed in San José that afternoon in 1974, he knew the next plane he would board was headed toward Golfito, near the border with Panama. He rented an airplane, a Piper Aztec, from a guy who owned a house on a golf course in the central valley. It takes about an hour to fly from San José to Golfito, and by the time the plane was over the Golfo Dulce, Danny saw breaking waves in the distance: white streaks that sliced through blue water, a misty spray above the hue, and both colliding with the green blanket of jungle spilling onto vacant beaches. This tapestry suggested that the stretch of shoreline was undeveloped: no trees had been cleared for homes, though some had been cleared for agricultural purposes; no people were working the waters; and no people were surfing. Inland there had been razing but there weren't any identifiable structures on the beach itself, just breaking waves, jungle, and ocean.

If this was today in Costa Rica, that kind of description would be undeniably appealing, but it was problematic for Danny. He needed some semblance of land owners down there, preferably with a large tract with a noticeable structure, because he had to be able to identify a property if he hoped to describe it to someone in Golfito. After the Piper Aztec skirted beyond Punta Burica, the thin strip of land that stabs the Pacific and forms the border between Costa Rica and Panama, he asked the pilot to double back and cruise north along the coastline again. On the second flyover, he spotted a small cut in the land that was cleared: it had a house and a crude-looking sawmill. Danny pounced.

"I knew it was an established farm, and to have an established farm means the owner has to have title to that property," says Danny.

Soon after the plane landed, Danny walked into a bar in Golfito, which was not so much a gritty port town in 1974 as a company town operated by United Fruit. Company towns mean that plenty of money flows through there at any given time, much of it spent on alcohol in dingy bars. Danny considered a bar an ideal location for finding strangers because drunks talk too much. He started talking with patrons on bar stools, rough-looking fellows who probably wanted nothing more than to kick the shit out of this gringo jabbering about a piece of land far away. But there are two types of people in this world: those who connect with people right away and those who don't. Danny connected with people immediately. And if they didn't feel the same connection, he had ways to make sure they did, one of which was that stacks of United States dollars always seemed to motivate people, especially in the southern reaches of Costa Rica. But at the moment, flashing wads of cash wasn't necessary. It turned out the owner of the property and its sawmill was one Claudio Lobo, known as Cullo, and he was sitting on the bar stool next to Danny.

"Where is your property in relation to the wave?" Danny asked in a mixture of broken Spanish and English.

"I got a spot out there, there are waves in front of my house, and there is a German who showed up and started surfing the waves. How much do you want to pay for it?"

"Well, I have to see it first."

"Then we'll go tomorrow."

"I was thinking we'd go right now."

Cullo escorted Danny, Danny's son, and his two friends to a nearby dock where they loaded a canoe with supplies and started navigating the tributaries that Kenny Easton had followed in 1963. When they reached Cullo's 250-acre ranch, Danny found what he had been looking for since leaving Southern California, and really what he had been dreaming of since Kenny spun those yarns.

"I could see waist-high waves. They were perfect, and they were wrapping around this point and right out in front of Cullo's property with its sawmill," Danny said. "Then I saw his dinky wheel that was maybe one meter across, a circular saw, and an old wooden table and other stuff. They were dangerous-looking things. I didn't want any of that stuff because they kind of scared me, this Mickey Mouse sawmill and all of his equipment, but I said I'd take the property."

Cullo's asking price was fifty thousand dollars.

"That is way too high. Make it thirty thousand. I'll give you ten thousand now and the other twenty thousand later when the paperwork is in order."

"Okay."

When they returned to Golfito, Danny gave him ten thousand dollars as a deposit. In the interim, he visited the public registry to begin the process of registering the land and hired an attorney to ensure the title was clear. With the title and registry process in motion, Danny returned to the sawmill property with his son and his friends. They camped on the beach and gazed at stars they couldn't see in Orange County because they were shielded by dense smog and an incessant glow of lights. They also packed their surfboards into the canoe and surfed. When they were finished camping, they returned to Golfito, where Danny found Cullo drunk in another saloon, paid him the remaining twenty thousand dollars, and walked him over to his attorney's office to sign the title. The title was officially in Danny's name, it was registered with the municipality of Golfito, and the 250-acre ranch near what would become the longest warm-water left-hand point break in the world cost him $120 per acre, a mere pittance compared to what oceanfront property went for in Orange County.

Over the next eight years, Danny continued to acquire properties in Pavones at a steady clip. By 1982, he had purchased 3,700 acres for a total of five hundred thousand dollars ($135 per acre). His land encompassed all four of the principal surf breaks and a fifteen-mile stretch of shoreline starting north of Pavones and ending in Punta Banco. If it sounds like Danny took advantage of the locals' ignorance and bought a paradise for next to nothing, sure, one could be convinced of that. But in his eyes it was nothing of the sort. The people wore rags and lived in stick huts with dirt floors; some huts were collapsed. The sturdiest of the huts would qualify as sheds in the backyards of dilapidated homes in Orange County. There were just three dozen families in the area, and everyone shared the same physical features, suggesting inbreeding. It really wasn't a far-fetched conclusion since there were only a few family names and nobody from the outside world was moving into town; intermingling was the only option.

There were no phone lines or electricity, no running water, no garbage service, no sewage system, no formal buildings, no local governance. Trash was everywhere, including rancid meat and feces, both human and animal. The stench intensified in the afternoon when the heat and humidity moistened the rubbish and boiled it. There weren't any roads connecting Pavones to the outside world, just paths suitable only for foot traffic and livestock. To commute to work on one of United Fruit Company's banana plantations, residents would either pile into boats and paddle to Golfito or walk through dense jungle to reach Conte, where there was a road. Many locals didn't bother working for United Fruit for the same reason they didn't attend school in Conte: the commute is too difficult. As for the condition of the land, there were ongoing fires, charred earth, and downed trees that were used to construct the ramshackle huts. What was virgin rain forest had been completely decimated and turned into a tropical cesspool.

"There were all these trees lying on the ground, dumped in the water, and I hated to see them cut down like that, these beautiful old trees, one hundred years old or more," said Danny. "It made me sick."

While others would reject such squalor, declare the people savages, and construct a fortified compound with armed guards and twenty-foot walls rimmed with barbed wire that was sharpened daily and confine themselves to the sweet waves, Danny did the opposite. He helped his new neighbors by immediately putting them to work. He financed everything: the materials, the jobs, the construction projects.

"Nobody really paid much attention to what he was doing," said fisherman William Mata. "I remember seeing yachts coming in and out of the area. I had no idea what was on them and didn't really care. Nobody else did either. Danny did lots of important things for Pavones."

Danny decided they needed new houses, but he didn't want to cut any more trees in the area, so he purchased lumber elsewhere in Costa Rica and transported it by boat to Pavones. To restore the forest, he planted tens of thousands of trees, including orange, cacao and avocado trees, all of which would produce fruit throughout the year to supplement the coconut and banana trees that grow like weeds. He hired agronomists from the United States and Costa Rica to monitor the reforestation process, including amending the soil to ensure quality harvesting from plants such as rice, corn, and peanuts. To get the existing soil and garbage and debris out of town, Danny had bulldozers, backhoes, and dump trucks shipped on barges to Pavones, where the machines would haul the junk out and deposit it somewhere that had refuse service.

"I employed everybody who was of working age," said Danny. "Of the ones who weren't old enough to work, I taught them how to drive tractors and taught them how to run machinery or other equipment. I even started a painting program for the women and children. I put them all to work, and they all loved me."

Self-flattery aside, it wasn't inconceivable that Pavones loved Danny, but the makeover wasn't complete. Since there weren't any roads and the government didn't seem interested in building them, Danny hired people to operate the heavy equipment and machinery to cut the road between Punta Banco and Conte. This is the treacherous red road that everyone who's ever been to Pavones has experienced. He financed the construction of the first school, church, and medical clinic, as well as the soccer field, a fish dock, and the cantina named Esquina del Mar, which was built before Costa Rica's maritime zone laws were instituted, meaning that it was built right on the beach with an unobstructed view overlooking the break. Until it was burned in 2011, there wasn't another beach bar quite like it in the world.

"I was the butcher, the baker, the candlestick maker," said Danny. "People came up to me with broken arms, all cut up, and I'd stitch them up and give them antiseptics."

In some cases, he did more than that. One night in 1982, Marvin, now a long-haired Pavones surfer with a rotting tooth, was in serious pain. He was thirteen at the time. He couldn't move, could barely speak, and nobody could help him. Danny, though, personally drove him on a motorized boat to the hospital in Golfito twenty minutes away. It turned out that Marvin had numerous blockages in his veins, which were affecting his heart.

"The doctor tell me that I die if I wait one hour more," Marvin told me in broken English. "I love Danny Fowlie. I will always love Danny Fowlie. He save my life."

Danny also built the Rancho del Mar, a sprawling estate on his original sawmill property, which became an exclusive boys' club. He'd fly in the most famous surfers in the world to surf his wave, and they'd stay at the Rancho del Mar, usually after knocking back a few beers at the Esquina del Mar. His ranch had multiple generators and all the cold beer and fresh fish you could ever want but that you could never have because you weren't important enough to be invited.

"The cantina was the entertainment capital," said photographer and filmmaker Spyder Wills, whose early footage of Pavones was featured in the 2006 film *Chasing the Lotus*. "Nobody was around. The waves weren't huge when I was there, although Rory [Russell] and Buttons [Kaluhio-kalani] promised me they could get big. But the waves kept wrapping around that point, and nobody was there. Fucking nobody was there, just iguanas crawling up the trees and down to the beach. It was perfect."

Danny's financing of these trips for Spyder and other surf photographers and writers led to pictures of and quotations from famous surfers playing in this magical place. These media gatherings continued for years, and Danny prefaced their trips like this: "You can't divulge the exact location; you can't even put the name of the wave; you can only say 'surfing somewhere in Costa Rica.'"

The journalists accepted his condition because, one, they wanted to surf the wave themselves as long as possible and, two, you don't cross Danny Fowlie.

"He was the boss man," Spyder Wills said.

"He imported people, surf stars like Gerry Lopez, who would come down and enjoy his private left," said Steve Pezman, publisher of the *Surfer's Journal*. "It wasn't known outside of a few surfers and I'm sure it was a magical time because surf travel didn't really start until the late seventies. It was always Danny's way to be popular and be loved. He no doubt enjoyed being this benevolent dictator. He surrounded himself with cultural figures with the trades to do work for him. He was kind of like the *patrón* [Spanish for boss]; he liked to be important. He also liked to test the loyalty because he wanted to see if you were attracted to him or the money."

When I interviewed Danny in 2011, I asked him what the final price tag was on his eleven-year reign in Pavones.

"I can't remember, and there isn't a receipt on my life."

The building projects, the exclusive boys club, and the famous surfers who sampled his world-class left made Danny feel special, but it wasn't long before the kingdom crumbled. One morning in 1985, when Danny was in Mexico, authorities raided his 213-acre ranch straddling California's Orange and Riverside Counties and claimed it was the headquarters for an international drug-smuggling ring, of which Danny was the leader. Authorities discovered that Danny didn't have great friends after all. Everyone confessed like songbirds in order to receive shortened prison terms or protect their assets. Authorities asked Danny to sing a tune.

"I said if that's what you're asking me to do you've asked the wrong guy. . . . I don't do that," said Danny. "The guys you're asking me to talk about, you don't talk about those guys."

So all of his friends in the United States sang tunes about Danny, who fought extradition from Mexico to the United States for six years. As he fought extradition, his empire in Pavones remained relatively intact. He held titles to his properties, and his friends were there taking care of them, which meant they were freeloading and surfing. But before he was sentenced to thirty years in prison in 1991, his empire vanished.

"We knew something wasn't right with this Danny," said one Tico who wished to remain anonymous. "He wasn't really into surfing, and we're from Costa Rica; we know what farms look like. And what he was doing didn't suggest he was a farmer. We kind of knew what he was up to, but nobody cared because it was Pavones, in the middle of nowhere, but we knew it could never last."

Many residents of Pavones and Danny's friends, including trusted confidante Al Nelson, believed that he would never set foot in Costa Rica again and would never be able to reclaim his land. As happens with all the well-known surf spots, the secret trickled out. As a result, more gringos arrived to surf a relatively empty, world-class left in paradise. And when these gringos were done surfing, they drank beers at the Esquina del Mar with Danny's friends. Some people thought it would be harmless to sell Danny's land with bogus titles to unsuspecting Nortes, and Tico squatters also claimed his territory and participated in the fire sale. Seriously, what would be the harm? They could make a few bucks, and Danny would remove the gringos, with force if necessary, once he came back. If that didn't work, Danny could show his original titles to the municipality in Golfito to prove he was the lawful owner, and the new occupant would have to give up the property.

Of course, it didn't quite work out like that because, well, people act funny when it comes to money. People sold lots in 1991 for ten thousand dollars that later sold for five hundred thousand dollars. But what his friends didn't consider—or what they didn't care about because they were making money off Danny—is that those unsuspecting Nortes who bought land from them would sell the land with bogus titles to other unsuspecting Nortes. They also didn't forecast the incoming squatter movement that endangered every gringo's life in Pavones. While Danny was in prison, his land was bought and sold so many times that those titles that were bogus in 1991 became legitimate by the time he was released from prison. Good luck getting a property owner who spent half a million dollars on an oceanfront lot to walk away from it because you wave a piece of paper stating you were the owner in 1985. Yet Danny would have to do just that because his 3,700 acres had been sliced up into small parcels and sold to the highest bidders—or stolen by the most violent of communist squatters—in the years he was gone.

"It became overrun by guys that wanted to make as much money as they could off my land, buying a piece and chopping it up like a piece of pizza," said Danny.

The benevolent dictator who ruled Pavones for nearly a decade returned to reclaim his land in the summer of 2005 when the town was entering yet another critical junction and he had finished serving eighteen years of a thirty-year prison sentence. That's the year *La Gaceta* and other media outlets began publishing stories about the tuna farms. Peter Aspinall felt the future of the town hinged on environmental issues related to the tuna farms, which threatened the wave and the local economy. Residents listened to Peter's concerns because nobody makes money in Pavones if something happens to the wave. But unlike 1974, when everyone supported Danny, not everyone was excited to see him return in 2005.

While these tuna farms Peter was preaching about sounded like a horrible idea, the town was nervous about the fallout from Danny's return. If Danny took his land back, who cared about a tuna farm? There would be nowhere to live. So while their ears were open to Peter's concerns, their eyes were fixed on Danny and what tactics he would use to reclaim his land. And then there were others who had their eyes and ears tuned to Danny at all times and ignored the tuna farms because they wanted Danny to disappear. After all, they would be on the receiving end of Danny's reclamation tactics.

Peter, though, wasn't convinced that he and Danny couldn't work together to fight the tuna farms. Towns can protest and complain all they want, but environmental battles are won or lost in the court room. You don't get into a court room without an attorney, and you don't get an attorney into a court room without money. Peter was confident Danny had money because, well, Danny always had money. But it wasn't clear how much money Danny had in 2005, or if he would even want to help save a town that turned its back on him and stole his land. Nevertheless, after Peter Aspinall hired Álvaro Sagot in 2005, he prepared himself for a fight with a person who had the governmental support of SETENA, the social support of the community, the scientific support of research, and financial support from one of Costa Rica's most successful tuna boat owners. Or at least that's what Eduardo Velarde thought.

8   Tuna Coast

Regardless of the resources on which the economy rests—farmed soil, grazed or browsed vegetation, a fishery, hunted game, or gathered plants or small animals—some societies evolve practices to avoid overexploitation and other societies fail at the challenge.
—Jared Diamond, *Collapse*

Coiba Island in the Gulf of Chiriquí off the southern Pacific coast of Panama is a sea horse–shaped island in what can only be described as a tropical paradise. Thick vegetation spills onto glinting stretches of beach, which provide an apron leading toward turquoise waters. But while its shape suggests a different marine animal, Coiba Island is all about yellowfin tuna. In fact, the entire coastline from Coiba Island north to the Golfo Dulce was once called the Tuna Coast. Peter Aspinall, upon building his ranch in the 1970s in the hills above Punta Banco, remembers the incessant blinking of tuna clippers out at sea; the glow from the sheer number of boats resembled a floating city. But over time, the glow dimmed because there weren't as many boats because there weren't as many tuna. Yet there were abundant numbers of yellowfin in the waters around Coiba Island, and so Manuel de Iglesia aimed his boats south and refocused his fishing efforts there. He didn't know it, but his boats were about to go on a tuna spree.

De Iglesia had licenses for three fishing boats to operate in these waters, and his typical yield was a combined 1,200 tons of yellow fin when his boats returned to port. At the time he visited Velarde in the marine park in 2003, de Iglesia was fetching $2,000 per ton of tuna, or roughly

$2.4 million, every time he docked. His boats made about seven trips per year and his gross receipts were between $20 and $60 million depending on the price per ton. He sold tuna to Sardimar, the largest cannery in Costa Rica, which cans tuna almost exclusively for export. Over lunch, Velarde wondered why de Iglesia had an interest in farming yellowfin tuna if his yields were so lucrative.

"He told me that he used to come back to port every thirty days, and now he comes back every fifty days," Velarde said. "He also said that yellowfin used to go for $600 a ton and now it is $2,400 a ton. The price was going up because there were no more tuna, and the ones he was catching were smaller. He knew he'd be out of business before long, so he wanted to know if there was any way to breed tuna before the last one was caught."

That hardly was a concern in the early 2000s around Coiba Island. Although nearly 180 local fishermen troll those waters for subsistence, the Panama government opened the waters to commercial fishermen. However, the tuna clippers decimated the fragile coral reefs surrounding the island with barbaric, destructive fishing methods that were new at the time. The tuna clippers caught fifty to one hundred tons in one loop of the island; this went on for months. Eventually, because of pressure from the local fishermen who were outmanned and lacked the size and capacity of the international tuna clippers, as well as from environmental groups, the Panamanian government issued a moratorium on yellowfin fishing around Coiba Island (it allows sport fishing because it uses less destructive fishing methods). That's when de Iglesia pointed his three boats north again, toward Costa Rica, but this time his destination was Puntarenas, where he would visit Eduardo Velarde, a well-known aquaculturist at a marine park.

One billion people rely on seafood as part of their daily diet, and 2.6 billion people get at least 20 percent of their animal protein from seafood. Since the 1970s, seafood consumption has consistently risen in tandem with overall food consumption. A 2005 study suggested that, on average, each person on earth annually eats thirty-six pounds of seafood. There are all sorts of edible fish in the ocean, but the most widely eaten is tuna. In 2010, commercial fisheries caught more than ten million tons of tuna for the global market. From sagging wooden shacks in West Africa to high-end sushi restaurants in Tokyo, people can't seem to eat enough tuna.

While humans eat more tuna than any other type of fish in the ocean, the average size of tuna caught in 2010 was about half the size of the average tuna caught twenty years previously. This is a troubling trend for two reasons: one is that since the tuna being fished these days are smaller in size and people are eating more tuna meat, meeting the demand requires catching at least twice as many fish, which, in turn, points to an increased likelihood of a precipitous decline in the number of tuna in the ocean; the second reason is that if the tuna are 50 percent smaller than before, fishermen aren't catching physically mature tuna but juvenile tuna that haven't spawned, so they are disrupting natural mating patterns and thereby also contributing to the decline in tuna populations. In contrast to the recreational fishermen, like those around Coiba Island, and traditional fishermen, like William Mata, commercial fishermen are catching tuna at a faster rate than the tuna can reproduce.

"It's a pity because bluefin spawn once a year and it's a cold species," Velarde said. "Yellowfin, though, is a tropical fish that likes to fuck all year long. Like people in tropical places, yellowfin are dancing and spawning all year long. There is no reason for yellowfin to suffer the same fate as the bluefin."

In *Four Fish: The Future of the Last Wild Food*, Paul Greenberg writes:

The conventions that govern tuna allow any tuna-fishing nation to fish in any other tuna-fishing nation's waters, provided the fishers stay within an overall quota of fish caught—a quota that no nation seems to have the resources or the attention span to adequately monitor or enforce. Catches from the high seas have doubled in the last half century, and much of that catch increase has come in the form of tuna. Moreover, because tuna cross so many boundaries, the way international tuna treaties are set up means that even when tuna do tarry in any one nation's territory, they are still technically catchable by any other treaty member nation.

Tuna is the most popular fish to the consumer and the least regulated fish in an industry that is difficult to regulate, and the reasons for both have a lot to do with tuna's characteristics. There are four dozen species of tuna, a name derived from the Greek *thuno*, which means "to dart." Of those species, the most heavily fished are bluefin, yellowfin, skipjack, and bigeye. The Greeks, who were the first to fish tuna in the Mediterranean Sea in second century AD, were obviously very perceptive. Tuna have been clocked swimming at more than forty miles per hour, and they are menacingly nimble, agile and twitchy. Not only are they faster than most ships, but they can outmaneuver and outdistance them. And their habitat encompasses nearly all the oceans. While these traits would seem to make such an unruly fish difficult to catch, particularly for ancient civilizations, tuna are rabid eaters and will bite at anything, including hooks without bait. Basically, they are not easy to chase, but they are easy to trick.

Despite the size of a specific tuna or the water temperature they prefer, all tunas have a similar body shape that is designed for swimming efficiently. Since they rely on movement to pass oxygen-rich water over their gills, a process that creates high metabolic rates (and a never-ending appetite), tuna can't stop swimming or they will suffocate. They also don't have any eyelids and are unable to close their eyes, and since stopping isn't possible, they sleep as water passes over their gills.

Carl Safina, an oceanic expert and tuna admirer, observes that "what allows a tuna to generate such dangerously explosive thrust, merely by wagging its tail, is a package of natural adaptations that exquisitely integrate specialized muscles, specialized circulation, and specialized external design. Virtually anyone who sees a living tuna is moved by the beauty of a life so energized and yet so mysteriously cloaked by the sea. Tuna provoke an intensity of interest that few other creatures engender."

About two-thirds of the world's tuna catch derives from the Pacific Ocean, which isn't surprising since the largest tuna-consuming nation (Japan) and the one with the most expansive commercial tuna fishing operation (Australia) are both in the Pacific. Of the species caught by commercial fishermen, bluefin is the most coveted because of its impressive size and quality of flesh. Bluefin, which swims in colder waters than the others and thus develops a higher fat content, has generated record prices at fish markets.

In January of 2012, a 593-pound bluefin tuna sold for a record $736,000 at Tokyo's Tsukiji Market, the world's busiest seafood market, where the equivalent of five million meals ferry through each day. A year later, a 498-pound bluefin sold for $1.76 million; this fish was auctioned for twice as much and weighed nearly a quarter less than the previous record-setting fish. By the time this book is published there will undoubtedly be another record set at Tsukiji because of the limited supply and high demand for the most prized tuna. While bluefin is the largest species of tuna, weighing several hundred pounds and often more than one thousand pounds, it's not necessarily the sheer size that attracts record prices and worldwide attention but the combination of size and quality of meat. Referred to as *toro* or *maguro* on menus, bluefin meat is succulent and has the highest body-fat content of any tuna, upwards of 15 percent. The excess body fat is the result of it swimming in deep, cold waters; other tuna species that prefer shallower, warmer waters have lower body-fat content.

Japan consumes about 80 percent of the 60,000 tons of bluefin caught worldwide. The country imposes no quotas on its fishermen because it denies the idea that the fish is in trouble—a peculiar stance considering that practically every study in the past decade suggests that the species is nearly extinct: the eastern Atlantic bluefin has seen its breeding numbers decline by 75 percent since the 1950s; the western Atlantic bluefin's breeding numbers are down 82 percent since the 1970s; the north Atlantic bluefin has declined 90 percent in twenty years; and while the Pacific bluefin is faring marginally better, experts largely agree that global bluefin tuna stocks are down 75 percent since the 1950s.

"The bluefin tuna industry is in the process of fishing itself to death," Greenpeace oceans campaigner Karli Thomas told *Japan Today*.

The International Commission for the Conservation of Atlantic Tunas (ICCAT) was established in 1969 to address the growing concern over the effects of the popularity of tuna in the United States and Europe. In all, there are thirty species that ICCAT watches. Tuna, however, has not been managed as originally intended. More than two decades ago, in 1991, Sweden proposed that the bluefin be listed as endangered, a distinction that comes with special protective status and becomes off-limits to fishing.

But the United States and Japan rejected Sweden's proposal, which came at a time when the fishing of bluefin hadn't even begun in earnest yet.

"What we have seen up until now, with both the exploitation of wild fish and the selection and propagation of domestic fish, is a wave of psychological denial of staggering scope," Greenberg writes in *Four Fish*. "With wild fish we have chosen, time after time, to ignore the fundamental limits the laws of nature place on ecosystems and have consistently removed more fish than can be replaced by the natural processes. When wild stocks become overexploited, we have to turn to domestication."

The earliest record of catching fish for food comes from around forty thousand years ago. The early methods were crude if not ineffective, and consisted of people attempting to grab fish with their bare hands. In time, fishing methods became increasingly more sophisticated, eventually including the use of spears and handheld nets and poles. Pole fishing, also known as rod and reel, with a line and reel attached to the pole and a hook attached to the line for snaring fish, is what most recreational anglers do. Recreational anglers are not interested in selling their fish. Some, in fact, are not interested in eating or even catching fish; they figure cold beers or conversation with friends or family is time well spent, regardless of the outcome. They cast with a smile whether they are on a boat in the Pacific Ocean, standing on the bank of a river in Montana, or sitting on a dock in Maine.

It's impossible to determine a reliable figure for the number of recreational anglers in the world, mostly because it's impossible to devise an accurate way of documenting those who fish in this capacity, but rough estimates present a liberal figure of one hundred to two hundred million people. As long as these types of fishermen catch fish with a spear, net, or pole—or even if they combine methods for increased efficiency—they won't exhaust the number of fish swimming on earth. The reason is twofold: first, they don't invest enough time extracting fish out of the water, and second, their methods for extracting fish out of the water are inefficient. Both parts of the equation allow fish to reproduce at a faster rate than recreational fishermen can catch them. But while there may be only a few hundred million people who fish for recreation, there is a much larger population that eats fish because it needs to, or eats fish because it likes to. Given such expectations, a different type of fisherman in terms of capability, efficiency, and philosophy is needed. This other type of fisherman is not interested in having a father-and-son bonding session on a river in the Rocky Mountains.

Commercial fishing involves people catching fish and selling them to others in exchange for money. One person invests time and money to catch a fish and someone else pays that person a specific amount of money for the fish. If the person who invests time and money into catching a fish doesn't catch a fish or can't sell a fish, that person becomes broke and is no longer a commercial fisherman; that person must find another occupation. So to keep from going broke, commercial fishermen have devised methods and modified equipment to ensure they catch fish.

Large-scale commercial fisheries as we know them today largely began in Europe, with fishermen going after herring during the Middle Ages and later cod in the 1400s and whales throughout the 1600s. The methods used were mostly the same as they were before, though their nets got bigger, their poles got stronger, their lines grew longer, and their boats grew larger and capable of housing more fishermen and storing more fish. At that point, fishing became one of the earliest segments of a globalized economy. From there, methods and equipment evolved to the point that the worldwide commercial fishing industry now generates $80 billion and employs two hundred million people (roughly the same as the number of recreational fishermen).

On any given day, there are four million commercial fishing boats operating in the oceans, a vast area that covers 130 million square miles, or 71 percent of the earth's surface. Of this total area, 64 percent is under no jurisdiction, which means it is not regulated by any specific country. This equates to an area one and half times the size of earth's land mass and results in a virtual free-for-all on the high seas. To expect the commercial fishing industry to police itself is like parents leaving their house to a group of teenagers they know will be throwing a party, stocking the cabinet with alcohol, leaving a box of condoms on the table, and expecting them all to behave.

Even in parts of the ocean where a country has jurisdiction, fishing and marine policies are unenforced—and that's assuming policies are in place. A country may not enforce its policies for two main reasons: either it doesn't care about what happens in its waters, or it does care about what happens in its waters but doesn't have the capability to monitor the situation, which kind of means it doesn't really care. Either way, those four million vessels pretty much do as they please, and the more fish they catch, the more people eat and the more money the fishing industry makes. From their perspective, the system works. If there are fewer fish, then they either need to spend more time fishing or devise better methods and more sophisticated equipment to increase their catch.

Many enjoy the money that flows through their country as a result of its fishing prowess. In fact, the leading fish-consuming nations subsidize commercial fishing companies in order to help them become increasingly efficient; nearly 40 percent of the $80 billion generated by the global commercial fishing industry is from government subsidies, with the largest subsidy coming from Japan ($5.5 billion). With governments committing a significant amount to support commercial fisheries, it's no surprise then that those companies have been influencing regulatory agencies. These agencies' responsibility is to design and manage policies that reflect the interests of commercial fisheries while balancing them with a serious effort to protect fish. Yet all too often these regulatory boards are comprised of those who are sympathetic to the commercial fishing industry and who reject proposals that contain a reduction in quotas or an elimination of destructive fishing methods so as not to be perceived by the industry as antibusiness.

"People ought to be worried about anybody who disregards the precautionary approach," Niaz Dorry, a former Greenpeace activist, told Paul Molyneaux for his book *Swimming in Circles*. "Every time the precautionary approach is disregarded, it is because somebody said I can't deal with these limitations and still make money. These people who want to pioneer aquaculture need to remember the Hippocratic Oath: first do no harm."

In Costa Rica, two government institutions that regulate fishing: the Ministerio de Ambiente y Energía, or Ministry of the Environment and Energy, manages inland fisheries, as well as subsistence and sport fishing; Instituto Costarricense de Pesca y Acuicultura, the Costa Rican

Fishery and Aquaculture Institute (INCOPESCA), meanwhile, deals with the more commercial aspects of fishing, including drafting legislation and managing resources such as aquaculture projects (inland and marine). INCOPESCA grants licenses for several types of commercial fishing operations, most notably shrimp and tuna, and to a lesser degree sardines. This is the agency that granted Manuel de Iglesia the right to fish tuna in Costa Rican waters—and it was the agency that would have to issue Velarde a fishing permit for the tuna farms.

The agency allows shrimp vessels to use the method of bottom trawling, which involves casting a net—some of them can be one hundred feet wide—into the sea and essentially scraping the floor of the seabed for the purpose of catching shrimp. As the boat moves, the net is dragged behind, scooping up everything in its path—essentially like a bulldozer plowing a field. The size of the net's mesh is small because it's designed to catch shrimp, but it also catches everything the same size or larger. Bottom trawling produces an exorbitant amount of what is known as "bycatch," unsought animals that are caught and of little value to fishermen. Bycatch often includes fish, dolphins, turtles, and sharks. Usually fishermen are only interested in the specific species they are fishing, so anything that isn't a shrimp in the net is discarded back into the water, rendered useless and usually unable to carry out its role as part of a functioning marine ecosystem. (Bottom trawling also rips up coral, sponges, and rocks on the seabed.)

The percentage of bycatch varies wildly depending on the study, but the World Wildlife Fund estimates that more than three hundred thousand whales, dolphins, and porpoises die each year from being entangled in nets. Many experts estimate that 80 percent of a shrimp trawler's haul is in the form of bycatch. Modifying the size of the mesh netting to match the physical characteristics of the intended catch can in some cases be a way to reduce bycatch, but since shrimp are obviously smaller than whales and dolphins and sharks, this specific modification will do little to reduce bycatch for shrimp trawlers in Costa Rica. Fishermen aren't really concerned with bycatch, but there is evidence to suggest that the method of bottom trawling is having an impact on the waters they fish.

The *Tico Times* reported that shrimp yields declined by more than 50 percent in a decade, totaling about 1,500 tons of shrimp in 1997 and only 700 tons in 2007. If the 80 percent figure is applied to calculate the amount of bycatch, that would equate to 3,500 tons of bycatch discarded into Costa Rica's waters in 2007. And that's the impact of just several dozen shrimp boats in a single year along a coastline that ranks sixty-eighth globally in terms of length. While Costa Rica is a minor player in the grand scheme of shrimp trawling, it still wastes an enormous amount of marine life in the form of bycatch; yet there have been some consequences for Costa Rica because of its shrimp trawling industry.

Between 2009 and 2012, the United States imposed a ban on Costa Rican shrimp imports after American inspectors felt that INCOPESCA wasn't effectively punishing shrimp trawlers who were not using a special device to prevent sea-turtle bycatches. (U.S. law requires any boat exporting shrimp to use this device.) Then in 2012, six nongovernmental organizations filed a motion with the Costa Rican Supreme Court to prevent INCOPESCA from allowing foreign shrimp trawlers in Costa Rica's waters (a resolution is still pending). INCOPESCA could be tougher on shrimp trawlers, but sanctioning other countries' vessels for unsavory practices in Costa Rica's waters might be viewed as hypocritical and perhaps cause a boomerang effect on a country that employs 25,000 Ticos in its fishing industry and whose fishing exports were valued at more than $138 million in 2002.

"Costa Rica fishermen are notoriously known around these parts as pirates out there on the high seas," says David Boddiger, editor of the *Tico Times*.

> They have a reputation for doing pretty much whatever they want, from exceeding quotas to illegal shark finning, where they cut the fin off a shark, keep the fin because it's valuable, and toss the carcass back into the water [where it usually dies]. And it's tough for the Costa Rica government to do anything about it because not only do they not know what's happening in another country's waters, they haven't been very good about knowing what's happening in its own waters. I mean, it wasn't until 2011 before our president shut down the private dock in

Puntarenas on the Pacific coast, where they were unloading all the shark fins for years, and started requiring all boats to be inspected at the public dock.

In addition to shrimp licenses, INCOPESCA issues tuna licenses, and there are about two dozen tuna vessels legally allowed to operate in Costa Rica's waters, predominantly boats from the United States, Mexico, Panama, and Venezuela. These boats are after the smaller tuna species like yellowfin and bigeye. To catch these tuna, the agency allows purse seining and long-lining. The first method involves setting a large circular net with an opening that can be pursed, or yanked closed, at the bottom, thus capturing everything within the net. For catching fish that usually congregate together, purse seining is an effective method. Tuna, however, are not that type of fish, so purse seining for tuna requires large nets that, like the nets used in shrimp trawling, result in a tremendous amount of bycatch. Moreover, purse seining produces even more bycatch when tuna fleets use fish aggregation devices (FADs).

FADs, which are illegal in Costa Rica but are used by foreign tuna vessels anyway, are floating mechanical objects with antennas. Fish avoid predators and believe there is safety in numbers; FADs are designed to send out signals to attract tuna, but by default they attract other fish as well. Before long there are all sorts of fish congregating around a FAD, which was placed there by the world's most efficient predator. When fish are detected around the FAD, a signal is sent to the tuna vessel, which then cruises over to the FAD, drops the purse seine, and hauls in its catch.

Since tuna are bigger than shrimp, the nets used to catch them are designed with larger holes, thus sparing anything smaller than tuna. A typical purse-seine catch without the use of a FAD is about a thousand tons, with two hundred to four hundred tons of that being bycatch, which includes juvenile tuna that has not yet spawned. The *Tico Times* reports that Costa Rica established satellite monitoring of FADs in 2009, but it may be that the illicit drug trade was more of a focus than illegal fishing practices. While strengthening detection and enforcement capabilities was a step in the right direction, the country doesn't have officials monitoring the boats twenty-four hours a day; officials are also usually off on weekends and holidays. But even if they worked around the clock, vessels can tamper with transmitter signals to make sure their FADs are undetected.

In addition to shrimp trawling and tuna purse seining, INCOPESCA permits the use of long-lining to catch tuna. Long-lining consists of using a single line, oftentimes more than eighty miles in length, barbed with as many as five thousand baited hooks spanning that distance. Floats are used to support the line, and both live and frozen bait fish are attached to the hooks. Considered by many to be the most destructive of all the commercial fishing methods, long-lining, according to World Wildlife Fund estimates, kills thousands of other ocean fish, whales, seals, dolphins, and sharks every year, all of which end up as bycatch. The WWF also reports that more than 250,000 turtles are caught by longlines and that 300,000 seabirds are killed by longlining; more than two dozen species of seabirds are in a threatened status because of long-lining. In all, 30 percent of the world catch of tuna is caught this way.

The last method approved by INCOPESCA—and the least used method because it yields the smallest amount of fish—is rod and reel from the deck platform of a tuna clipper. Since the tuna vessels operating in Costa Rica are foreign and unload their catches on foreign docks, there is no way to track the amount of tuna extracted from the country's Exclusive Economic Zone (EEZ). This zone, where countries have sole rights to their marine resources, usually extends out two hundred miles from a country's coastline. Reliable shrimp and tuna catch figures are difficult to find, but a recent study by the University of British Columbia stated that from 1950 to 2008, shrimp trawlers in Costa Rica unintentionally caught more than 870,000 tons of sharks, rays, and boney fish as bycatch; half of that tonnage was discarded unused.

While these fishing methods are largely considered the driving force for the alarmingly low bluefin tuna numbers today, one must remember that someone is catching this tuna, fattening this tuna, and distributing this tuna for one reason: someone is *eating* all this tuna. There is no clear culprit in the pie chart of blame for the decline of bluefin tuna, but citizens hope that regulatory agencies do manage these sorts of things. And with studies indicating that between 80 and 90 percent of the world's total bluefin tuna stock has been depleted due to overfishing, the International

Commission for the Conversation of Atlantic Tunas (ICCAT) has come under attack. The problem with this organization, as with INCOPESCA in Costa Rica, is that its hands are tied and the rope around its wrists was placed by those interested in making money off fish. In other words, the entities making money off fishing in Costa Rica are the ones expected to regulate how much money can be made.

"Things don't move too fast in INCOPESCA because the people from the private sector, who also belong to the commercial fishing sector, are on the board of directors," Herbert Nanne Echandi, INCOPESCA's executive president from 1998 to 2002, told the *Beach Times* in 2008. "There's always a lot of pressure on the board of directors from the commercial sector."

In 2007, scientists recommended that in order to start restoring the amount of bluefin tuna left in the ocean, ICCAT must institute an annual quota of 15,000 tons; instead, ICCAT imposed a quota of 30,000 tons—and the actual catch that year was 60,000 tons. These figures suggest the inefficiency of regulatory agencies that manage the seas, both in the Atlantic Ocean and the Golfo Dulce. These agencies set policies that encourage fishing, perhaps even overfishing, and are helpless in enforcing their protective policies and punishing those who disregard them.

"Tuna fishing can no longer continue being practiced as it has been practiced for the last ten, fifteen years," Robert Mielgo told Richard Ellis, author of *Tuna: A Love Story*. A former tuna fisherman who created a consulting firm to assist tuna farms in becoming more sustainable and law abiding, Mielgo pointed out that "if we continue, it's the end of the sector as such—because of pure greed. The more we overproduce, the less price for the fish. The time is no longer of debating: the empirical scientific facts are on the table. The question is how are we going to regulate, how are we to punish, how are we going to control?"

Maybe farming tuna would save the species.

By the late 1980s, fisheries were collapsing in Port Lincoln, Australia, the epicenter of bluefin tuna fishing. Situated along a bay in the western part of the country, in the state of South Australia, Port Lincoln developed the country's largest commercial fleet of tuna boats; they were capable of catching as much tuna as the ocean could throw at them and distributing it to Japan, their best customer. In previous decades, they had done just that. But by the late 1980s, Port Lincoln was teetering on the edge; its fishermen were so effective that they overfished southern bluefin tuna. Tuna became scarce: boats were coming back lighter, some were coming back empty, and what had been a way of life for decades was coming to an end. But out of the ashes came something known as tuna farming, an experimental way of catching and fattening fish. It combined cutting-edge science with new fishing methods and sophisticated equipment. The result was the most efficient and lucrative commercial fishing system the world had seen, maximizing profit in the classic exchange process between commercial fishermen and consumers.

In 1989 fifty young tuna were captured and held in Port Lincoln for observation by Australian fishermen and Japanese scientists. The tuna were transferred to feeding pens, where they would be fed until they reached a sufficient weight to be sold. From there, the process would be adjusted: taking into account market price, the value of the Australian dollar versus the yen, and the size of the tuna, they would be kept in the feeding pens for several months to a year before being sold. According to Ellis, when the tuna are considered big enough to be slaughtered, a platform is lowered into the pen and divers in wet suits prepare to kill the fish. One diver shoves the fish onto a ramp while another grabs its gills and hauls it partially out of the water. After a metal spike is pounded into its brain, another metal rod is rammed down its backbone to ensure the dying tuna will not tense up and spoil the tender meat. This particular method of killing tuna in pens and preparing them for distribution is considered more humane than a method once used in the Mediterranean Sea. Starting in Croatia, Port Lincoln tuna barons introduced tuna farming to the region in the 1990s; by 2000 every country on the Mediterranean had offshore tuna pens. In some of those pens, tuna were corralled into the corner and shot with rifles.

In the 1996 book *Tuna and the Japanese* by Takeaki Hoiri, it was reported that the idea of tuna farming came from a Japanese tuna auctioneer who went to Australia to find people to catch tuna and put them in a tank, where they would be fattened for a few months, killed, frozen, and shipped to Japan. This may be true, but the system was refined in Port Lincoln, where setting up a tuna farm was relatively inexpensive; the fishermen had the boats, and it cost about $75,000 to place a pen with nets, buoys, and anchor in the water. The one tricky part was finding the tuna to bring back to the pens to be fattened. Initially, tuna were caught with baited hooks and transferred to the pens, but that method often resulted in the tuna flesh being compromised. Then a Port Lincoln fisherman implemented the idea of capturing juvenile tuna by purse seining, which, as we have seen, requires large nets and results in a tremendous amount of bycatch.

Before tuna farms, commercial fishermen were mainly interested in catching adult tuna that could be immediately sold. But with tuna farms, any size of tuna would do, which was a good thing from the point of view of fisheries faced with a scarcity of adult tuna. Now, with the benefit of hindsight, we know that purse seining large quantities of juvenile tuna instantly effectively strips them of their ability to ever reproduce and is thus a very effective way to deplete a population. Of course, that wasn't a concern in the 1990s when tuna farming transformed Port Lincoln. There, most were more worried about where to stash all the money that was being generated; after all, the town has the most millionaires per capita in Australia.

Fisheries preferred this new method of tuna farming to the old methods of tuna fishing, not because it would help preserve the population of tuna but because it made them a more valuable commodity. Able to control feeding schedules and distributions, fisheries could gain control and leverage in the Japanese markets. In Australia, and then later in the Mediterranean Sea, farm owners could keep their tuna in pens until it was time to sell, taking into consideration recent fluctuations in the value of the Australian dollar against the Japanese yen, and the current prices for tuna. If the exchange rate was favorable, tuna were shipped; if it wasn't, they stayed. If tuna was commanding high prices in fish markets, tuna were shipped; if prices were lower, they stayed.

"Figure you're a buyer," John Norton, a fish buyer, told Paul Molyneaux, author of *Swimming in Circles*. "I come to you with my wild product. Sometimes I can supply you, sometimes I can't. Maybe the price'll be high, maybe low, and the quality is all over the map. Then I offer you an aquaculture product, consistent supply, consistent quality, and consistent price. What are you gonna buy?"

As a result of this newfound control by fisheries, profits exploded. From 1994 to 2001, the total export value of the bluefin tuna industry in Australia increased 560 percent, from $45 million to $252 million. By 2006, the industry earned an estimated $300 million. Similar figures were reported in other parts of the world. In 2004, the Spain-based Fuentes group reported $160 million in sales, but one independent researcher believes the operation hauled in closer to $250 million. In the first nine months of 2011, San Diego–based Umami Sustainable Seafood reported $56 million in sales from its farms in Mexico and Croatia. In Mexico, where tuna farms began popping up by the late 1990s, national tuna exports have generated anywhere from $80 to $90 million annually.

As Ellis wrote in his *Tuna: A Love Story*, "Capturing half-grown tuna, fattening them, and selling them to Japan was a cash cow for tuna farmers, but a tragedy for tuna."

The unquestionable leader in tuna farming in Europe is the Spanish-owned company Ricardo Fuentes and Sons, whose Japanese partners include Mitsubishi. The Cartagena-based company controls about 60 percent of the region's bluefin production; industry experts estimate its annual profits at more than $200 million. Most of the company's interests are in the countries dotting the Mediterranean, although it received a concession from Panama to start a yellowfin farm in the early 2000s. Perhaps that was a clear indicator that the company was aware of the dwindling supply of bluefin on its home turf and needed to diversify—or maybe it was just a way for the boss to give his sons something to do.

Although the patriarch of the business is Francisco Fuentes, it was his sons who procured the concession in Panama. The Fuentes family; the owner of Corelsa, an aquaculture supply company that had access to big tuna-farm cages; and Miguel de Iglesia were investors in what was to become the first yellowfin tuna farm in the world, although it was originally supposed to be in Panama, not Costa Rica. The location for the farm was supposed to be Puerto Armulles, basically around the corner from Pavones on the Panamanian side of Punta Burica.

"But these guys couldn't agree on anything," Velarde said. "They were all investing a shit ton of money and all they did was fight. These were spoiled kids trying to figure out what to do with poppa's money. Instead of buying a boat and some cages to get started, they bought a yacht to play with. I heard through an associate that the three investors for that project were on a yacht with tinted glass, music, and they were drinking and partying with poppa's money. It was like who was going to be the king of kings. It was the three kings, and there can only be one king. They couldn't figure out who would rule the Panama tuna operation."

Despite holding the concession, the three kings could never agree on how to proceed or how the money would be allocated and invested. In the meantime, Panama revoked the tuna farm permit over environmental opposition, but really because it was a shoddy operation with hot-headed investors and never had a chance from the start. De Iglesia, however, remained committed to creating the world's first yellowfin tuna farm, but it wasn't going to be in Panama. Over lunch with Velarde in Puntarenas that day, he decided it would be in Costa Rica.

"Manuel de Iglesia says, 'I don't know anything about breeding tuna, I just know how to catch them,'" Velarde reported.

It didn't work in Europe with saving the bluefin, but I told him let's do it differently here, and the only way to do it differently is to breed them from an egg. He sounded interested and agreed to invest a percentage of the profits toward that research. It took me sixteen years from when I spawned red snapper in captivity to where they could be produced commercially. So he was going to pay me to be a general manager and also give a percentage of the profits to spawn and grow these little critters, which is very expensive.

Velarde saw it as a blessing that the three kings couldn't come to an agreement. Their Panama project was going to operate in the same fashion, and with the same fishing methods, that led to the collapse of bluefin in the Mediterranean: by fattening what they caught in cages and selling them. Velarde would focus on breeding tuna from eggs, which had been his goal the entire time; more important, in his mind, was that he would be responsible for saving the tuna species before it was fished to death.

With Panama no longer an option, the next logical choice for de Iglesia was Costa Rica, where Velarde knew how to navigate the bureaucratic process because of his snapper and shrimp businesses. De Iglesia committed $3 million for start-up costs, which not only was the estimate to get the cages in the water but also covered the paperwork challenge: obtaining a concession and other necessary permits, hiring researchers for the environmental impact statement, and employing social workers to conduct surveys from whatever local communities were nearest to the tuna farm location. The company's name would be Granjas Atuneras, or Tuna Farms.

"This was my opportunity to make tuna a business, to protect the species, to put Costa Rica on the map for aquaculture, although it would take time to develop the science to spawn them. The country had tilapia farms on land, my shrimp and snapper farms, but this was different because these were floating cages in the ocean. Tuna clippers nowadays get small tuna. Not only are they catching less, they are catching smaller fish. They don't get a chance to spawn, and this is what I wanted to do. And I found the perfect place."

That place was Danny Land, but what Velarde didn't know was that Danny Fowlie was about to be released from prison and was preparing to reclaim his territory. And as Velarde already knew, there can be only one king.

9   Law and Order

It was all so businesslike that one watched it fascinated. It was pork-making by applied mathematics. And yet somehow the most matter-of-fact person could not help thinking of the hogs; they were so innocent, they came so very trustingly; and they were so human in their protests—so perfectly within their rights! They had done nothing to deserve it; and it was adding insult to injury, as the thing was done here, swinging them up in this cold-blooded, impersonal way, without a pretense at apology, without the homage of a tear.
—Upton Sinclair, *The Jungle*

The coastline between Punta Burica and Peter's ranch in Punta Banco is laced with waterfalls, gray sand, and booming waves. It is the true end of the road in Costa Rica, nowhere to go in your car but back where you came from. From a gravel turnaround near a Dutch-owned hostel, the mode of transportation is either on horseback or one's feet. One can walk the fifteen miles to Panama, to the sliver of land that is Punta Burica; there might not be a more scenic beach stroll in the entire country. At low tide men fish rocky inlets; a Guaymí indigenous teenager rides a horse, the hooves leaving behind imprints in the sand; and the hills at Punta Banco become mountains, reaching almost 2,300 feet above sea level, creating a hulking, verdant shelf that drops precipitously into the turquoise hue. At high tide the water envelops the beach, cloaking the sand, and has forced unsuspecting beach strollers to escape into the hills to avoid being consumed by the violent ocean. Even on the calmest of days the ocean is agitated, as if being powered by an underwater engine. And in some ways, it is.

The shelflike cliff is a canyon wall bordering the ocean's eastern edge. Just a few miles from shore, the water depth measures nearly one thousand feet. To the north, at the entrance of the Golfo Dulce near Punta Banco, the water depth is less than three hundred feet. Inside the gulf, it reaches a maximum 693 feet. This underwater topography has created one of five tropical fjords in the world. If drained, the Golfo Dulce would look like a giant bathtub, with its rim and mouth higher than its center, creating a situation where anything that flows into the Golfo Dulce might not flow out. However, nobody knows for sure as there's never been a comprehensive current study, because, well, there was never a reason to have one done until Velarde's tuna farm project.

The tuna cages would be located about one and three-quarter miles from the mountainous shelf, at a depth of 165 feet; that is the maximum depth divers can dive without a decompression chamber. Each cage would hold up to 120 tons of tuna; the project would start with four cages and grow to ten cages at full operation. In all, the concession area granted by SETENA was three miles in length and a mile and a half wide, which would allow more space for additional cages in the future.

"It seems like a large area on land but, on the ocean, it's not even a dot," Velarde said.

Manuel de Iglesia's three tuna clippers usually haul in a combined thirty-three thousand tons of tuna every year, some of which is adult tuna and some of which is juvenile tuna that hasn't had a chance to spawn. Although he sells his entire catch to Sardimar, his agreement with Velarde was that he would provide between 1 and 3 percent of his annual catch, or between 330 and 990 tons of tuna each year, for Velarde to fatten them in cages; he would also direct a percentage of the profits to research and development of breeding tuna from an egg and pay Velarde an annual salary of one hundred thousand dollars. De Iglesia was fetching two thousand dollars per ton from Sardimar to grind the tuna into cans; Velarde estimated that by fattening the tuna to ideal sizes and meat quality for sushi distribution, he would fetch twenty-five thousand dollars per ton. At 120 tons of tuna per cage and close to 500 tons spread over four cages, the tuna farms' annual gross revenue was projected to be $12 million per year, with 10 percent set aside for research and development. If the project reached full build-out at ten cages, it would gross more than $25 million annually.

Once the cages were installed, the process would be rather simple: when de Igelsia's tuna clippers reported a catch, Granjas Atuneras boats would meet the clippers at sea, transfer a portion of the catch to smaller boats, and transport the tuna to the floating cages, where they would be deposited and fattened for mass distribution.

"I was going to take five hundred tons a year and put it in cages, grow them, and then sell them for sushi," Velarde said. "It was either going in the can or in the cage. If I wasn't involved, it was all going in a can. Now I had a chance to take a little bit of what was already going in a can and try and make enough money to learn how to breed them from an egg. It wasn't going to deplete the species any more than it was already being depleted because his tuna was already going to the can."

While the potential revenue was there, the project's costs were sizable: four cages at $1 million per cage, increasing to $10 million for ten cages, and $6 million in working capital, for a total cost of $10 million. Velarde, however, figured he would need $3 million in start-up costs, which de Igelsia agreed to invest. Initially, he wrote a check for $250,000 to cover Velarde's salary and the costs of conducting studies to obtain the necessary permits, including the social study of the community.

"It was a perfect location. The mountains come very steep to the ocean, and the ocean keeps going very sharp down and that creates very fast, very heavy currents, which is good," Velarde said. "You need deep oceanic movement. From a scientific standpoint, it was the best location in the country. And another thing, it's an Indian reserve so nobody can build anything there. There won't be any type of development there because of the terrain, it's too rugged, and so I thought there wouldn't be any complaints from potential developers who had ideas for a project there. It's in the middle of fucking nowhere. I couldn't see a negative."

Nobody argued that the naked coastline wasn't the best location from purely a scientific standpoint for a tuna farm, but there were others who certainly felt there were negative aspects to the project. First, the opposition felt that Velarde didn't fully gauge the social and biological effects of the project. These were what provided the framework for the opposition mounted by Álvaro Sagot, the high-powered environmental attorney. And these were also the issues that the international surf community eventually adopted in its public relations campaign. But Velarde only gave marginal consideration to the NIMBY (Not In My Back Yard) movement he encountered.

"I knew that Golfito and that area is the most depressed area economically in Costa Rica," he said:

> Girls have children very young, kids don't go to school. There are basically two industries: bananas and African palm oil. I also knew it was a communist area of the country that expelled the Americans, Chiquita banana [formerly United Fruit], so what is left today is an economically depressed area that was in need of help. I thought the tuna farm would help this area and provide jobs and provide a brighter future, so that was the social interest. I thought my problem was going to be that this area is a heavy drug area and heavy surfer area, and I knew there would be problems. Drug guys don't want development; they want it as poor and hush-hush as possible. They don't want all this activity and trucks coming in and out, and neither did the surfers there. These people don't want to be bothered. I knew a lot of people down there felt that way. I also knew beforehand that Mr. Aspinall wanted this area to stay pristine. But I didn't specifically worry about how to keep their Tarzan jungle pure and pristine. I was thinking much bigger than them and their comfort; I was thinking of a bigger good for Costa Rica and for nature. When you do something of this magnitude, you can't please everyone.

According to the environmental impact statement submitted to SETENA in 2004, the year after Granjas Atuneras became an official company, Velarde had formulated encouraging employment projections for the tuna farm: during the first two years, there would be altogether 104 jobs at the processing plant located in Golfito and at the site of the tuna cages floating in the water; by its third year of existence, there would be 178 jobs at the two locations. Moreover, the EIS stated the project would indirectly create an additional two hundred positions in the first two years and more than four hundred by its third year of operation. These indirect employment figures were wide-ranging and rather far-reaching, but they mentioned an increased workload and revenue for restaurants and hotels, local mechanic shops, construction companies, even the airport since planes would fly freshly fattened tuna for distribution to North America and Japan.

"The cages themselves don't require a big working force, but it's a project that really would move money and people, the most in that area since Chiquita bananas," Velarde said. "The biggest working force is in the processing plant, maintenance for the boats and cages, trucks hauling the fish from the processing plant to the airport."

Environmentalists immediately questioned the projected direct employment figures.

"He was going to teach the junkies in Golfito how to dive and provide everyone jobs? Yeah right," stated Randall Arauz, founder of the turtle protectionist group Pretoma. "The types of jobs created by a tuna farm require mostly skilled labor; these people would have to be brought in or they would be have to be trained. They weren't going to hire anybody but a few people locally in Pavones or Punta Banco, yet they were the people who would suffer from the impact of these farms. It didn't add up from our point of view."

Regardless of the accuracy of Velarde's employment projections, in an area where unemployment is nearly 35 percent, any mention of new jobs has a tendency to convince the people that need to be convinced. In March of 2004, Velarde met with Golfito officials, touting the employment figures and introducing the project. While there wasn't a single representative from Punta Banco or Pavones, everyone in Golfito unanimously supported it. But extravagant employment projections would not be the focus of the opposition. Instead, the basis for their case would be other questionable aspects of the EIS: the project's effect on marine animals, including nationally protected turtles; the effect of currents on where metabolic waste from the tuna farms would end up; and the support, or lack of it, for the project from the communities closest to the tuna farms.

"We're scientists, we're not a bunch of tree huggers," Pretoma founder Arauz said.

> Eduardo comes out and says this is like tomatoes, we just farm them. If we run out, we will just farm them. Then we come out with scientific information suggesting otherwise, that the farm would deplete the species. That's great that he wanted to breed them, but that's not what this project was about and we had to evaluate the project for what it was, a project to fatten tuna and make lots of money while depleting the species by overfishing the tuna. Not to mention the current study and the surveying of the community was a joke. We, at Pretoma, wanted to see a real environmental impact statement. We didn't want to see some bullshit with a University of Costa Rica stamp on it. To some people that has credibility, but if we can, we will shoot it down. SETENA should have done it themselves, but that's when we stepped in.

Upon retaining Álvaro Sagot and trusting Pretoma to focus on the project's technical problems, Peter Aspinall investigated the community support claimed in the EIS. During October and November of 2003, Granjas Atuneras interviewed residents to notify them of the project and give them an opportunity to comment or ask questions. Velarde hired the University of Costa Rica, the country's most respected educational institution, to handle the interviewing of residents. There were four people in all who conducted the studies, two of whom identified themselves as students; they drove UCR-owned vehicles into Pavones over a period of several weeks. The UCR workers presented residents with a written questionnaire, encouraging them to ask questions if necessary, since much of the population is illiterate, and then asked the interviewees to sign the questionnaire after it was completed.

Before the UCR workers interviewed residents, Velarde visited the fish house to notify the local fishermen's association. William Mata is certain that it was presented not as a notification of what *would* happen but as a hypothetical project that *could* happen. Nevertheless, Walter Mendoza, the association's president at the time, told Velarde he had the full support of the fishermen.

"Eduardo Velarde is very intelligent and knows the ocean. That is what he does for his work," Walter told me in Spanish. "But the whole town thought that I took money, and that Eduardo Velarde was bad, that he couldn't be trusted. I was in the minority. The farms wouldn't affect us, it wouldn't hurt tourism here. It could be a tourism attraction. It wouldn't affect surfing either. These were all lies Peter Aspinall and Pretoma and the lawyer told people. The cages wouldn't even be seen. The currents wouldn't be affected because it is so deep right there, and Eduardo did a current study."

After several days of interviews in the area, Velarde was satisfied with the community responses that were returned. Combined with the endorsement from the local fishermen, that part of the equation was complete. He did exactly as the law instructed him to do for this project. In a sweeping declaration, the EIS announced the entire community was notified of the project and supported it. The EIS listed everyone interviewed, highlighting their signatures on the written survey. There were thirty people interviewed in all, which is a small sample size for an area of several thousand, but SETENA ruled it a sufficient amount. Aspinall was less concerned with the number of people than their identities: he recognized half of the names; the other half he didn't.

"The other ones didn't live in the area anymore or were never residents," Aspinall said. "In a few cases they interviewed government employees who were stationed along the Pan-American Highway for just a few months. These people don't represent our community. As for the others, I knew the other people who were living here and visited each of them to ask them if they had been interviewed or if they supported the project. In every case, they said they hadn't."

Under Costa Rican law, companies have to inform the public and the community of any new project. According to the EIS, Granjas Atuneras did that in the fall of 2003, which, coupled with technical aspects of the study, is why SETENA granted the environmental permit. It's also why the environment minister, Carlos Manuel Rodriguez, didn't get involved: because the project wasn't illegal. Although legally Granjas Atuneras complied with each requirement, Aspinall felt that how the information was gathered could not produce a true reflection of his beach community.

As Aspinall began knocking on doors, all those listed in the EIS as being interviewed told him they were never told about a tuna farm; they only remembered being told by college workers they were being interviewed for a project in connection with the University of Costa Rica. They remembered being asked questions like: Do you think there are enough jobs in the area? Do you think there should be more employment in the area? Would you like to make more money? Would you like to see more tourism in the area? Are you happy with the general direction of the community? Do you like the level of education in the area? Would you like to see improved education? Is the environment important to you?

"And they used the answers to those questions to conclude the community wanted a tuna farm," Aspinall said.

> People were very angry because they felt deceived, that they were misled. They thought they were being interviewed by the University of Costa Rica, which they were, but nobody mentioned anything about a tuna farm. In some cases, some people said they were never interviewed and were shocked to see their names listed by the company. In other cases, people said they never signed any paper and accused the company of forgery. Another problem is some of these people can't read or write, and people felt the company took advantage of people's lack of education and were tricked into trusting these people because they were from the University of Costa Rica. I also found out that Eduardo told the fishermen that it was going to be a snapper farm, which would be of interest to them because they already fish snapper a lot, so that is why they supported it. Every fisherman I talked to other than Walter told me it was going to be a snapper farm.

This was, of course, useful information that Aspinall provided to Sagot, but the flow of information didn't stop. He began investigating rumors that Walter Mendoza and his son Jose Gonzales, known as "Pepe," collected *propinas*, or payments, to pay off the other fishermen to support of the farms. It wouldn't be entirely surprising. After all, offering a *propina* is a method Velarde used himself to get his first job in Costa Rica. William Mata told me several years later, while rubbing his fingers together, that Walter accepted *plata*, or money, to spread a positive message about the farms.

In 2007, at the Universidad para La Paz, or University for Peace, a bilingual university in Costa Rica, a student researched the tuna farm conflict and wrote a thesis about the project. The student interviewed twelve prominent community members who agreed to speak if they remained anonymous. Of the twelve people interviewed, six stated that Walter and Pepe had received payment from Granjas Atuneras; one of the interviewees who said the two received payment admitted to being Walter's nephew. A few of the interviewees said they were in support of the project until they talked with others and learned what Peter Aspinall was now learning.

Velarde dismissed this as rumor-mongering in an uneducated community.

"If you had a small army of NGOs with their teams of lawyers backed by a lot of money spreading the idea in a small community that apples are poison, and one guy with his son with no money defending the idea that apples are good for your health, that's the real picture of what happened concerning our idea of how to save the tuna down there. I never told them it was a snapper farm. I was honest from the beginning."

Peter was skeptical of the rumor that Walter and Pepe accepted a bribe from Velarde, and he never definitely established any nefarious behavior involving Velarde and the fishermen.

"You have to careful with what you say because people have been killed for things they say here," Aspinall said. "That's extreme but it does happen. I heard Walter and Pepe would be paid one hundred dollars each time boats had to be driven to the cages, and that makes more sense they would agree to that because one hundred dollars is a lot of money to people here."

Although Aspinall wouldn't categorically rule out a possible bribe, he had stronger and easier-to-prove arguments accumulating in his and Sagot's corner. Though in his midfifties, Aspinall walked in the searing heat and humidity nearly twelve miles round trip to and from the town of Conte deep in the Guaymí Indian Reservation where there aren't any roads, only trails. He wore khaki shorts and a blue collared shirt, tied in such a way above his belly button that his stomach cooled as he walked along muddy trails through the bug-infested jungle. He was curious if the Guaymí had been notified of the project.

"It took me hours," Aspinall said. "I was tired and sweating by the time I arrived. I walked right into a meeting of about one hundred Indians, including the chief. I got lucky because sometimes it's impossible to get them together. I was a little nervous because it's not polite for just anybody to walk onto Indian land without permission. But I felt it was important to find out if the government ever notified them."

While indigenous people account for only 1 percent of the country's population, the Guaymí represent nearly two-thirds of the voters in the district of Pavones. Usually confined to the hills between Pavones and the Panama border, the Guaymí found it objectionable that the government would allow Granjas Atuneras to install a tuna farm project in the waters near Punta Banco, which is part of land designated for the Guaymí, without notifying them. The government never asked their permission or even bothered to consult with them about the tuna farm project. Doused in his own sweat that afternoon, Aspinall confirmed they weren't consulted. The Guyamí, who have fished the pristine waters near Punta Banco for centuries, believed the project was an invasion of their sovereign land. The government, though, wasn't technically required by law to notify the Guaymí of the project because, by law, it's not their land—and this project was in the ocean anyway.

The Guaymí are the earliest known inhabitants in this part of Costa Rica, settling in the area sometime between 800 and 1500 A D. They had once roamed from present-day Colombia north through what is now Costa Rica. But like many indigenous groups in Latin America, the Guaymí's population dwindled, and their land was taken from them as a result of the Spanish conquest, that four-hundred-year reign that lasted from the end of the fifteenth century until the end of the nineteenth. In Costa Rica, the Guaymí population hovered around ten thousand for most of the twentieth century, which is where it stands today. (More than 150,000 Guaymí live in bordering Panama.) In 1977, the government passed legislation to establish Indian reservations. It was a nice gesture considering Costa Rica has one of the lowest indigenous populations in Latin America; its Central American neighbors with far higher percentages of indigenous people have treated their natives far less fairly. Costa Rica's reservations are sequestered on the country's extremities on the Pacific and Caribbean coastlines. The law states that natives have the right to stay in self-governed communities, but the government retains the land titles. This legislative loophole has resulted in companies being occasionally able, with the blessing of the government, to exploit Guaymí land for resources, usually either for minerals or lumber. It was completely legal, if a bit insensitive, for the government to trump the Guaymí's complaints by flashing the titles to their land as its defense. Still, not notifying the Guaymí was another error made by Granjas Atuneras and SETENA. And in the court of public opinion, perception is often the strongest evidence.

When he left the reservation that day, Aspinall walked the six miles back to Conte where his white truck was parked along a gravel road. Now that he had collected stories of forgeries and accusations of outright lying on the part of Granjas Atuneras and learned of the company's failure to notify the Guaymí, the EIS assertion that the tuna farm had community support seemed disingenuous or outright false. With that angle handled by Aspinall, it was hunting season for the technical issues in the EIS. Next up for target practice was Pretoma, which took aim at the project's current study and what it felt was outright negligence of its impact on nationally protected turtles that use the area as a nesting site. By the time Pretoma was done shooting at the EIS, Velarde's investor was concerned, and reports surfaced of collusion between SETENA and Granjas Atuneras.

Pretoma's office is located in the San José suburb of Tibas, three miles from the city center, but seemingly a million miles from the cracked side-walks, the orchestra of honking car horns, and the stained concrete of the capital's buildings. A dull, gray church beside a pleasant park with squirrels scurrying about, metal swing sets, and flowering rose bushes are appropriate symbols of Tibas's humble offerings. Past the cemetery and less than a mile from the park, Pretoma's office rests on a quiet corner, with metal gates guarding it from the street, among a row of modest houses. It would be an ideal place to call home, and that is why Arauz converted part of his house into an office for what was to become the principal sea-turtle protection group in Costa Rica.

Funded entirely by private donations, the nonprofit group was founded in 1996; its first conservation project was a sea-turtle nesting site that year in Punta Banco. Research suggests that four species of sea turtle inhabit the area: the green, the leatherback, the hawksbill, and the olive ridley. More than fifteen thousand turtles hatch annually on the beach in Punta Banco; the waters there include the area that Velarde had pegged for the location of the tuna farms. Most of these hatchlings are of the endangered olive ridley species, but there are hatchlings from green and hawksbill turtles, too. Poaching turtle eggs is the main culprit behind the olive ridley's demise. All four species, however, are victims of bycatch from trawling and long-lining because they are often caught in nets and snagged by hooks.

Poaching turtle eggs was declared illegal in Costa Rica in 1996, yet one study has reported that poaching went up 30 percent after the law was enacted. Turtle eggs are considered a delicacy. Usually consumed in a drink, they're said to act as an aphrodisiac and provide medicinal benefits. Although these benefits have been questioned by experts, the demand for them has created an expansive black market. At night, it's not uncommon to come across small gangs of machete-wielding egg poachers on Costa Rican beaches, scooping up and bagging hundreds of eggs. In extreme cases, poachers simply can't wait for the mothers to hatch, so they slice open the belly of a pregnant mother nesting on the beach, take the eggs, and leave the mother to bleed to death on the sand.

Each egg, which is roughly the size of a ping pong ball, is sold to distributors for about fifty cents and can be purchased at bars through-out the country. The airport bar in Golfito, for example, sells them for about two dollars; it has a handwritten note taped to a shelf indicating whether turtle eggs are available that day. In one very prominent case, officials stopped what they believed to be a drug boat trolling the waters off the Caribbean coast. When they inspected the boat, they found more than one million turtle eggs on board with a street value of five hundred thousand dollars. As with harvesting tuna, stealing eggs before the turtles are able to hatch and reproduce results in a massive depletion of the animal's population. Even if the poachers are somehow magically elimi-nated, turtles are threatened by commercial fishermen. In 2013, nearly three hundred olive ridley turtles washed ashore on the beach between Punta Banco and Pavones. According to the *Tico Times*, tests showed mucus and water in their lungs, suggesting their deaths were caused by forced submersion, most likely from long-line fishing. Despite the inherent challenges, Pretoma fights to protect turtles anyway.

Beginning with the site in Punta Banco, Pretoma added three more throughout the country in an effort to protect the turtles and reduce poaching. At the Punta Banco site alone, it collected nearly 150,000 eggs from 1996 to 2010, with about an 80 percent success rate for the hatching of those eggs. However, during the period when Velarde was collecting data for the tuna farm project, Pretoma's monitoring efforts were elsewhere. Thus, whereas Pretoma collected an average of 8,448 eggs at Punta Banco in 2003 and 2004, it collected 16,959 eggs at San Miguel, and 12,076 eggs at Playa Caletas. (Its fourth site, Corozalito, wasn't monitored until 2009.)

Pretoma created a program where volunteers would be given free housing at an open-air house in Punta Banco and assist a full-time employee to help protect the turtles. It even provided some financial and logistical support to one university graduate student who wanted to conduct research on sea turtles in the summer of 2012. However, the student admitted that she was rather unimpressed with the turtle numbers during the six weeks she was in Punta Banco. In fact, she would go weeks without seeing one.

"I actually think this is a perfect location for a tuna farm," the student concluded. "I am not in favor of tuna farms but this is a good location in terms of least amount of impact because there aren't many turtles here as compared to many other places in Costa Rica, including as close as Carate on the other side of the Golfo Dulce."

Velarde concurred with the graduate student's conclusion; he even used Pretoma's own numbers when selecting his site for a tuna farm.

"I used Pretoma's numbers, there were the least amount of nesting turtles on the Pacific coast," Velarde said. "I even offered to buy one hundred thousand turtle eggs and give them back to Pretoma. Besides, turtles aren't kamikazes, they aren't going to go into the cages saying, 'Eat me, eat me,' and killing themselves by banging into the cages. I was providing rational arguments and these other people used irrational arguments against me."

While Arauz admitted the turtle numbers are significantly lower there than in other parts of Costa Rica, that wasn't the argument Velarde presented in the EIS. "He's acting like he's doing us a favor by wiping out those turtles," Arauz said.

> We have the research on three hundred to five hundred turtles nesting every season, and we collect thousands of eggs every year. The thing is the law says turtles are protected. It doesn't matter if it's one turtle or a million turtles. If it's one turtle, you protect it the same as if it's a million turtles. You can't say these turtles are less important here, that's just the way it goes. But the reality is there were lots of holes in the environmental impact statement, and it didn't take us long to find other problems. It was poorly written and didn't have the technical information one would need. It wasn't exhaustive, they were reaching conclusions that there was no way they could reach from the information they were providing. The turtles were one thing, the lying about the community support was another, but the main thing was the current study and where all the metabolic waste would go, not to mention the threat of diseases spreading.

In 2003 Velarde sought out the leading scientists and researchers for his EIS. He hired the country's most respected social worker to hire people to conduct surveys in the community and he hired Dr. Omar Lizano, who is considered the most respected marine biologist in the country, for the ocean study. During a one-week span, Lizano studied the currents in that part of the ocean for a total of three days. His findings regarding low-, mid-, and high-level currents in the EIS seemed to confirm Granjas Atuneras's argument that the metabolic waste and spread of diseases would be minimized because the currents flowed "out." In total, Velarde spent $250,000 of Manuel de Iglesia's $3 million that was earmarked to cover the costs of the getting the project's cages into the water. A big chunk of that was for the current study, and Velarde believed it was money well spent.

"It was static like a swimming pool," Velarde said.

> We calculated the amount of tuna shit that we were going to have there. Do tuna shit in a bag and take it somewhere else? No, they shit in the fucking ocean. And when fish squirt, it dilutes. It's not like a

goat, it's solid, but it's a squirt and it's watery. It's not like I was going to unload tons of dump trucks of shit and put it on the shore. Nobody lives there anyway. There are no fishermen who fish there, there is no tourism, and the science said it was not going to pollute and kill anything. Even if the shit did go somewhere and wasn't diluted, which is impossible because it dilutes, it is also eaten by other animals. It will be disseminated. The researcher stated I wasn't going to pollute. Now I am not going to pollute, I am not going to kill turtles, and I hired the very best social worker with the University of Costa Rica to talk to the community. I can't be involved with any of that, these are people telling me this information and I have no influence.

Arauz, however, wasn't so sure.

Since the Golfo Dulce is essentially a giant bath tub, he was concerned that currents would send tuna feces into the Golfo Dulce, where they would wash ashore, affecting beachfront hamlets and destroying ecosystems there. There is some anecdotal evidence supporting the argument, something almost any Pavones resident can confirm. Since the area is a heavy drug-trafficking zone linking South America and North America, metal containers full of drugs and other debris constantly wash ashore in Pavones and Golfito. The containers are dumped over the side of the boats beyond the mouth of Golfo Dulce and somehow flow into the gulf. Also, some fishermen routinely litter at sea, and it's not uncommon to see a pile of garbage floating beyond the mouth of the gulf, and then see that same pile of garbage change locations multiple times over the next week. If the surface currents can send boxes of drugs into Pavones, it's reasonable to assume that they can do the same with tuna shit. Randall Arauz argued that currents are complex and that a conclusive study of them would take more than a week.

"What about the dry season? What about the wet season? What about La Niña years? What about El Niño years?" Arauz asked. "At the very least you should have a one-year study; he paid a guy to do a study over three days. That's not enough. But since this guy was from the University of Costa Rica, it means something to SETENA and the government. Whenever there is a University of Costa Rica stamp on something, people think it's legitimate. And Omar Lizano is very good at what he does. He just didn't do it for long enough in this case."

When I contacted Dr. Lizano, I asked him about the nature of his research, including the scope and cost. He affirmed the type of current study completed, and he respectfully declined to state his fee for his services. When I countered by asking specifically if the duration of his study was sufficient for a project of this scope, he didn't respond.

The tuna feces debate, however, advanced when Arauz pressed Velarde for an answer about potential problems caused by the food tuna would consume in the fattening process. Tuna are fed with sardines and anchovies and typically consume twenty pounds of smaller fish for every pound of their own weight. It doesn't take a mathematician to understand that human efforts would eventually deplete the smaller fish species in an effort to feed tuna's voracious appetites. More importantly, Arauz was concerned about the threat of viruses and diseases spreading from the sardines and anchovies into Costa Rican waters.

According to a study conducted by Surfrider, the California surf activism group, "ocean fish farms can amplify and spread deadly diseases and parasites into natural environments. To address these threats, farm operators often apply drugs and chemicals, sometimes with subsequent harm to wild animals." The report further stated that chemicals such as pesticides, antibiotics, and fungicides used at cage sites can be carried outside the farms: white spot disease, a highly contagious and lethal ailment, nearly destroyed the shrimp farming industry in the 1990s. In *Swimming in Circles* Paul Molyneaux reports that one researcher found white spot virus in 70 percent of the shrimp he pulled off supermarket shelves in Hawaii; the spread of parasitic sea lice from farms to wild salmon has resulted $5 billion losses per year; and in 2012 the Food and Drug Administration reported more than one hundred human illnesses after a salmonella outbreak was linked to yellowfin tuna distributed in restaurants and grocery stores.

For the tuna farm project, Velarde would transport sardines and anchovies from Peru, their leading supplier in Latin America, to the cages near the Golfo Dulce. While there is a threat of spreading viruses and disease from one marine area to another, Velarde planned to wean his tuna off sardines and anchovies and introduce them to a dry food made with corn, soy, and fish meal in an experiment that would help decelerate the depletion of sardines and anchovies, which are used as fishmeal for other farmed species.

"It's always a concern, but you have a sanitation minister that does certification in Peru," Velarde said. "Listen, I don't want to bring something that is going to harm my fish. If I bring sardines and anchovies and my fish get sick, I lose money, I can't lose money, and I don't want to lose money. So that argument right off the bat was stupid because, like it or not, products of the ocean are going from one country to another more than any other type of meat product. It was a concern, but it was my concern."

Randall Arauz and Velarde spoke about their respective arguments to resolve the matter outside of court.

"Randall told me if we find something wrong, we're going after you," Velarde said. "I told him, tell me what I am doing wrong, I want to do it right. Pretoma gets funded to create problems where there aren't any. If there is nothing to fight, there is no way for them to get money. He didn't want to work with me."

Arauz viewed things differently.

"I do want to say he turned out to be a cool guy, and he treated me with a lot of respect even though we didn't agree," Arauz said.

He had lawyers, they were rich, but he was very polite and a lot of times when I meet with guys like that, they can be mean. We had strong debates, he was a gentleman, but we just couldn't agree on anything he wanted to do. Just in general during the Óscar Arias administration, there was an aperture for all this foreign money coming in, for gold, for petroleum, for tuna farming, whatever. Tuna farming, it was in vogue during those years. SETENA is highly politicized. And when these institutions become highly politicized, science goes in the back seat. You provide all the science, but there is already a political mandate. So you have a biologist from the University of Costa Rica, it has credibility and SETENA says yes. The problem is they aren't being technicians, and they aren't being biologists or scientists; they are following a mandate. And they have to abide by the mandate.

In the fall of 2005, with little chance of coming to an agreement outside the courtroom, Pretoma, in conjunction with the Punta Banco Association, filed a lawsuit against Granjas Atuneras in the Constitutional Chamber of Costa Rica's Supreme Court. At the time, Granjas Atuneras had the environmental permit from SETENA and the water permit from another government institution and was waiting on the fishing permit from INCOPESCA, which rarely denies a permit for a pro-fishing venture, particularly if the project involves the largest supplier of tuna to the country's largest tuna cannery. If Granjas Atuneras was awarded the fishing permit, it could have the cages in the water by the end of the year.

By July of 2006, the Supreme Court accepted the case for review, but it would take nearly a year before there would be a ruling and the opposition would get its day in court. In the meantime, as was the case with other environmentally contested projects in Costa Rica such as the oil drilling project in the Caribbean and the Las Crucitas open-pit gold mine, Granjas Atuneras moved forward with its plans since it had the support of the government. And a month later, in June of 2006, INCOPESCA issued the final necessary permit, a fishing permit, with six of the group's nine board members voting in favor of the farm and three voting against it because of environmental reasons. Velarde thought it was interesting how the lawsuit was against SETENA and INCOPESCA, not Granjas Atuneras.

"They knew they were never going to beat me, Eduardo, in court," because I complied with the law," Velarde said.

Because if I lost, they knew I was going to sue their asses. This was a big project, and Pretoma and Mr. Aspinall and Mr. Sagot are smart, so they decided to go against the person that gave me the permit, the government. They thought the government was sloppy and that they could beat the government; they didn't figure that I was going to be backing up the government, arguing that aquaculture is good for Costa Rica, and we did that. At the beginning of all of this I met with Carlos Manuel Rodriguez, the minister of the environment, who asked about the environmental and scientific aspects of the project. He liked what he heard. He is the highest environmental government worker in the country, a country that is about the environment. This project was then scrutinized everywhere in this "green" country, and yet I still got all the permits. The government liked the project, thought it was environmentally smart, and so the minister signed the permit. He didn't have a pistol to his head.

From the time that Pavones's first non-Guaymí settlers acquired land under the country's homesteading laws, Pavones has always represented opportunity to outsiders, and in some cases that opportunity has turned to exploitation, whether on the part of land speculators, squatters, or tuna farm operators. But in this case, the opposition would align with the one person who had deep pockets and who could pay Sagot's sizable lawyer bill—or who the opposition still hoped could. Yet, some people consider this person to be the biggest Pavones exploiter of them all: Danny Fowlie, who was released from prison the same year Pretoma filed a lawsuit in the country's constitutional court. Danny would eventually learn more about the tuna farm project and even consider it an avenue to reclaim his turf.

10   The King's Exit

To me, the thing that is worse than death is betrayal. You see, I could
conceive death, but I could not conceive betrayal.
—Malcolm X

Of all the Danny Fowlie stories, my favorite is about how he left Pavones
in 1985. One day, legend says, a plane buzzed overhead. Hanging out of
the side door was Danny, who tossed wads of American dollars into the
humid air. It was raining bills, and the dark cloud looming overhead
was Danny. Residents were on their knees, reaching toward the heavens,
pleading with him not to leave, but, if he must, showering them with
money was a decent consolation. As their knees were muddied and their
outstretched arms were feathered by floating hundred-dollar bills, Danny
promised them he'd be back one day. And with that final message, the
plane curved north toward San José, enveloped by the clouds and moving
out of sight forever. Residents cried, feeling as though a lover had gone
off to war, wondering if he would ever return.

"He was our Pablo Escobar," said one Pavones resident, referring to
the Colombian drug lord who was loved by the impoverished majority
whose communities were ignored by the government but improved by
Escobar, albeit with profits from cocaine sales.

Contrary to that anecdotal whopper told by his Costa Rica–based
lawyer to an author writing about drugs in Central America, Danny
Fowlie, the self-proclaimed King of Pavones, left of his own accord with
little fanfare. One would think a lawyer's story is somewhat credible—or
at the very least rooted in evidence—but as is the case with Danny and

those connected with him, fact and fiction have been blurred to the point where only one thing is clear: nobody knows the truth, not even Danny himself, for his mind is so scrambled and warped from a life of betrayal that the remaining working parts create an alternate reality consisting of what he wishes were the truth. However, I will do my best to make sense of a confusing trail of deceit, drugs, and money that spanned the globe and created a mythological surf folk hero who lived out his final years in a crumbling casita in Mexico, too broke to buy a fridge, desperate to be remembered for anything other than what most everybody remembers him for.

The dethronement began on March 1, 1985, when authorities completed a two-day raid of his 213-acre ranch straddling the Orange and Riverside county lines in Southern California. Danny had visited the ranch in late February and then left for Mexico, unaware that a drunken blunder several days later would be the first domino to fall in dismantling one of the country's largest drug-smuggling rings. His ranch manager, an inebriated Wayne Westmoreland, was arrested in the early morning hours of February 28 in South Laguna for allegedly firing a gun inside his house, according to the *Los Angeles Times*. When authorities arrived, they found two plastic bags, each containing about twenty pounds of marijuana. A further investigation uncovered $73,000 in cash, guns, a small amount of hashish, and what a deputy told a reporter were "numerous ledgers and bank records." Westmoreland, who was charged with possession of marijuana for sale, confessed to deputies that he managed a remote ranch off Ortega Highway in the chaparral-studded hills east of Laguna Beach; the ranch was owned by Daniel James Fowlie, the King of Pavones.

The *Los Angeles Times* reported that a sixteen-person SWAT team stormed the ranch and arrested two more people, recovering $23,000 in cash, fifty rifles and shotguns, three automatic weapons, a money-counting machine, a precision scale, and packaging machines and cardboard boxes. The paper also reported that the team found TV shipping cartons and fabric softener sheets, which were determined in court to be a way of transporting drugs and masking the odor of marijuana. There was, however, no marijuana found at the ranch. One of the two people arrested that day at the ranch was Robert Pellegrom, a Dutch citizen and Danny's right-hand man who entered the Federal Witness Protection Program after providing information about the ranch's true function. Two other men who had prominent roles in the enterprise, Ron Gates and Joseph Cooper, also became government witnesses and provided additional details on the vast organization. Given their testimony, it is obvious that Pavones's benevolent dictator from 1974 to 1985 had been living two lives.

Danny's Leather Gypsy handbag business, which he sold for $3 million, had manufacturing offices in the early 1970s in Tijuana, Mexico. It's unclear exactly how he linked up with one of Mexico's principal drug lords because Danny remains tight-lipped about that portion of his past. U.S. attorneys believed that as early as 1971 Danny met with Rafael Caro Quintero, cofounder of the Guadalajara cartel, about smuggling marijuana into the United States. Danny denied that early of an involvement, saying that he was still heavily invested in his real estate holdings and his leather handbag business. But perhaps his denial is connected to his wanting his storybook discovery of Pavones in 1974 to remain as pure as possible. Regardless of the exact timing of the 1970s meeting in Mexico, by the time his ranch was raided in 1985, authorities estimated that Danny's organization had smuggled at least fifty-three thousand pounds of marijuana from Mexico and trafficked it through Rancho del Rio in Southern California. One of the government witnesses was Danny's ledger man, who testified the organization grossed anywhere from $75 to $150 per pound of marijuana. Another government informant revealed that Danny's supplier was Javier Caro Payán, who was a cousin of Rafael Caro Quintero and the drug boss of Baja California, Mexico, a desert peninsula where Danny had Leather Gypsy offices at its northern end and where he owned land in Cabo San Lucas at its southern end.

A few local authorities believed Danny's earliest link to drug trafficking was during the late 1960s when he was involved with the Laguna Beach–based Brotherhood of Eternal Love, a group of drug smugglers and recreational users inspired by Timothy Leary, a former Harvard psychology professor. Danny was suspected of being part of the group's drug distribution sector, which included marijuana, LSD, and hashish. One of the group's most active members was Mike Hynson, a close friend of Danny's, who gained international fame as one of the two young surfers profiled in the 1966 film *The Endless Summer*. Hynson declined to speak about Danny's involvement with the brotherhood, but Danny vehemently denied being part of drug trafficking at that time.

"I didn't supply them with any drugs, but I knew they were around and hung out with them," said Danny, who claimed that his connection with the group was limited to partying and surfing with Hynson.

The Brotherhood of Eternal Love was dismantled in 1972 following the arrest of Leary and forty-five other members. Danny was never arrested, and soon after, he sold his Leather Gypsy business and became the principal landowner in Pavones. If Danny intended to move his family to a surf paradise and live in relative anonymity, which is the story he clings to, his entrepreneurial spirit wasn't suppressed for very long. People with money, it seems, have a magnetic connection with each other.

Not long after arriving in Costa Rica, Danny connected with Robert Vesco, a slick-haired, mustached fugitive financier from the United States who was hiding in Costa Rica. By the early 1970s, Vesco was wanted for securities fraud in the United States after swindling investors for $224 million. He was also a wanted for making an illegal $200,000 contribution to President Richard Nixon's 1972 presidential campaign, presumably to get Nixon to end the investigation against him. Although that didn't happen, Vesco found protection in Costa Rica under President José Figueres, whose personal bank account enjoyed deposits in excess of more than $300,000 from Vesco. Vesco's companies also invested $11 million into Costa Rica, much of it in businesses that Figueres's family members owned. Costa Rica didn't have an extradition treaty with the United States at the time, so Vesco lived comfortably under the protection of Figueres. By the late 1970s, Vesco had more than enough money and was looking to downsize his empire just as Danny was just looking to expand his.

"Vesco was a multimillionaire, but Pepe Figueres took so much money for him to stay in the country that we always joked that Pepe turned Vesco into a millionaire from being a multimillionaire," Danny joked.

After arriving in Costa Rica in 1974 and buying his first oceanfront ranch in Pavones in front of the world-class left, Danny started buying Vesco's properties, including a half-million-dollar palatial estate in San

José with a pool, laborers, and a high wall surrounding it. Vesco also tried to sell Danny his wife's Mercedes for thirty-five thousand dollars, although he didn't realize that Danny knew that particular model could be purchased in the United States for eighteen thousand. Danny told him he didn't want the Mercedes, but Vesco was committed to liquidating some of his assets. He wanted to play a coin game with Danny where he pitched a coin against the wall and if Vesco called the correct side, heads or tails, Danny had to pay the full thirty-five thousand for the car. If he didn't call it correctly, Danny could have the car—for free.

"This guy snookered so many people, and I knew that he was an expert penny pitcher," Danny said. "I told him let's flip the coin and he calls it in the air. He didn't like that too much. So I said then let's do it this way then: I will take you down to Pavones and the one who catches the most waves in ten minutes is the winner. He had the same chance of catching more waves than me in ten minutes as I did pitching pennies with him. So we decided to flip the coin. I won."

Vesco introduced Danny to Norman LeBlanc, Vesco's financial advisor and planner. LeBlanc, another swindler who was linked with a heroin dealer and stole more than $50 million from Vesco, handled Vesco's business interests in Costa Rica. LeBlanc began handling Fowlie's business interests there as well, and these were rapidly increasing following his land purchases in Pavones and the San José area. Vesco fled Costa Rica in 1978 and ultimately landed in Cuba, where he died in 2008. Danny assumed his role in Costa Rica's underground empire following Vesco's departure. While Danny nostalgically recounts the story of finding Pavones solely to create a surf paradise for his kids, employing every local, and building the town's infrastructure, those who knew him best contend those acts weren't entirely altruistic.

"He wanted to own his own fiefdom somewhere in the world, and he wanted to be an emperor, and in his own weird mind he saw that in Pavones, because he had the money to buy land and there were nothing but poor people down there who he could easily control," said Al Nelson, a childhood friend of Danny's who became linked to Pavones's tortured history after Danny went to prison.

Surfing was part of it, but the reality is his ego got the best of him. He liked hanging out with Vesco, liked the cars, the lifestyle, he couldn't get enough of it. One time I took Dan to the airport because he was flying to meet Vesco in Nicaragua. We were running late, and Dan got pissed . . .

I don't have any evidence of this other than my own speculation, but I suspect he got into big-time drug dealing after meeting Vesco. It makes sense to me because Dan always had money, always gravitated toward money, but things got really out of control after he went to Costa Rica. The thing is Dan is the biggest loser in the history of mankind, and the reason is very simple: he was a guy that was great at anything he did, so he had no reason to go into the drug business. He got too big, and Dan didn't know when to quit. Maybe none of us would.

Given a link between Vesco and drugs, including an indictment in Florida, Danny landed on the radar of the Federal Bureau of Investigation and U.S. Custom agents because of his close association with Vesco, who was already under surveillance. It simply didn't make sense that Vesco's empire in Costa Rica, which he established after fleeing the United States with more than $200 million, was assumed by a surfer whose largest business venture was a hand bag company that sold for $3 million in the early 1970s. Something didn't add up about Vesco's replacement, so the FBI began tracking Fowlie.

"I don't think Vesco was that big a figure in the drug trade at the time, some dabbling and some connections might be the extent of it, and my impression is that Fowlie didn't need his help too much," said Michael Fowler, coauthor of *Bribes, Bullets, and Intimidation*, which chronicles the drug trade in Central America.

As authorities began tracking Danny, he brushed them off and decided to show off his wave in Pavones and his growing empire instead.

"I'm never going to get caught. I am bigger than the U.S. government," Danny told Al Nelson.

"He was always kind of waving a flag and daring them to catch him," said Steve Pezman, publisher of the *Surfer's Journal* and fellow surfer from the Laguna Beach area.

Al and Danny both grew up in the La Jolla area, although Danny is six years older. They met in the early 1950s, when Al was a teenage surfer who admired Danny and others in the Windansea crew, but the two drifted apart over the next quarter century. While Danny served in the Korean War, surfed big waves in Hawaii, and started his abalone diving and Leather Gypsy businesses, Al went to law school at the University of California, Davis, and continued surfing in Hawaii, landing back in the Windansea area only in the early 1980s. Pat Curren, the Windansea surfer and famous big wave rider in Hawaii whose father brokered Danny's real estate deal in the 1950s, visited Al one day. They reminisced about various people from the past. When Danny's name came up, Pat told Al about Costa Rica and Pavones. Al remembered the first time he met Danny, back when he had a taxi business, and he wasn't surprised to hear that he was expanding his interests internationally.

"Dan was always out there doing something, he was always a little ahead of the rest of us," Al recalled.

We were just the dummies drinking wine where he always had some project going. Dan was always admired for being a guy that went out there in the world and did things. He was a tremendous diver, good surfer, built surfboards, a good waterman; he was just always around the water. So Pat, who had already been down to Costa Rica and was impressed, told me Dan had asked about me and wanted me to come down. I was going through a time in my life where I didn't know what I was going to do. Pat and I had done a lot of traveling together, so we went down there and I started to see what Dan had built down there, which was pretty neat. But it was obvious where the money was coming from. He once lost thirty thousand dollars and laughed it off like it was no big deal. His ex-wife told me he'd spend a million dollars a month sometimes. It was no secret that he was in the drug business, but he never got Pat or me involved in that. He just wanted to share his life with his old surf buddies. We'd stay at his condos in San José, then fly down to Pavones on one of Dan's planes, stay at the ranch and hang out at the cantina, then come back. It was a really special time, but things started to change and we started seeing less of Dan. He was always in Mexico or in the Netherlands, doing what Dan does, which was okay until there came a time where he never came back and we were left down there to sort everything out.

As it turned out, Al's first few years of surfing and hanging out in Costa Rica coincided with the crescendo of Danny's drug business. The reason he started seeing less and less of Dan, who'd started going by "Dan" instead of "Danny," was because his business was expanding. While Dan wouldn't admit to the precise date of his arrangement with the Quintero drug organization, its maturation period was reached by the early 1980s and continued until 1985 when Rancho del Rio was raided. There is evidence that the relationship started as early as 1978, when Dan met Ronald Gates, a carpenter, at a party in South Laguna. The two became friends and began hanging out on the sprawling ranch, usually either skeet shooting or riding motorcycles. Dan then hired him to build a warehouse. Gates testified in court that during one of their stints at the estate, Dan moved a metal table, and Gates saw a hole opening onto an underground stairway, which led to a room that was ten feet tall and thirty feet long. According to Dan's ledger man, Joseph Cooper, the room was used as an underground storage facility to hide tons of marijuana.

Cooper testified that he was also instructed by Dan to set up a bogus container company headquartered in Tucson, Arizona, where tanker trucks carried ten thousand pounds of marijuana to a rented warehouse before it was transported to Rancho del Rio, where the marijuana was then distributed throughout the western United States and Canada. But a mishap on the organization's first night of operation nearly thwarted Dan's career as major drug dealer. On that first night, two tanker trucks arrived from the border at Nogales, but the entry door into the warehouse was too low and the trucks couldn't clear the opening to get in. According to court testimony, Dan, being a quick thinker, deflated the tires and drove the trucks into the warehouse. From that point on, he ran a meticulous business in which those types of errors never happened again. Ledgers were kept to the penny, and Cooper said counting all the money became a difficult chore, although he had no problem accepting drug profits that went unreported to the Internal Revenue Service.

Cooper and Gates received reduced sentences for providing information that led to Dan's arrest. The same deal was offered to Robert Brook, who was responsible for distributing Dan's marijuana in Canada. Brook, like Dan's right-hand man, Robert Pellegrom, disappeared into the witness protection program after providing testimony that helped bring down Caro Payán and Caro Quintero, the Mexican drug suppliers. The *Los Angeles Times* reported that in exchange for information leading to arrests, the government allowed Brook to keep $1 million in assets from his drug profits, including a house in Laguna Beach, two Mercedes-Benzes, a BMW, and other property and assets in Canada. Dan, however, received no such treatment.

As poetic as his lawyer made his 1985 Pavones exit seem, with money flying through the air, Dan admitted to me he did no such thing. Although his son Dan Junior spent more time than his father did in Pavones, the elder Fowlie looked for ways to invest his money, or, as authorities believed, ways to launder his drug money. Either way, Dan didn't show is face again in Pavones after 1985. With Rancho del Rio serving as the headquarters, things ran smoothly until it was raided that year. In total, more than thirty tons went through the underground storage area, and Dan was regularly receiving lump sums of $250,000–$300,000 for his role in the operation.

He formed an oil shipment company called Tencoil Europa. Based in the port city of Rotterdam and also claiming offices in Laguna Beach, the company was flush with cash, as can be the case with oil companies. But following the raid of Dan's ranch, a Dutch detective who assisted U.S. authorities discovered that Tencoil Europa never secured a single oil shipping contract. Witnesses, though, claimed to have seen several hundred thousand dollars, in cash, flowing through the Rotterdam offices. While court testimony exposed Tencoil Europa as a shell company designed to launder drug profits, Al Nelson believes that Dan probably intended to become an oil baron.

Tencoil Europa reported oil contracts from Nigeria, and Al recalled a story about Dan's visit there to secure a deal. Through intermediaries who were connected with oil suppliers in Nigeria, Dan was asked to bring $1 million to begin negotiations and cement Tencoil's first deal. He flew to Nigeria with a briefcase of cash, stacked perfectly and amounting to $1 million. He sat at a table with two strapping African men who placed weapons on the table and proceeded to tell him, according to Al, "Okay, you have twelve hours to leave the country." Dan left without an oil contract and $1 million poorer.

"He is not academically smart, but he is very street smart, although he was still naïve in many respects," Al said. "He was the King of Pavones but that didn't matter in Africa. That was a lesson learned. In Pavones, he could pay those people off because they were uneducated and liked what he was giving them, whether it was money, Rolexes, or clothes. He surrounded himself with people who wouldn't question him. His former wife asked him one time, 'Why do you keep hiring these losers to work for you?' And he told her, 'Well, that's the only people who will work for me.'"

With millions of dollars flowing through Tencoil and invested in land throughout Mexico and Costa Rica, Dan could financially withstand the authorities seizing his assets in the United States. But with enough witnesses and informants testifying to authorities following the 1985 raid of his ranch, which he steadfastly contends was purchased with legitimate money from real estate dealings and his Leather Gypsy company, Dan was officially on the run. According to court documents, he told two confidantes in a 1985 meeting in Rosarita Beach, Mexico, that he would never return to the United States; he even instructed one of them to haul his trailer and boat to Mexico. So he was well aware at that time that U.S. authorities were circling him like sharks on chum, and he knew that everyone in the operation was talking to authorities to save themselves. Well, everyone but his two sons, Dan Junior and Gus, who were also involved in the family drug business. In 1989, the two sons were arrested and pled guilty to unloading five thousand pounds of marijuana from vans at Rancho del Rio; they received minor prison sentences. In all, six people were arrested and charged in connection with the organization, and a few more informants disappeared into the witness protection program, but Dan continued to elude justice outside of the United States and became even more emboldened.

He says he can't recall the exact chain of events that led to his leaving Pavones for the final time. He wishes it was after drinking a beer at the cantina after a two-minute surf ride—but he knows that didn't happen. The truth was he was feeling heat even in Costa Rica and returned to Mexico, where he also had multiple residences, including one in Cabo San Lucas, another end-of-the-road location known for its surf. He successfully escaped his captors for two years but was arrested in 1987 in the Mexican surf town of Puerto Escondido, home to a wave nicknamed the "Mexican Pipeline." Perhaps it would have been fitting if his international surf and drug journey started, more or less, at the long, tranquil, soulful wave of Pavones and ended at a violent, no-nonsense break in southern Mexico, but that wouldn't be accurate.

Dan was apprehended by Mexican authorities and faced forty-nine drug-related felony charges, although these would be reduced to twenty-six by the time he eventually entered a U.S. courtroom. Before that, Dan used his connections, power, and money in Mexico to avoid extradition. After being arrested in Puerto Escondido, he was transferred to a prison outside La Paz, 140 miles from his spacious beachfront pad in Cabo San Lucas and the territory of drug lord Javier Caro Payán, who, authorities believed, supplied Dan with marijuana.

After Dan was transferred to the La Paz prison, U.S. authorities visited him, seeking information about his suppliers, including Caro Payán's cousin, Rafael Caro Quintero. Dan didn't talk. Even when he was baited with deals similar to the ones his former associates received, basically a reduced sentence and/or entry into the federal witness protection program, Dan didn't talk.

"The people I was dealing with, they aren't people you talk about, at least not if you planned to live, and I wanted to live," Dan told me in 2013. "Of course I knew things, I know lots of things, but I told them you're wasting your time with me."

Dan suspected that, more than uncovering the entire drug smuggling enterprise, the actual reason the authorities wanted him to squeal was that Caro Quintero was accused of plotting the kidnapping, torture, and slaying of Drug Enforcement Agent Enrique "Kiki" Camarena on February 7, 1985, a few weeks before Dan's ranch was raided in Orange County. Another man, pilot Alfredo Zavalo-Avelar, was also kidnapped and killed. Both bodies were found at a ranch about sixty miles north of Guadalajara, where Camarena was kidnapped in broad daylight as he left the U.S. Consulate office to have lunch with his wife. Camarena was taken to a house on the outskirts of town and tortured for hours; doctors were even on hand to keep Camarena alive as his captors physically beat him. They also interrogated a DEA agent who once destroyed a marijuana plantation in northern Mexico, resulting in a $50 million loss for Caro Quintero's business. When they had heard enough, Camarena's skull was crushed like an egg shell, according to court testimony, and Caro Quintero fled the country a day later. In plain view of Mexican authorities, Caro Quintero boarded a plane at the Guadalajara airport. His next stop: Costa Rica.

There were reports that the plane Caro Quintero used to flee was also occasionally used by Dan, who admitted only that he and Caro Quintero used the same pilot to fly their personal private planes because the pilot's reputation in Latin America was a good one. Dan never said if that same pilot was used in this particular incident. Still, the FBI, which had been tracking Dan for years on account of his relationship with Vesco, believed Dan purchased marijuana, as well as smaller amounts of cocaine, through Caro Quintero and his associates.

Michael Fowler, coauthor of *Bribes, Bullets, and Intimidation*, said that Caro Quintero may have visited Dan in Pavones after fleeing Mexico and becoming a fugitive in Costa Rica. Dan denied that they ever met in Costa Rica. Authorities, though, believed they in fact did meet because during their search for Caro Quintero, they visited Pavones and spoke with a woman who picked Caro Quintero out from a photo; this woman was aware of what Dan looked like because he was the King of Pavones.

When I asked Dan about his role, he denied involvement but did comment on Kiki: "He was a dirty DEA agent, and that doesn't go over too well in Mexico."

Within weeks of fleeing, Caro Quintero, who had his own extensive network in Costa Rica, was arrested in Alajuela, a tranquil city outside of San José, and returned to Mexico where he awaited trial. In 1989, he was sentenced to forty years in prison for his role in the killings of Camarena and Avelar. In all, twenty-five people were sentenced to prison for their roles in the crime, but Mexico refused to extradite anybody to the United States. Diplomatic relations between the two countries became strained, mostly because an audio recording played in court revealed that the kidnapping, torture, and murder of a DEA agent involved several Mexican officials. Although Mexico wouldn't extradite Caro Quintero, U.S. authorities still arrested several Mexicans in California for their involvement in the killing.

As much as they tried to get him to help them bring those responsible for killing Camarena to justice in exchange for a reduced sentence, Dan didn't let out a peep during their visits to the La Paz prison where he was held. His obstinacy notwithstanding, relations between Mexico and United States were further strained when it became obvious that Dan really wasn't in prison at all.

During Dan's three years in a Mexican prison fighting extradition, he was routinely granted four-day furloughs. He usually spent that time sport fishing in the cerulean blue waters off Baja or conducting business a few hours away in Cabo San Lucas, where one of his companies was financing the building of a shopping center. With Dan's jeep usually parked outside the prison, it was clear that he was slowly, but surely, getting out of prison. Even when he was actually in prison, one U.S. agent based in Mexico told the *Los Angeles Times* that his was the "country club of Mexican prisons." Dan Weikel, who covered Dan's extradition battle and subsequent court case for the newspaper, reported that "in prison, Fowlie wears his own clothes, usually jeans and flannel shirts. He is on a first-name basis with the staff, and the atmosphere in the prison yard is more akin to a city park. To help him take care of businesses on the outside, his Jeep Cherokee is parked on prison grounds and he has hired an errand boy for four hundred dollars a month."

His prison lifestyle cost him thirty thousand dollars a month, according to Al Nelson, who occasionally visited Dan. Despite the exorbitant cost, it seemed to be paying off.

"They kinda' let me do what I want around here now," Dan told Weikel in an interview for the article, which was published in March of 1990.

Two months before that, a court in Mazatlán rejected the United States' extradition request because it ruled that such an act would violate the

Mexican Constitution. After his 1987 arrest in Puerto Escondido, the extradition battle had been waged continuously, but after three years, it started to look as if it would be unsuccessful. Despite having sworn testimony from all the major players in Dan's drug operation, all of whom were lined up to testify in court, federal prosecutors had essentially given up on ever apprehending him because they couldn't convince Mexican authorities to hand him over.

So it is little surprise that Dan was particularly brazen when Weikel visited him in 1990. With his growing confidence, Dan granted Weikel an interview because he thought it would be a golden opportunity for him to discredit Orange County sheriff Brad Gates for illegally seizing his Rancho del Rio property in 1985. Dan agreed to be interviewed under one condition: any story about him was not to be published until after he won his extradition case and was granted freedom, which, he anticipated, would happen any day now.

"I thought he was fairly clever in concealing stuff, and he was in denial on a lot of what I was asking him, what his involvement was even when it was obvious he was involved," Weikel said. "About Rancho del Rio, this sprawling ranch of river rock and timber, cottages and a big barn, he claimed it was a small vineyard that had immature vines. The huge underground tank, he claimed this is where he stored the grapes. He really believed his story. Maybe that was part of his cover in Pavones: 'I am an established member of the community, but hey, I'm doing this stuff as well but how can you come after me? I am a great guy.'"

"Personally I liked him," Weikel added. "On one level, I would have liked to have him as my dad. He was an outdoorsman, he surfed, he fished, he just had a lot of interests you would have as a kid. I also surfed. He was also a decent artist who once painted a picture of an owl for the president of Mexico while in prison. But there is a flip side to this guy, and that was he was a dope smuggler, a tax evader, all of this kind of stuff."

Dan did indeed paint something for Carlos Salinas de Gortari, the Mexican president from 1988 to 1994, but it's unclear if it was done with or without a wink. Although he repeatedly denied such accusations, Salinas was accused of fraud and corruption and of being in cahoots with the Mexican drug cartels during his six-year term. Perhaps it was just a matter of coincidence, but Dan successfully fought extradition and lived comfortably in a Mexican prison during the time Salinas held office. That was about to change.

Weikel returned from Baja bubbling with excitement at the idea of writing this amazing story he had uncovered south of the border. His editors briefly entertained Dan's request to stall publication, but he was foolish to think journalists would operate on his time schedule and demands. By the end of that month, Weikel's article about Dan living it up south of the border while he was supposed to be in prison was published in one of the largest newspapers in the country.

"I am not surprised," a San Diego attorney who specializes in Mexican law told Weikel after he read the article. "It sounds to me like he's got the kind of benefits that money can bring you. And, if that is the case, he is going to have to keep paying for them."

U.S. authorities certainly weren't amused when they read how the United States' most wanted drug trafficker was marlin fishing off the coast of Baja, dining on fresh fish and knocking back beers, sometimes with Mexican government employees. Once discouraged, U.S. authorities were reenergized because they had new information to ratchet up their pressure on Mexican authorities, including information on Salinas, who spent much of his presidency defending himself against claims of being in bed with drug cartels. But even Salinas could not defend his country's behavior as exposed in Weikel's article.

"The government had almost given up trying to get him," Weikel said. "The extradition, it was clearly dragging on and it was unclear what was going to happen to him. He was slowly getting out. They had been working on the case for a long time, but they were discouraged. But when federal authorities read my story, they were angry. They felt they had new ammunition."

Four months after Weikel's article was published, in July of 1990, Dan was extradited to the United States. The same court in Mazatlán that had denied his extradition request seven months earlier granted it, deciding that his extradition didn't violate the Mexican Constitution after all. It was believed to have been the first extradition from Baja California to the United States since the 1890s. One day Dan was marlin fishing; the next he was handcuffed on a plane heading toward John Wayne Airport in Orange County.

On July 10, 1990, Weikel reported, Dan pled not guilty to twenty-six felony charges, including money laundering, income tax evasion, and conspiracy to smuggle 53,000 pounds of marijuana into the United States. Within a year, at the age of fifty-eight, and following a six-week trial, he was found guilty on fifteen of the twenty-six felony counts, including possession of marijuana with the intent to distribute, conspiracy, illegal transfer of currency outside the United States, and operating a continuing criminal enterprise. He was sentenced to thirty years in federal prison and fined $1 million.

"Dan likes to play games," Al Nelson said. "He can't admit he's ever done wrong in his life. He wants people to think he's the good guy and that he served time because these assholes rolled over him to get a reduced sentence, which is true, but they rolled over him because he was the boss. There are always two Dans, and I remember him interviewing with that reporter. I told him 'Dan, your ego, you just told a story that is going to get you in the end.' The president of Mexico was denying giving preferential treatment to drug prisoners who had money, and then Dan goes and talks with the *LA Times* about getting preferential treatment. It made no sense other than that Dan's ego got the best of him. He didn't know when to stop."

The government, which never found more than an ounce of marijuana at his Rancho del Rio property and almost exclusively used sworn testimony from drug dealers looking for personal parachutes, was ecstatic. The verdict provided closure to a twenty-year investigation into a massive drug enterprise, which they believed started as early as the late 1960s with the Brotherhood of Eternal Love. In 1989, before he was even convicted and was still in a Mexican prison, U.S. President George Bush used Dan's Rancho del Rio, which had long been seized and later was purchased by the Orange County Girl Scouts, as the backdrop for a nationally televised news conference on the war on drugs.

"Many of you know the history of the ground we stand on," Bush was quoted as saying in the *Los Angeles Times*. "It was the core of an international marijuana and cocaine smuggling ring. How many lives—how many families—how many hopes and dreams have been destroyed with these chemical weapons of death and destruction: drugs?"

When I interviewed Dan twenty-three years later, almost to the date of his conviction, he vehemently denied his role as a mastermind or ring leader, so strongly it sounded like he still believed, somehow, that he wasn't involved and was swindled by others. He still viewed himself as a surfer dad whose family business inadvertently led to him and his two sons receiving prison sentences.

After being charged with twenty-six felony counts, Dan sat on a bench outside the courtroom when Weikel and an FBI agent handling the case walked past him. Dan recognized Weikel and, in what the reporter interpreted as a rather threatening tone, said to him, "I hope one day I can return the favor to you." The agent asked Weikel if he wanted to take the threat any further and file formal charges. Weikel declined, stating he wanted the agent to remember that comment should something happen to him in the future. Nothing ever did.

"Drug dealing today is a violent business, but Fowlie wasn't violent," Weikel said.

> I heard his reputation was not for violence, but I think he could have hurt me had he wanted to. He was just part of this group of pot smugglers back then. These guys were characters. There was the Coronado Company down in the San Diego area, and they were surfers and watermen just like Fowlie's group. They weren't killing people; they were just smuggling pot from Mexico and were groups run by charismatic characters that wanted a certain lifestyle. They wanted to travel and surf, but these guys were ambitious, and Fowlie was especially ambitious. I am not sure if he would have had gotten in the drug business that we have today, it just wasn't his style; it was different times back then.

Dan didn't know it at the time, but in 1991 he had bigger problems on his hands than a reporter who, he felt, burned him by publishing a story prematurely. With his assets in the United States confiscated, what he had left was basically limited to the 3,700 acres he owned in Pavones. Little did he know that since his disappearance in 1985 and his time in prison, his land had been overtaken by organized mobs of squatters and an all-out war was occurring there. After being betrayed by drug-dealing associates with whom he didn't have a long history, he would now have to entrust childhood friend Al Nelson with helping him reclaim his land—all the while himself being behind bars at Terminal Island, a federal correctional institution south of Los Angeles that once housed gangster Al Capone.

11 Jungle Invasion

The best revenge is to live on and prove yourself.
—Eddie Vedder, musician and surfer

What happened next in the saga of Pavones seems impossible to fathom and sounds like the farthest reaches of fiction. Yet as hard as it tilted toward utter bullshit, the truth needle repeatedly snapped back to fact because, somehow, this really did happen: a confluence of events, which occurred in three countries and less than two months apart from each other, flooded a surf town at the end of the road of Costa Rica, a forgotten town that doesn't appear on some maps, and scarred it to the core. There is no way to make sense of all it except to describe how it happened.

In March of 1985, Dan was in Rotterdam as Pat Curren and Al Nelson, shirtless and tanned from the equatorial sun, remained in Pavones. The previous month, on February 7, Dan's marijuana supplier killed a DEA agent in Mexico, fled to Costa Rica, perhaps visited Pavones, and was apprehended a few weeks later outside of San José and was sent to a Mexican prison. While that was happening to his supplier, Dan's ranch was raided, and by early March his drug enterprise was beginning to crumble. Pat and Al, in the meantime, were being tickled by the charms of the down-south lifestyle. The surf was good, the beer was cold, monkeys crawled in the trees, and a whale passed in the Golfo Dulce, its spout blowing a mist of water on the horizon.

Al and Pat probably wouldn't have known this, but also in March of 1985, the United Fruit Company officially ceased operations at its headquarters in nearby Golfito, ending its near century-long stranglehold in Costa Rica.

The closure followed years of labor disputes that were encouraged by Cuba, which financed a Communist-backed labor movement deriding the company's exploitation of its workers and its propensity to send profits overseas. It was a process, Communists argued, that benefitted foreigners at the expense of Costa Rica, which seems like low-hanging fruit in today's global economy. Resentment, however, had been growing since United Fruit's arrival. Costa Rica was the first country to produce bananas for export, although there were only a few thousand acres dedicated to farming bananas in the early 1880s. Then, in 1883, the government enacted a law declaring all national products to be free of export taxes. It was no coincidence that United Fruit reaped the benefits of this sweetheart tax loophole, which, after all, was created strictly for Minor C. Keith, the company's founder.

In the previous decade, Keith's uncle had made an agreement with the government to build a railroad from San José to Limón, a Caribbean port city where United Fruit's headquarters were initially established. The government fell behind on its payments for the railroad right at the time Keith inherited his uncle's assets following his death. In an effort to continue with the railroad project, Keith borrowed money to complete construction. As a show of appreciation for not sending Costa Rica into default status, the president gave Keith several hundred thousand acres near Limón to grow bananas, issued him a lease on the railroad, and, most important, enacted that law that created a banana republic.

The railroad wasn't much of a moneymaker in terms of passenger traffic, although it did infuse other foreign capital into the country. Keith's banana business, on the other hand, became quite lucrative. By the time United Fruit's headquarters moved from Limón to Golfito in 1938, the company was the largest employer in Central America, with more than ten thousand employees. Valued at more than $200 million, it never paid a single cent in export tax to the national treasury. It was nice racket indeed, but it didn't come without its hassles. In the mid-1930s a major labor strike shook the country's Caribbean coast. The government intervened and settled with the workers, but United Fruit didn't participate in the process and ignored the deal struck between the government and the workers. Thus, another labor strike began a month later, and it was then that United Fruit considered a move elsewhere, perhaps a place where the locals would be happy to have a job at all. Golfito, the principal city in Costa Rica's poorest region, became that place.

As they did in Limón, profits mounted in Golfito, but leftist governments throughout Latin America encouraged employees to regularly strike in an attempt to improve their working conditions. As Cuba's presence in the region strengthened in the 1970s with the support of the Communist Soviet Union, and Cuba began training Costa Ricans to fight these sorts of labor battles, United Fruit decided the disputes had become so untenable that it was no longer worth the hassle to conduct business in Costa Rica.

When United Fruit closed in 1985, Golfito fell into the doldrums. A town once rife with stately mansions and manicured streets once again became one of the most depressed cities in Costa Rica, and it has never recovered. Overnight thousands of people were unemployed, and the Communist-backed labor soldiers were stuck in a steamy jungle and without a cause. Shortly thereafter, as fate would have it, drug-related events in Mexico and the United States led them to turn their attention a few miles south where two gringos sipped beers in Pavones. A town made up of ranchers, fishermen, and a few surfers, where nobody was employed by United Fruit, Pavones was about to feel the impact from others losing their jobs at the company's headquarters in Golifto.

Al and Pat were watching the afternoon pass when suddenly a plume of dust billowed above the jungle road, and a white bus rumbled toward the cantina and the soccer field. There was never much traffic in those days, but the arrival of a lone bus wasn't out of the ordinary. It gave Al only a slight pause as he sipped his beer. Then another bus rumbled down the road, and another, and another, and Al did put his beer down; this was out of the ordinary. Al and Pat, gringos lost in paradise, looked at one other and their growing eyes said it all: we're in big trouble.

The busses stacked up like jets on a crowded airport runway, blocking the road into town. People started exiting the busses. From Al's vantage point, he saw the serious look on their faces before he saw their guns and machetes. There were five hundred of them, Al estimated, and they didn't say hello. They immediately started chopping down trees, burning houses, and putting up fences on property that wasn't theirs. A few busses left, only to return later, stocked with provisions and more people. A small army had raided this sleepy surf town that was previously only known to a select few outsiders.

"I could tell these guys weren't fooling around," Al said. "They just took over the place, and we didn't know what was happening. We were the only two white people around. We were there to surf, stay at our buddy's place, and wait for him to come back."

This incident marked the beginning of what became a more than decade-long period in Pavones's history known as the "Squatter Wars." It probably would never have escalated if the King had been there, but Dan was in Rotterdam masquerading as an oil baron, and within a few years he was in a Mexican prison. Al, meanwhile, wanted out of Pavones. Although there weren't any telephones, he found a ship-to-shore radio, and using repeaters on mountaintops, he coordinated with San José. He couldn't reach Dan, but he did reach Dan's lawyer. Al described the current events, and authorities were notified.

"We were told it's too dangerous to stay, and they needed to get us out of there, but when they tried to get us out, they said the squatters blocked the road and they couldn't reach us," Al said. "Police came and there was a shootout and people were killed. Jesus Christ, we were just there to catch a few waves. We didn't know what the hell was going on. We're hiding out and then a truck got through on a second trip, and we finally made it safely back to San José."

When they reached San José, Dan was still in the Netherlands but was informed of what was happening to his kingdom. He contacted his financial advisor, Norman Leblanc, who packaged Dan's land holdings into various corporations based in Costa Rica and Panama. By April, Leblanc had used his connections to successfully evict the squatters who arrived the day Al was sipping beers, but they returned a few weeks later, and Leblanc's power was marginalized in what became a squatter onslaught, more or less backed by the government. As much as this invasion didn't please Dan, he was more concerned about the fallout from the raid of Rancho del Rio the previous month, primarily because his associates were squealing to authorities and a warrant had been issued for his arrest.

He couldn't return to the United States, and now he couldn't return to Costa Rica. Al left San José and returned to the United States, but Dan encouraged him to move to Cabo San Lucas, Mexico, where he could surf and live at another one of Dan's places. He would be safe there. Al thought that was a fine idea.

When Al arrived at Dan's beachfront property in Cabo, Dan was still preoccupied with what was happening in Orange County, and remained relatively uninterested in events in Pavones. He might have been more interested had he known squatters had taken it over, including all 3,700 acres of Danny Land. Although they couldn't win their labor dispute with United Fruit, the Communist could focus on enormous tracts of unoccupied land, supposedly owned by a gringo drug dealer who had recently been arrested and was out of the country, possibly forever.

While this wasn't what Costa Rica intended when it crafted its home-steading laws, the Communists hijacked the spirit of the law and saw an opportunity to claim unoccupied land as their own. The fact that they were invading a gringo's land was all the more satisfying since gringo-owned United Fruit had just left thousands jobless down the road in Golfito. Dan didn't know that was the motivation at the time, but regardless, he figured that his dutiful followers would stop anyone from taking the King's land, which, in fact, they were powerless to do; in some cases, they even aligned with the squatters and participated in the takeover. Dan's focus remained on eluding the authorities, so Al's focus was on surfing more untouched waves in Cabo. Things continued in this fashion until Dan was arrested in 1987 in Puerto Escondido and was transferred to the prison outside of La Paz. It was there that Al visited Dan and proposed a plan to save his land in Costa Rica.

"It was costing him a lot of money to stay in prison there, and the prison workers don't want to lose that money, so we agreed I'd go back to Costa Rica and see what was going on," Al said. "He had lots of money in Mexico, and really felt his land was gone in Costa Rica, and was only concerned about fighting extradition and staying in Mexico. So I went down there and the *precaristas* [squatters] had taken over everything. Hundreds of families were living on his land, and the government was flat-out saying that Dan Fowlie is a criminal and they don't give a shit about his land. So the government is supporting the squatters in taking over his land, and they aren't talking to me because I'm nobody."

"But I look at these thousands of acres of land, prime beachfront and ocean view land," Al continued,

and I know it will be valuable one day. I know Dan is going to need money, and as his friend, I can't just stomach to see this happen. Regardless of how he bought the land, that's his land, he bought it, it belongs to him. I come back from Costa Rica and suddenly his two sons get arrested, and basically the whole family is in prison. So I visited him in jail again and told him I will fight for you, but here's the deal: You're the bad guy, and the government is allowing them to take over the land. The only way we can do this is for you to turn all the land over to me, the good guy, but you have to transfer the land to me. The government might take the land, but they will have to pay me for it and then I can give it to you. That's the law. Or if I can keep the land and get these squatters off the land, I will hold onto the land and give it back when you get out. His only option was to trust me because his two sons were in prison, and there was nobody else to fight for his land.

Dan wrote letters in prison informing Norman Leblanc and others that Al was in charge of his land. What Al discovered upon arriving in San José is that Dan had left a tangled mess of a paperwork trail behind, one that required months, even years, of untangling. There was an initial meeting with Leblanc, who was holed up in a stuffy apartment in a seedy area of San José where he smoked cigarettes and bet on horse races. From prison, Dan had instructed Leblanc via telephone to switch the land into Al's name. The initial hurdle was that most of the 3,700 acres were wrapped into small corporations and, following Leblanc's recommendation, Dan's name wasn't attached to them. Instead, other people were labeled as presidents, either locals living in Pavones or those who Dan felt were trusted associates in Costa Rica.

"Dan understands the streets, but he doesn't understand the law," Al said.

He always tried to stay away from his name being on paper. It's like you want to buy a house and you don't have the money, so you have your grandma buy the house but the title is in your name. Twenty years later she says it's her house, not yours. She's right in that she paid for the house and you didn't, but that's not how it works legally if her name isn't anywhere to be found. It was a mess. The corporations were in disrepair, books were missing, and paperwork was missing. He made all these people as presidents, lawyers and secretaries and farmers in Pavones, and I had to find each of them and show them the letter Dan gave me telling them that I was the new owner.

Most of the people bailed out and turned it over to me because they just wanted their names off his land after what had happened to him. Others told me to fuck off and they didn't have to give it back because their name was on it, and legally it was their land. There were a few problems like that, but after a while I was able to get everything into my name. After thirty flights down there, and spending thousands of dollars of my own money, and spending hundreds of hours to figure this out, I followed through and got Dan's land back but under my name.

With Danny Land now in childhood friend Al's name, there was just one little problem: Dan eventually said he didn't authorize Al's takeover of his land. Dan said when they met in 1987 in prison, he wrote a letter that only gave him power of attorney and stated that Al was the manager of his land. In fact, he explicitly wrote that Al Nelson was not allowed to buy or sell any land.

"I wrote a letter saying all of this, but I made a mistake when I wrote a letter for this sniveling, crooked son of a bitch," Dan said of Al. "There was too much white space under the letter, and so Al doctored the letter and wrote more after he left that allowed him to buy and sell my land. He's a lawyer and knew how to doctor documents for his own gain. That's what happened. I never gave him my blessing to take over my land. I just needed somebody to manage it while I was away to take care of the squatters."

Al contends this is pure fantasy, a story concocted in Dan's own mind.

The scary thing about Dan is, and this has gotten worse as he's gotten older, he believes his own bullshit stories. He is correct in that there was space left because it was a ten-page letter with his signature on the bottom of the last page. He told me in case you need to do something in my name I am leaving you this space and you can fill it in. But then he told me what I really needed was a power of attorney in Costa Rica to do anything in his name. So I flew to Mexico City and it took me seven days, going to a different office each day, to get notary verification, and after all this red tape I went to Costa Rica but never needed the power of attorney. The letters were all I needed, and I became the owner like he wanted so he could get his land back.

These differing versions of the story could have been sorted out in one of two ways. The first involved the original letter written by Dan in prison, but neither Dan nor Al could produce it because it was presumably in the hands of Norman Leblanc. The other way was finding Norman himself, but that was impossible because he put a gun to his head, pulled the trigger, and splattered his brains against a wall. With those options exhausted, it was unclear who was the real owner of the land. But at the time Dan Junior was released from prison and visited Pavones, the elder Fowlie had no idea what was happening to his land because, according to Al, everything was fine.

When Dan Junior reported back to his father, who was still serving time at Terminal Island in the United States, he had a horror story to tell: squatters were everywhere, encouraged by the government because the owner had abandoned his property. What land Al had been able to protect after becoming the legal owner by forging papers, he had since sold for a mere pittance, and now a litany of crooks were selling land they bought for pennies on the dollar to unsuspecting buyers. Plus, he said, the government was ignoring the murders and arsons and gun violence stemming from the land disputes. Basically, his son told him, it was a chaotic land grab.

When Al and Dan agreed to whatever they agreed upon that day in 1987, Dan considered himself the owner either legally on paper or through a handshake agreement with Al that his name would be on paper again one day in the future. And it's true, Al successfully managed to stave off most of the squatters and reclaim his buddy's land, but it's what happened next that became an impossible web to untangle.

"When Danny left the area, it's important to understand that Costa Rica is prone to squatters," said Steve Pezman, publisher of the *Surfer's Journal*. "That whole area became a zone of contention, a squatters' lot. People started scrambling to get some, because it was unclear who owned what. It settled down as people staked out their turf and assumed ownership. The whole intrigue is how the land got cut up and managed after Dan left. Al Nelson had a role in that, but Dan entrusted Al. Dan has his version of what happened, and Al has his version, but I would trust Al over Dan. They are not friendly; they are two bull male sharks swimming in a pool. They avoid each other."

Regardless of whether Al or Dan was the legal owner, Dan was powerless and remained stuck behind bars until 2005, when he was released from prison. The Al-said/Dan-said war of words lasted until 2013 when I interviewed them both in Cabo San Lucas, by which time they were somewhat friendly again and the land squabble had abated. But what transpired in Pavones during the years after their 1987 meeting in a Mexican prison was anything but friendly. Not knowing—and not caring—who was the actual land owner, people did whatever they wanted; they killed, and the government did nothing to stop things from spiraling out of control. The fog separating fact and fiction grew thicker as violence erupted in the jungle, creating a lawless surf town in a forgotten corner of Costa Rica, which one writer had dubbed "the Switzerland of the Americas" because of its reputation for peace and neutrality.

On a drizzly afternoon on November 13, 1997, a mob of squatters entered the property of American Max Dalton and surrounded him. About four years earlier, Dalton had purchased an oceanfront piece of property that originally belonged to Dan and probably still did, yet he brokered a deal through Al Nelson to gain title and live out his final years in the Costa Rican jungle. Dalton visited the municipality in Golfito numerous times in the previous few years to start the process of evicting squatters. They were always evicted, and they always returned. He was accustomed to occasional confrontations, which were usually accompanied by threats from the land invaders. On that day, threats were turned into action.

Squatters released cattle onto the property to irritate the seventy-nine-year-old Dalton, as was their wont, although this time around they wanted matters to escalate. The squatters had become so emboldened over the past decade, mostly because their influence stretched to the highest reaches of the municipality of Golfito, that they had actually formulated a murder hit list, and they started ticking names off it. Everyone on their list was a gringo, because gringos, they felt, were obstructing their opportunity for peaceful residency in the area. Al Nelson's name was on the list, and so was Dalton's when the squatter mob surrounded him after he attempted to rid his property of the cattle.

First-hand witnesses there that day were squatters, with the lone exception being Dalton's farmhand, who was nearby but wasn't privy to the exact chronology of what happened. All he heard were gunshots, and when the mob broke, two bodies lay dead in the mud: Dalton and fifty-five-year-old Álvaro Aguilar. Both men were armed. According to the *Tico Times*, the squatter witnesses testified that Dalton fired the first shot, which hit Gerardo Mora, the leader of the squatter movement, in the hand, and that, in turn, prompted Aguilar to fire at Dalton. Aguilar's shot mortally wounded Dalton but not before Dalton fired a shot that killed Aguilar. The chain of events seemed unlikely from the outset, but the only witnesses were squatters. Dalton was alive after being shot, but the squatters watched patiently, waiting from him to bleed to death.

Later, while in Pavones, Allan Weisbecker, a writer, discovered that Dalton's murder was a premeditated attack planned by Gerardo Mora with the help of a Municipality of Golfito executive. Mora, the writer concluded, shot Dalton, shot Aguilar to fit the squatters' story, and then shot his own hand to cover all angles of the story, which would be scrutinized in an investigation by the Organismo de Investigación Judicial (OIJ), Costa Rica's equivalent to the FBI. According to Weisbecker, municipality executive Jimmy Cubillo gave the squatters an oceanfront piece of land to build an icehouse—land that Cubillo knew was occupied by Dalton. Thus, the squatters had an extra incentive to kill Dalton. All they needed to do was to create a situation where the murder would seem to be an accident. But it was no accident that squatters living in tents on Dalton's one-hundred-acre property released cattle toward Dalton's home to spark a gunfight.

The OIJ, however, concluded in February of 1998 that evidence supported the squatters' story that Dalton and Aguilar killed each other. Dalton's family was outraged at the agency's findings, and, seeking a solution to a larger problem, they elicited the assistance of high-level government officials in the United States. Jesse Helms, chairman of the Foreign Affairs Committee, and California Democrat Dianne Feinstein pressed the issue even further, demanding that Costa Rica end the violence in Pavones.

The United States Embassy, responding to complaints from the roughly two dozen Americans who lived in Pavones at that time, accused the Costa Rican government of failing to protect Americans from violence, as well as pointing to the local authorities' incompetence regarding, if not complicity in, the murder of Dalton. By the end of November, the U.S. State Department issued a warning advising Americans not to visit the area. The warning stated: "Operating with impunity, the squatters continue their attempts to intimidate U.S. citizens in the land [Pavones] area, occupying their land, threatening them with death and reportedly cutting water supplies to their land." Oddly, the travel advisory did nothing to stop the flow of surfers from visiting, mostly because after Dan went to prison, one of the world's best waves was no longer a secret, and getting a chance to ride it was worth a little danger. Although the travel warning did little to deter surfers, politicians increased the pressure on Costa Rica to find those responsible for Dalton's death by threatening to cut off aid to the country. Costa Rica maintained that the impoverished squatters were just seeking the rightful, peaceful takeover of land under the country's homesteading laws.

But according to an article in the *Tico Times*, the U.S. Senate released a fact sheet on Pavones, denying that the squatters were impoverished *campesinos*, and asserting instead that they were organized professionals who were seeking to appropriate land without paying for it. Mora was arrested on manslaughter charges in connection with the Dalton case, but was eventually released due to lack of evidence and remains to this day a large property owner in the area.

While the double murder may have been the focal point of the Squatter Wars, they started with the invasion of squatters in 1985. Although gringos occupied Dan's land following the invasion, thereby preventing any legal opportunity for squatters to homestead, the squatters encroached on the land anyway, with the result being a nearly constant see-sawing of two sides staking out turf on disputed land. Under Costa Rican law, citizens who remain on an unoccupied piece of land for three months begin to accumulate rights. After one year, it is nearly impossible to evict them. After ten years, they can legally register the property as their own. By the time Dan was released from prison in 2005, it had been twenty years since he last occupied his own property. However, squatters contend that Dan was always the true owner and wasn't present.

The first major incident in the Squatter Wars occurred in 1988 when squatters stormed Rancho del Mar, Dan's signature piece of property fronting the sawmill surf break; this was where Dan purchased his own private wave from Carlos Lobo in 1974. Fourteen years later, squatters burned buildings to the ground and started to approach the adjoining property. According to Weisbecker's book *Can't You Get Along With Anyone?*, a gun battle ensued between the squatters, on the one hand, and, on the other, Lobo and expatriate Owen Handy, who successful staved them off. Then, in 1991, a mob of squatters left the town center, walked across a bridge spanning the Rio Claro, and advanced toward the land of surfer Peter Noeldecken, which was probably another piece of Dan's property. As the mob approached, some on horseback, Noeldecken's caretaker gunned down squatter Hugo Vargas, killing him instantly. Weisbecker writes that the squatters quickly retreated but burned down three houses in the process, and then surrounded the cantina and screamed for revenge. (There is a stone monument in Vargas's honor near the bridge.)

A year later, in 1992, armed squatters stormed the municipal building in Golfito and demanded a better handling of the land dispute. Because the central government took no action against the gun- and machete-wielding citizens for storming a government building, the squatters interpreted the non-action as a justification of their behavior—or maybe of the government's cowardice. Either way, there was no law governing the area. It stayed that way until Mora murdered Dalton, and then roughly a month later, in December of 1997, James Pospychala was stoned by forty squatters, including women and children, after he tried to dismantle a squatter camp. Pospychala escaped unharmed, but shortly thereafter his house was burned by squatters. In January of 1998, Senator Jesse Helms requested that the Inter-American Development Bank (IDB) withhold a $70 million loan package to Costa Rica until more progress was made on the land conflict. Magically, the land disputes diminished. The stoning of Pospychala punctuated a thirteen-year warring period that Americans could no longer ignore. They put immense pressure on the Costa Rican government to find those responsible for killing Dalton, or at the very least to find a way to eliminate the violence.

In the Costa Rican government's defense, the Americans were asking it to perform an impossible investigation to figure out who was the legal property owner of the disputed land in Pavones. If Dan Fowlie was the legal owner, then technically he abandoned his land when he fled, and therefore it was available to squatters because it was an absentee landowner situation. But if Dan wasn't the owner and Al Nelson was, their agreement that started in 1987 took years to complete, during which time squatting had already begun. Moreover, how could it really be determined on which specific date Al assumed legal ownership of Dan's various properties, since they totaled almost four thousand acres yet were wrapped into a handful corporations based in Costa Rica and Panama? Such circumstances might justify the government's hesitation to get started with the investigation; they don't justify the government's ignoring the land disputes for thirteen years, while Ticos and foreigners were murdered and attacked. Yet, the fact is, the government did nothing, and vigilante justice prevailed.

Nevertheless, Costa Rica's IDA encouraged homesteading on unoccupied land as a means to improve it, and since it considered the land unoccupied, it supported the squatters' takeover. As they acquired property rights, the squatters prematurely sold land to unsuspecting gringos, who then sold it to other unsuspecting gringos. Nowadays, there are more bogus titles floating around Pavones than raindrops in November. Some of those gringos in Pavones were no choir boys. There were land crooks, cocaine dealers, brothel owners, and one guy who was selling babies on the black market. Dan himself issued a warning from prison about the land thieves. Here's what he wrote in a four-page letter to the Municipality of Golfito in 1996, which was later published in the *Tico Times*:

> When I return to Costa Rica, I will take aggressive legal action against those who are involved in these illegal and unauthorized sales and transfers. During the past 10 years, while in jail, I have hired or assigned different lawyers, accountants, administrators, and supposed friends to help me maintain my properties in Costa Rica. I have given these people thousands of dollars to pay all the necessary taxes, lease payments and legal fees to defend my property rights. I have been swindled by all of them. All have abused my trust and have committed various forms of fraud, selling or transferring titles of my properties, leases and machinery.

As much as Dan's letter attempted to document the illegalities of the land transactions, all it really did was strengthen the squatters' case with the IDA. If Dan himself admitted the land was acquired through illegal methods, then the land should be given to the squatters because it was unoccupied by the true owner. In other words, it wasn't the true owner who was evicting them or trying to evict them; it was an imposter illegally acting as the true owner. Therefore, the contested land was available for squatting after all. It was a flimsy but effective argument accepted by the IDA, which was uninterested in fighting for the property rights of a convicted drug dealer or sticking up for the sketchy characters either associated with him or acting on their own behalf.

With Dan's letter backfiring on him and essentially giving the squatters full property rights by the end of the millennium, the violence subsided for the most part, even though some tensions between Ticos and gringos remained. The land was divided up to most everyone's satisfaction, new gringos were coming in as the world-class wave become more and more popular, and some of the newer residents were respectful folk looking to build a small business or retire. The town started to have a different feel to it, but it still had troubling shaking ghosts of its past.

"Almost every gringo down there has a checkered past. They are hiding there from drug deals or whatever," Al said.

They have the lowest forms of human life down there, and, boy, there are some bad actors. I don't trust anyone down there. I don't know anything about the new people coming, but I know the old people and all of them will screw you in a second. Now the local people are incredible thieves because they saw how these outsiders do things and think that is how the world works. They will steal the shirt off your back and tires off your car if you slow down too much. Beautiful place, but it's got some real problems. The fact is it's a place down in the jungle with no police and all this crap can go on, but it works down there.

As Al saw it, "A lot of the problems go directly back to Dan"—to his involvement in drugs, to his leaving, to his not having his land squared away and instead having it in so many people's names. Had he not operated the way he did, the land disputes would not have gone on or escalated. "So as much as Dan should be credited with building everything down there and the good things he's done," Al added, "he also should be blamed for the bad things that happened after he went away."

Was he the King of Pavones? According to Al, "The reality was he was king to a bunch of undereducated people in Pavones. He had a hundred and fifty times more money than they did and he could buy them and all the punk surfers around his son. But you walk out into the big lights, without the money and power, and a real man wants to talk to you, and you're a nobody. That's what happened when he went back to Pavones."

12 Pura Vida

No one is useless in this world who lightens the burdens of another.
—Charles Dickens

Before Rancho del Rio was raided, Dan was rich and powerful, and it seemed that every decision he made was the right one. After his ranch was raided, it seemed that every decision he made was the wrong one: not sorting out the paperwork mess in Costa Rica during the two years he was on the run, giving the interview with a *Los Angeles Times* reporter that led to his extradition, and writing that letter to the Municipality of Golfito from prison, thinking it would help his cause. But perhaps the worst decision of them all was returning to Pavones in 2005 after being released from prison.

More interested in settling scores and band-aiding mistakes from his previous life than creating a new one, Dan walked through a chain-link fence and past the white sign of Terminal Island a free man. Credited with three years served in a Mexican prison, as well as a year served while awaiting trial in the United States, he served a total of eighteen years of his thirty-year prison sentence. He entered Terminal Island a muscular, tan, fifty-eight-year-old man with a full head of blonde hair and many connections. He walked out in 2005 as an unemployed, unrepentant seventy-two-year-old former drug smuggler who looked two decades younger. Yet his favorable genes couldn't mask the fact that his connections, money, and power had dried up like a river in a drought-ridden desert.

"Eighteen years in prison is a long time, especially in the older half of your life," Al Nelson said.

Maybe his mind went crazy, but what happened next was about money, not our friendship. For all the millions of dollars he had, he never lived high on the hog. . . . He never had the flash that some drug dealers have. Sure, he had jets going down to South America, or he'd go to Thailand for Thai sticks, but basically he was a simple guy. If you give him a beer and a joint, he's a happy guy, that's Dan. People think he must have rat-holed some of his money before he went away, but he the truth is he was broke when he left prison.

The kinds of paperwork issues that compromised his land in Costa Rica also plagued his land in Cabo, where hundreds of acres along the beachfront north of town had been carved up and sold over the years. As in Pavones, Dan's land in Cabo was in another person's name, and that person spent his own money to pay taxes and keep the land while Dan was in prison. The land had been purchased by Dan and a Mexican drug dealer (who later disappeared) and split fifty–fifty. Since Mexico doesn't have squatter laws, Dan's land near Cabo wasn't subjected to the same fate as his land in Pavones, although it was sold off over the years for various reasons while he was in prison. The tumbledown casita (his former care-taker's place) has become his permanent residence after prison; one of his ex-wives lives in a larger house on the property. He arrived in Cabo after leaving Terminal Island primarily to settle a score with Al, who still resided less than a half mile away in a concrete abode overlooking the Pacific Ocean. This house had been built on a lot that Dan gave Al in return for Al's seeing to his affairs, before the land disputes in Pavones erupted.

After Dan's son Pequeño revealed to him that Al was selling his land in Pavones for pennies on the dollar and not protecting any of it, Dan became outraged, and when he was able to leave Terminal Island, he immediately called Al. Al informed Dan that any land that wasn't overtaken by squat-ters was still in his control and that he would transfer the land to Dan's name once Dan paid him a nominal fee for retaining the land. Dan cut him off and barked that he was a liar and that he wouldn't pay Al any-thing. Convinced his childhood buddy betrayed him, Dan threatened to bulldoze Al's house.

"He was just belligerent and ridiculous," Al said.

I told him I want to settle this damn land deal, we don't have to be friends, but we have to talk. He said, "No, we don't. I am going to have you put in prison the rest of your life." That's a pretty heavy statement, so I asked him, "You mind telling me what the charges would be?" He replied, "Mismanagement of land, stealing my land," and then he said he was going to bulldoze my house. I just had to laugh. The problem is he believes what he's saying. When I showed him documented proof of something, he said the most incredible things. I told him "Dan, you wrote this letter, you gave me this letter, and this is where it says you gave me the land. Look, the letter is right here and, look, here is the paperwork for your land." Then he tells me, "That's a forgery." It's pretty hard to talk to someone like that. He was convinced in his mind that I sold all of his land and screwed him, but the reality is I am still the owner of his land that wasn't taken by the *precaristas* [squatters]. He found that out later after we became friendly again, but we didn't talk for about six years after he got out of prison, even though we lived down the road from each other.

After Dan threatened to bulldoze Al's house, Al contacted Dan's parole officer in the United States, informing him that Dan was in Mexico and that Dan had physically threatened him. Al said that if he turned up dead in Mexico, Dan should be a suspect. While Al believed that Dan really was a teddy bear and wouldn't hurt anyone, he knew that Dan hired enforcers when necessary. Apart from that, he was flabbergasted that after serving eighteen years in prison, Dan had a passport in a matter of months and was traveling across international borders. These were details his parole officer didn't seem overly concerned about.

For his part, Dan said he never physically threatened Al, but he's killed him many times in his own mind over the years.

He should die for what he's done, but I've spent enough time in prison. He wanted all this money for defending my property, and now he was extorting me to get my own land back. He said he spent seventeen years defending my property and wanted me to pay him, but I told him, "Wait a minute, you went down there for a week or ten days at a time, you got drunk in the cantina, and you sold my property. The only reason you have any money at all in life is because of me." Al is basically squatting on my property in Mexico. I gave him the land he's living on and then he tells people that if he dies in Mexico, I am the one who killed him? This guy is no good, but I didn't have time to deal with him. It would be tough to beat this guy with his lawyer talk and forged paperwork. I finally told myself, "Look, I might be able to beat this guy in court, but the clock is ticking. I am in my seventies, I don't have time to spend ten years in court settling this thing, so I'll go down there and settle it myself."

Al wanted to advise Dan that returning to Pavones was a mistake, but their conversation didn't last long enough; a childhood friendship that lasted five decades was finished over a classic case of greed and deception.

"I couldn't make him understand that he needed to go through me to get his property back," Al said.

His power was gone, his influence was gone, but he didn't know it and it was sad to see what happened next. He still thought he was King, he didn't realize things changed down there in eighteen years. The squatters weren't going to give him his land back. And the land the squatters sold to gringos, they weren't going to give him his land back either. They didn't give a shit he was once King. But, see, that's Dan. He thinks he can do things his own way, and he still believed he was the man. He doesn't realize he was only the man because he had money, but the money was gone. He was just an old man to those people.

In May of 2005, just about the time when Pretoma successfully stalled the Granjas Atuneras project in court, and Peter Aspinall hired high-powered environmental lawyer Álvaro Sagot to represent the community and build its case, Dan showed up in Pavones. Contrary to what legend promised, he didn't return in a plane buzzing overhead and showering residents with hundred-dollar bills. Instead, he came in a rental car with Pequeño and his Costa Rican lawyer. There were also several off-duty police officers accompanying Dan's group, for no other reason than as a way to document the visit's details and have official reporting of what he did while visiting. While there were numerous properties to investigate, the two most important ones were the cantina, the most beautiful place on earth to drink a beer and watch the waves roll in, and the original sawmill property Dan bought in 1974 when he camped underneath the stars with his sons and where he later hosted surfing's biggest stars.

Dan arrived at the soccer field and walked over to the cantina. Blue and white with a concrete floor, the cantina had a ping-pong table placed randomly on the floor, but Dan walked over to the row of wooden stools anchored to metal posts. Several white, rusted fans sputtered under the wooden ceiling, whipping hot, humid air into his face. Above him, on the second floor, was a row of basic rooms that served as the town's hotel before other establishments were built. The cantina offered cold showers, a shared bathroom, a bed, four walls, a door, and spitting distance to a world-class break. Dan was proud to have built those surfers' quarters, but he wasn't there to reminisce about the good old days. He wanted to speak with Chico Gomez, a Tico who had been in charge of the cantina when Dan disappeared in 1985. Gomez eventually sold the beach concession to a gringo; Dan claimed the gringo illegally obtained the concession from Gomez.

While Dan was in prison, Al paid for the concession but not maintenance. Since the cantina was in the country's maritime zone, where property can't be owned but can be leased if built prior to 1980, no one actually owned it. Al discovered the cantina situation was a typical Dan Fowlie-esque deal, which meant it was a paperwork quagmire. Originally, Dan put the cantina's beach concession in Chico Gomez's name, but his family suffered financially as they awaited the King's return.

"Chico is a good guy who would never do harm to Dan," Al said.

He and his wife are running the cantina for Dan while he's in Rotterdam or wherever. Well, a business needs money to run. It wasn't making a ton of money anyway, but it needed upkeep like paint, a new septic system, and a generator (since there was no electricity). Chico would come to me and say, "Al, I need money from Dan," but I didn't have that kind of money and Dan is in the Netherlands, and then he's in

Mexico. The whole time Dan wasn't giving Chico any money. Chico gave me a letter one day explaining all the problems with the business, and he asked me to give it to Dan. Dan saw the letter but never answered Chico's letters. So Chico started putting his own money into the business. It was costing him too much and since his name was on the concession, the only way to recoup some of his losses was to get rid of it. He had no other choice.

Dan saw things differently and demanded an explanation. But he didn't get the explanation he wanted from Gomez, and, according to sources at the scene, he threatened Gomez's son. Gomez told a *La Nación* reporter that Dan even threatened to harm other family members if he didn't return the land. Dan, though, denies threatening anybody during his visit.

"I had a peaceful time there," Dan said.

Seriously, Chico Gomez's son is thirty-eight years old and six-foot-four and 250 pounds. How can a seventy-two-year-old man threaten somebody like that? This story only came about because a gringo down there who is on my land and wanted me gone got everybody excited and made up this bullshit story. He said I was armed, but I wasn't armed. I paid a guy from the government to come with me to verify that I wasn't armed and that nobody would plant something on me like drugs or whatever. I know there are people who don't want me around because they never thought this day would come, but it was the gringos who didn't want me there, not the Ticos. I was there to make peace with the people I love. They wanted me there.

Dan's versions of events, however, contrast with others.

"Again, everything that comes out of Dan's mouth is full of half-truths," Al repeated. "Dan claims he didn't threaten Chico, but what he doesn't tell you is that he hired two goons, L.A. gangbangers, to do the threatening. So, yeah, technically he didn't physically threaten Chico and his family. He only gives people a little bit of the story. He never gives people the whole story."

Dan's story that the Ticos were happy to see him contained shreds of truth. While some locals were in fact excited to see him, one source who talked with the *Tico Times* and who wished to remain anonymous described Dan's return this way: "I have not seen Pavones with the potential for violence so near the surface since the early 1990s as in those few days he was here. The squatters could turn to violence if Danny comes back and says he will move them off the land."

Dan never encountered the squatters, and violence never erupted because his visit didn't last more than a week. Sources, though, told me tensions were bubbling despite Dan claiming it was a peaceful visit.

"If he ever comes back here, the squatters are going to kill him," said one long-time local. "It's not just the gringos that don't want him here."

Yet in Dan's mind, it was a successful visit: he just wanted to remind everyone that the King was back and that he intended to reclaim his property through legal means. Others saw it differently, expecting intimidation tactics like those Dan used on Gomez. Either way, Dan left Pavones without resolving anything land-related, including his sawmill property, which was under the possession of Patrick Weston. Dan blamed Weston for single-handedly concocting a fairy tale about his brief yet turbulent return in 2005, basically so Weston could provide the government much-needed ammunition to keep Dan from returning in the future. Weston, who once paid a bribe to the Golfito mayor for a concession and then documented the bribe as a way to expose the mayor as a corrupt government official, was a former cocaine dealer, according to Dan, and someone who illegally acquired possession of his sawmill property.

"All of these gringos are scared to death of me coming back," Dan said. "Patrick Weston is a liar. He told the Costa Rican government that he doesn't know me and never met me as a way to separate himself from me so he could steal my property, but that is a lie. We know each other. He definitely doesn't want me back."

Shortly after Dan left Costa Rica in 2005, the country's immigration director prohibited him from returning, pending the investigation of the threats he allegedly made against Ticos at the cantina. Later that year, he was officially banned from Costa Rica and considered persona non grata. As he did with his land disputes, he has continued to fight for his reentry into Costa Rica. Using video showing a tranquil visit to Pavones and testimony from friends, who claimed he didn't threaten Gomez, as well as video documentation of the improvements he made to area during the

1970s and 1980s, Dan fought for reentry from a stucco garage in Cabo San Lucas, but with little success other than padding his lawyer's pockets.

"I was in the government when the decision was taken," said Carlos Manuel Rodriguez, the country's environmental minister who was issuing the tuna farm permit in 2005, when Dan was expelled. "Unless there is another decision by the government that I don't know about, I think it will be impossible that he will be let back in," he added.

> The truth is he left legal ownership and power of attorney to a lot of people who are bandits and who are unreliable people. And there were problems with double selling of his property and Ticos and foreigners fighting; there were many problems. Nobody knows Danny, nobody remembers him anymore . . . that was a long time ago. The government does have the authority, through immigration laws and policy, to keep him from coming back. They didn't want him to come back because of his background, that was the main reason. It is true Danny lost everything, he lost things through the people who he left in charge there, most probably some of the legal powers given to different guys. They did wrongful, unfair and illegal things, most probably, but the legal system allowed it to happen. But to go back now and change things is very complicated because of the legal process, in terms of proving those things, and it really wouldn't be beneficial in terms of the social situation. Now things are really peaceful, I would say, and nobody is pushing for that to happen, nobody wants to bring that up again. It's been very peaceful since everything settled down, between all the different conflicts and land conflicts. Everybody has moved on.

Everybody had moved on except for Dan, who continued to operate as though the contested land was still his. He filed liens and criminal complaints against the property and Al, respectively, which further muddied the situation and has prevented Al from selling the land or transferring it to Dan's name. But then Dan's delusions had one positive outcome: they helped the town in its fight against the tuna farms.

With Dan refusing to believe that squatters legally owned some of his land, or that they had the right to sell some of it to others, or that Al held legal title for his remaining land, Dan took the position that he owned all of the land, and soon after he was banned from the country, he donated it all to Parque Pavones del Pacífico, an environmental group that is essentially Dan's alter ego.

The Parque Pavones del Pacífico website states:

> Our mission is to manage the conservation, reforestation, and development of the greater Pavones region. Focusing on needs of local residents and environmental concerns for the area, we work in the Pavones community to ensure a brighter social, economic, and ecological future for the people of Pavones. By donating much of his Pavones land to Parque Pavones, Daniel Fowlie (principal owner and developer of Pavones) has ensured that the miles of beachfront property he purchased in the area in the seventies and eighties will be preserved, reforested, and developed in a manner that benefits local, national, and global humanitarian interests.

Given that the Parque Pavones del Pacífico website was a static website that was quickly created as a means to an end, linked to other propaganda websites created by Dan, this testimonial was obviously a ploy intended to convince the government to grant Dan reentry into the country. Parque Pavones del Pacífico was supposed to demonstrate that Dan cared for the environment and the people of Pavones and wanted positive things for Costa Rica. Predictably, those around him chalked up this latest enterprise to an aging and mentally deteriorating ex-convict who couldn't accept reality and was unable to adjust to a life outside prison where he wasn't King. Here Dan goes again, they said, another one of his fantasies—a fictional environmental group that exists only in his own head and has been donated land by a person who was the landowner only in theory.

Dan, though, believed that if he created enough websites about himself, then somehow all of the information on them would be true. Regardless of what was fact or fiction, though, the reality is that , without Parque Pavones del Pacífico, the tuna farm opposition group may have never gotten its day in court.

In June of 2006, INCOPESCA issued the final necessary permit to Eduardo Velarde. Six of the nine board members voted to approve the world's first yellowfin tuna farm, one that was modeled after tuna farms in Australia and in the Mediterranean Sea. This project could now legally happen, and it placed Costa Rica at the forefront of an aquaculture breakthrough at the global level. With the fishing permit in his possession, Velarde had six months to begin operations. With his investor already committing $250,000 for the studies required by law, it was now time to buy the cages, modernize the processing plant in Golfito, and begin training divers to maintain the cages. If everything went according to plan, Velarde was going to give himself an amazing Christmas present: becoming the brains of a cutting-edge aquaculture project.

Although Velarde figured a lawsuit was forthcoming because that was threat posed by the opposition, he knew that a company could continue with its project until a court injunction stated otherwise, as had been the case with Las Crucitas and the offshore drilling project in the Caribbean. While proceeding was certainly a risky endeavor because any monetary investment would be lost if the project were halted, Velarde intended to do just that, now that he was equipped with the fishing permit, the environmental permit, and the water permit. In his mind, the project couldn't be stopped. He had the support of the federal government, and although a lawsuit could be filed, it was unclear when, or whether, the Supreme Court would accept the case. It was also entirely possible that if it did, by the time the court accepted the lawsuit, reviewed the material and made a ruling, the project would have matured to the point where the research and development phase of breeding tuna from an egg was progressing. At that point, Velarde would have an even stronger case that the tuna farm project was good for the environment.

"I was ready to go, and I was very excited," Velarde said. "These Tarzan jungle people weren't going to get their way. All they had were stories, but I had the better arguments."

Since mañana is the busiest day in Costa Rica, Sagot's opposition group led by Peter Aspinall was indeed working in a difficult timeframe. There was credibility to its complaints of forgeries and deception, to its claim that the current study was incomplete, and to its assessment of the project's potential hazards to nationally protected sea turtles, but there was one problem: none of this information had been packaged into an official lawsuit that had been reviewed by the court system. And even then, the review would also have to hear Velarde's arguments, and this meant the process would take more time. After all, the opposition's claims were serious: they suggested collusion between Velarde and sectors of the government or at the very least negligence and ignorance on its part. Any ruling would not be made in haste, but then the process had not even begun since nothing had been officially submitted to the court. Sagot would have to modify his tactics, as well as speed them up. As he did in the Las Crucitas case, Sagot suggested the public outcry angle.

Within a week of INCOPESCA issuing Granjas Atuneras a fishing permit, a group consisting of ten different organizations, including environmentalists and fishing and tourism associations with businesses headquartered in the Golfo Dulce area, filed an official complaint against the Ministry of the Environment and Energy, which oversees SETENA's actions and also issued the project's water permit. The group promised to file a lawsuit in the near future.

"I had no idea what this tuna farm was all about, we had to learn everything, but we all agreed we didn't want it," said Denise Echeverria, spokesperson for the Vida Marina Foundation, one of the organizations listed in the complaint.

> There were already illegal things that had happened. The community was never notified, nobody gets *La Gaceta* down there, and then people said their signatures were forged and they never were interviewed, which would also be illegal things. We felt we had a good case, but it became a massive effort. Pretoma handled the sea turtle part of things, I worked with Peter Aspinall for the community and social angle, and Álvaro Sagot did the legal angle. When we started notifying the public of all these illegalities, people started to listen.

In the days following the complaint, Sagot filed a lawsuit on behalf of Pretoma and the Punta Banco Association with the Constitutional Chamber of the Supreme Court. The court immediately accepted the case for review, but the hearing and ruling wouldn't come for nearly a year. In the meantime, Sagot encouraged mounting a public relations opposition that spanned far and wide. Include anybody that has power and influence, was his suggestion. Peter Aspinall visited with teachers and schools and other community groups in the Golfo Dulce. By the end of the month, he had collected ten thousand signatures on a petition denouncing the project. This figure, which represents roughly 90 percent of the region's total population, amounts to a much more accurate sample size for gauging the community's view of the project than the few dozen interviewees listed in Granjas Atuneras's EIS.

Those signatures, combined with signed affidavits from community members who said that they were never interviewed—or in the most extreme cases, who said that their names were forged—were tucked into Sagot's file. So were the turtle studies from Pretoma as he built the case against Granjas Atuneras. The paperwork was sufficient to open the eyes of the Supreme Court justices, but it was time to work the media angle. Sagot groomed opposition members on specifically what to mention during the media barrage, which sabotaged Velarde's plans to start buying cages.

"The company abused the population and it was asserted by the company and SETENA that the people were in favor of the project, when this was not true," Sagot said.

> They also cited the names of people with their identification documents saying that a sector of the population had positive reasons for the project and this was not true. In fact I am a notary public who got records where these people said they had never been interviewed. SETENA acted badly because it did not assess the many aspects required. For example, there was no information on the management of organic waste solids removed for cleaning tuna cages. It was mandatory to explain where this would go. It did not discuss anything about a possible problem of mass death of tuna in a cage. Nor did SETENA assess social impact for the people of Pavones, where they live off tourism. The area needs to be protected because it is a tourist resource for the natural beauty and rich biodiversity. These were all part of the complaints.

The media onslaught started when Peter arranged to have several busses packed with residents of Pavones and Punta Banco drive nine hours over crummy roads to San José. Once there, they protested at a park downtown in front of the national assembly. Senators heard the commotion, and several walked outside to visit with protestors, who then proceeded to denounce the devilish acts of the great enemies: SETENA, Granjas Atuneras, and its leader, Eduardo Velarde. Within days of the protest, a congressional commission launched an investigation into the project. Peter went on national radio programs to discuss the company's unscrupulous behavior. Randall Arauz at Pretoma was also interviewed by television news cameras. By August of 2006, it became a national story and was being framed as a scandal that required immediate attention.

"It was fucking ridiculous," Velarde said.

Every time they interviewed somebody from Pretoma or Peter Aspinall or some other NGO, they were in a bright room or there was beautiful scenery behind them. Then when they interviewed me, I had a black background and I looked horrible and mean. If I didn't know me, I would hate me and think I was the devil too based on what I saw. I can't imagine what other people were thinking. When that started to happen, it was obvious the media was sympathetic to the opposition, and I refused to do any more interviews. I was never put in a positive light or given the opportunity to explain my side of things. It was always about a protest there, surfers whining here, why Eduardo Velarde is the devil, why the other guys are angels. I couldn't win, and my investor got nervous. He saw all the articles and television news stories. I just told him to wait for our day in court when our arguments would be heard.

The opposition didn't know it, but its objective of creating enough controversy to stall the project had succeeded. Manuel de Iglesia still earmarked the money for the project's first cages, but he didn't authorize spending more until the case was resolved in court.

"No investor likes a scandal," Velarde said. "We were being made to look evil before even having a chance to defend ourselves. It was totally an unfair thing to do."

As the allies mounted in the opposition's favor, another key member joined the small army following the media surge.

Sequestered to his rented stucco garage in Cabo San Lucas, Dan Fowlie read online about the brewing tuna farm battle. Still unable to return to Costa Rica, the former surfer and waterman believed this would be a great cause to kick-start the efforts of Parque Pavones del Pacífico, and perhaps give him a chance to help the town he once controlled.

"These tuna farms are no good. Everything gets caught up in those nets, and it's not good quality meat," Dan said. "They are basically feeding them inside a swimming pool; their mouths are all open and sucking up their own feces. Anything that hurts animals or turtles and nature is against my foundation's principles. Anything that damages the community of Pavones is against my principles."

Dan contacted Peter Aspinall and expressed his desire to join the battle. Although they hadn't talked for decades, Peter had a soft spot for Danny. In the 1970s, when Peter was expanding his farm into what is now his Tiskita Lodge, a sparkling showpiece of a jungle lodge, Dan used the bulldozers that helped build Pavones's roads and other infrastructure to clear trees and build an airstrip. Dan hated ripping out the palm trees for a runway because he adored them, and he knew Peter hated it too. Dan agreed to clear the land because it would allow Peter's mom, a pilot, to fly in and see her son more often. That was reason enough for Dan to cause environmental damage, but he replanted trees elsewhere to compensate for the ones he destroyed. So when Dan disappeared and the Squatter Wars ensued, Peter was sympathetic to his land being sliced up, as Dan described it, "like a Marie Callender's pie."

"Danny's land was complicated because it was part of a big scam," Peter said. "The scam was organized by these people saying they were poor farmers who came into the area and then invaded his land and took possession. The law said the government could appropriate land only if it was suited for agriculture. Most of Danny's land wasn't suited for agriculture, it just wasn't that good, and the government should have never appropriated his land and given it to squatters, but they did. It was too bad, because Danny really did a lot for the community."

When Dan contacted Peter in late 2006, an opportunity presented itself for them to work together again. Dan wanted something, anything, to change public perception of him following his controversial visit in 2005, and Peter and the opposition needed something they believed Dan had: money.

Every environmental battle requires a coordinated group that seizes media interviews and organizes public protests, but those are free activities, or at least relatively inexpensive ones. Sagot and his sterling reputation as an environmental attorney were not inexpensive. His price tag: twelve thousand dollars, which, although cheap by United States standards and certainly a discounted rate because this was one of Sagot's preferred cases, seemed a near impossible amount to raise in one of the country's poorest regions.

"Pretoma gets funded by making a lot of noise and getting in the newspapers," Velarde said. "They created this story of Pavones as a small town going up against this huge company that wants to come in and destroy their town. What huge company? It was me and my son, who also does aquaculture, that's it. The community was told to think a certain way by Pretoma and Álvaro Sagot. Everything went sour before I even had a chance to explain myself."

Pretoma organized a surf contest in September of 2006 that generated a little over five hundred dollars. That money went to Sagot. Private donations brought in a few thousand more. That money went to Sagot. Still, the town needed more money. A fundraiser festival denouncing the tuna farms held after the surf contest was a loosely organized affair, which is to say it was fabulously unofficial—even by Tico standards. For those who were unable to attend the protest in San José, there was a local one where several hundred people congregated under sun-drenched skies, but it failed to attract anybody from Granjas Atuneras or the government to hear the complaints. As is the case with most gatherings in Costa Rica, the protest resembled a party more than a protest. Ticos and gringos banged on drums and sang to nobody in particular. They danced in the muddy streets. A group of boys played soccer. Banners hung between tree trunks and had a clear message: "Save the Golfo Dulce. No to the Tuna Farms," but it wasn't a fundraiser as much as it was an excuse to party, and Ticos never run out of excuses to party. It was a unifying moment, to be sure, but the sun rising has long been justification for a party and bringing Ticos together. The event made just enough money to throw another party, which the community hoped would bring in more money to give Sagot.

Costa Rica's national slogan is "Pura Vida," which literally translates to "pure life," but it has additional meanings and usages. If one Tico asks another Tico, "How are you?" the response will often be "pura vida," meaning "all good" or "living great." If a Tico sees something inspiring or amusing, the reaction is also likely to be "pura vida." The phrase can be used to say hello and goodbye. It can even be a polite way of expressing a difference of opinion, as in "we agree to disagree." These events, attended by Ticos and gringos, were pura vida moments for the community, but what wasn't pura vida was that Pavones was unable to reach its goal of raising funds for Sagot to fight against a Granjas Atuneras legal team that was surely making more than Sagot's twelve-thousand-dollar fee. With a court date looming, the town was five thousand short and risked losing the one attorney who could save the area from the tuna farms.

"Even though we were struggling to come up with the money to pay the lawyer, the one thing this tuna farm battle did was bring the community together," Peter said. "Everything else that's happened in the area, like the land conflicts and the squatter issues, had always divided the community. But this was something that unified everybody. We didn't know whether we would win or lose in court, or if we would even have a lawyer in court, but the community working together was a positive development. And it was a nice to see people do what they could with the money, but it wasn't enough. We needed more money."

One day, before walking into the Supreme Court to learn of his community's fate, Peter received a letter. Inside was a check for five thousand dollars from Parque Pavones del Pacífico, enough to cover Sagot's expenses.

"We're going to beat these tuna farm guys in court, I just know it," Dan said.

13   Judgment Day

This is a court of law, young man, not a court of justice.
—Oliver Wendell Holmes Jr., former U.S. Supreme Court justice

In the spring of 2007, with Sagot fully paid and after several years of squabbling, representatives from both sides walked into the Supreme Court building east of downtown San José. Rose bushes lined the concrete path leading toward the glass double doors of the six-story building. Costa Rica's three-striped white, blue, and red flag fluttered on a pole erected in a plaza; a bronze statue of a warrior in the right corner of the court building symbolized that this faded brown building, one of many in San José that needed a good scrubbing, was a defender of justice. The constitutional wing of the Supreme Court's stated mission is "To protect human dignity and rights in all their forms, guaranteeing the supremacy of constitutional norms and principles and of international and community human rights law in force in the Republic."

Members of both sides passed through the doors and walked into the courtroom through a stained wooden entry. Behind a bench at the far of the room were seven justices. In front of them was a clear divide: two different tables, two different sets of seats, separated by a wide strip of carpet. Eduardo Velarde and his lawyers moved toward one side and were dressed in black freshly pressed suits. Álvaro Sagot was also wearing a suit, and flanking him were environmentalists, biologists, and community members. Pretoma's Randall Arauz wore casual attire, khakis and a collared shirt, as did Peter Aspinall. They situated themselves on the other side of the divide. In all, there were perhaps two dozen people in the courtroom.

Velarde had prepared a presentation about the tuna farms identical to the one he had shown Golfito officials several years prior. The justices listened to his extravagant employment figures for the impoverished area, how the project would save tuna from depletion, how it would be good for Costa Rica. The justices' reaction, according to Peter, "was like they were trying to be sold something by a salesman. They kind of rolled their eyes." Velarde continued, explaining how the project would function, including how the tuna would be caught and transported to the cages. His choice of images to illustrate this process was his first blunder, not from a practical or legal sense but an emotional one. On the screen flashed beautiful, large tuna that were being yanked onto a fishing vessel.

"I think his presentation and the image of the tuna helped the judges get a picture of this industry and realize that this is an industry," said Vida Marina's founder Denise Echeverria, who was present and smiled when she saw that image. "If they didn't understand the size of this animal, its dimensions, then it would be difficult to have a picture in your head of what exactly this project was. That video presentation helped a lot in that respect, that this was something huge and that it wasn't one farm but a bunch of farms in the same spot."

While the justices were amazed at the size of a tuna, Velarde moved on to the law that required him to notify the community and gauge their support of the project, and in a rather confident tone, he explained that he had hired independent researchers from the University of Costa Rica to interview community members, including fishermen, and that the results had been overwhelmingly positive. He explained that he had hired the University of Costa Rica's Omar Lizano, the country's leading marine researcher, to conduct the current study, which concluded that metabolic waste would not impact the Golfo Dulce because the currents flowed away from the gulf. And as he also noted, all of this material had been packaged into an environmental impact statement, at a cost of several hundred thousand dollars, and was approved by the country's governing bodies for fishing and the environment.

It was a clean, professional, and thorough presentation, but it was also a sterile one, given with little emotion. By the time he was through, the justices seemed unmoved. Velarde didn't add a dimension that the justices hadn't already known from reviewing the EIS themselves during the past year. After Velarde finished, the court moderator thanked him for his presentation and asked him to return to his seat.

"And now we will hear from the president of the Punta Banco Association," the moderator said.

"The justices all shook their heads and paid attention, and to me that showed how important the community angle was to them," Peter said. "They knew we had come from way down in the bottom in Costa Rica and they wanted to hear right from us, from the community."

Members of the community explained that there had been no transparency and that Velarde had never informed the community about the project. They also claimed that the government never notified them of the project, emphasizing that an announcement in any newspaper, let alone an obscure one like *La Gaceta*, wasn't proper notification in an area where newspapers weren't circulated at all and where there was no Internet access. They also denounced the project because it would negatively impact sea turtles. Returning to Velarde's statement that the tuna farms had community support, they claimed that the company, not the university's independent workers, had selected people to be interviewed from a voting list pinned to a public school wall; they also pointed out that half of those people didn't live in the community and didn't represent the community. The justices' heads cocked sideways and their eyes got bigger when in they heard in addition that some community members who were named in Velarde's report said that they were never interviewed at all and, in some cases, that their signatures were forged. The following statement, which was submitted to Sagot and translated into English, was submitted to SETENA in the days leading up to the court appearance, and a copy was made available for the justices:

The complaint to SETENA was accompanied by affidavits from many locals' "alleged" interviews where under oath they said they were never interviewed about the project or something similar. . . . At least thirteen residents of the area declared under oath: "I've never been interviewed or formally identified as a pollster or interviewee on the Tuna Farm Project. We learned that our name was on the EIA submitted to SETENA but insist that we never filled out any questionnaire related to the project."

This was exactly the type of information the justices were seeking. Of course, they were aware of the two sides' arguments and complaints prior to that day in court, but now they were hearing from the community members themselves, not reading a lawyer's fancy written language or reviewing an activist agenda covered in the media. Apparently convinced that nefarious behavior had occurred, their disdain was directed primarily at SETENA for its disregard of citizens' claims of forgery and deceit, as well as for its approval of the EIS with nothing more than a cursory glance at the environmental impact. It was obvious the community members had been groomed by their lawyer beforehand, but that didn't mean they weren't telling the truth or that the justices wouldn't be moved by their testimony.

"They take me to the highest court on this baloney shit," Velarde said.

They said say we are going to kill tuna, but the tuna is going in the can anyway. They say we're going to kill these turtles, but we've used Pretoma's own numbers and this was not a highly visited area for sea turtles. They said our tuna is going to shit in the ocean and pollute their beaches, but the current study didn't say that. They say it's going to hurt tourism, but in other places tuna farms are good for tourism. Mr. Aspinall could buy a few boats and charge his customers at his jungle lodge for something else to do like go see the tuna swimming in the cage. These people were tricked by Sagot to say they were never interviewed or we made up signatures, but we took pictures of the people interviewed. How can you say you weren't interviewed when there is a picture of you being interviewed? That's why the court threw out those claims because they saw they were bogus.

These people were like ants in their thinking. A guy in Pavones who has never been out of Pavones can't look at the big picture. It is a sin that Sagot and Pretoma didn't allow them to see the big picture.

The more you travel and study, the more you have a responsibility to help the world. Joe Blow in the mountains or in the jungle doesn't have that responsibility. God gave me more tools and education and I have more, so my responsibility to help the world is greater. But Sagot and Pretoma blurred the picture, and it's sad what they did to those people.

Overarching arguments aside, both sides were confident when they walked out into the darkening sky that afternoon. A few months later, on May 9, 2007, the court made its ruling and based it on a critical error in the EIS regarding the current study. Out of the thousands of words and hundreds of pages in the EIS, it was a series of sentences about where the currents flow that troubled the justices. Although Dr. Lizano's data revealed that the currents in that area would flow away from the Golfo Dulce and out into the sea, the wording in the EIS was that the currents flow "to the coast." This was an offshore project, a few kilometers away from the naked coastline south of Punta Banco, and "to the coast" doesn't mean "to the Golfo Dulce," but the ambiguous language of the current study was enough to hiccup the process. After hearing both sides, the court ruled to suspend the tuna farm project until the precise direction of the currents was determined. As the *Tico Times* reported, the court sought to "guarantee beforehand, with reasonable certainty, that the metabolic waste resulting from the farm will not cause environmental damage."

Velarde chalked up the decision to a clerical error in the EIS and told the *Tico Times* that "It's an error in three sentences. It's easy to clarify."

The court also required SETENA to interview the residents listed in the EIS as supporting the project again, as well as to interview additional residents to paint a more accurate picture of the community's feelings on the project. After the court ruled, both sides claimed victory: Velarde said he could easily fix the confusing nature of the language and Lizano's current study by rewriting the results in such a way that would leave little doubt as to the currents' direction; the opposition, meanwhile, believed that the justices recognized that the community had been deceived and that they understood the need for a comprehensive current study that tracked trends over several years, not just for a few days. In reality, neither side won.

The opposition didn't have the financial capability to procure its own current study, while Velarde did, and usually whoever pays for a study gets the desired results. Velarde, however, had a bigger hurdle to clear. With the precedent set that the Golfo Dulce and the surrounding area is a delicate ecosystem with a complex geography, Pretoma could successfully attack any conclusion from a current study—or at the very least make a strong enough argument that a proper current study should take years to complete, thereby postponing the project even further. Moreover, the opposition was successful in turning the entire community against Granjas Atuneras, as well as the government, by reversing what was stated in the EIS, so there was little chance that SETENA interviews of residents would yield anything but vitriol for Velarde and the government. Alas, the government could delay the interview process until after the current study language was revised because, remember, mañana always is the busiest day in Costa Rica. By that time the project would have already continued because the scientific argument is what troubled the court. It was obvious the community was aware of the project and the government approved it, so requiring SETENA to interview them was more a nice gesture, a stern order, than a requirement for the project to continue. And that's what happened.

SETENA didn't interview residents, and within a year of the court ruling, Velarde submitted a revised version of his EIS to SETENA. On November 6, 2008, SETENA issued a resolution recommending that the project continue, "based on the existing environmental impact study, other documents provided by the developer and one new outside report," according to the *Tico Times*. The paper also reported that two months earlier, SETENA asked Dr. Lizano's department at the University of Costa Rica for its "technical criteria" for the tuna farm and that the information was submitted to the agency within two weeks. After SETENA recommended that the project continue, which wasn't quite a disregard of the court's ruling but certainly not a real attempt to uphold it, Pretoma appealed and stated that an independent study should be conducted on the Golfo Dulce. SETENA rejected Pretoma's appeal, stating the project should continue and, as the environmental agency governing for the country, it can decide which studies are sufficient.

"Randall at Pretoma told me they have their permits, they have the support of the government, and they are going to put their nets in," Peter said. "Once they put their nets in, we won't get them out."

With Velarde having the upper hand and the opposition at an impasse in terms of strategy, it was time for Pavones to take things to the next level. Amazingly, it had been ignoring the trump card the entire time: a town with a world-famous wave that relies on surf tourism was threatened by an aquaculture project. It's an argument that hadn't been fully presented despite its being used numerous times in other surf environmental battles worldwide. Up until this point the opposition was national, but that was about to change.

14 Saving Waves

There is a higher court than courts of justice and that is the court of conscience.
—Mahatma Gandhi

Early in 2009, after SETENA disregarded the court ruling and stated the project could continue, Pretoma hired Andy Bystrom, an American who was given the keys to the Pavones–Tuna Farm awareness campaign. When he learned of Pavones's surf history and the importance of surfing in general to the country, he knew he could shift the focus of this campaign and take it to the global level. Andy, with his light skin and blonde hair, fits the stereotype of a gringo headed to Costa Rica to make a change; those qualities don't always endear themselves to Ticos. He took frequent trips to Pavones, making the eight-hour drive from the San José suburb of Tibás several times a month to familiarize himself with the town and develop a relationship with its citizens. This continued for nearly two years although there was a possibility that, at any moment, Granjas Atuneras trucks could barrel down the dirt road with equipment or pens could be dropped in the water. Despite his concern for the community's well-being, Bystrom wasn't a preacher-man like Eduardo Velarde. When he arrived, he asked questions and didn't make declarations. While Velarde said, "This is what I am going to do with the tuna farms, do you want to help me?" Bystrom's pitch was "What do you want for your community, how I can help you?" The difference paid dividends in the community's response to a concerned, educated gringo arriving on their doorsteps looking to help.

"My first impression when I visited was 'Oh, my God, we can't destroy this place' because it was kind of untouched," Bystrom said.

Other parts of Costa Rica are pristine and beautiful, but there was something obviously a little different here. But it really doesn't matter what I think. I have no connection, I am from the United States, I was basically there as a tourist, my agenda doesn't matter. And Americans are kind of symbolic of everything that's happened down there, both good and bad, so locals can be a little skeptical of outsiders. At the end of the day, it's about what the people wanted. Lots of people went down there and promised things, but the same problems are still there: the lack of education, lack of employment, lack of buy-in to what's happening in their community. But everybody is very aware of what they have there, it's unique and it's at the end of the road, and a lot of them don't want to leave even though they could make more money elsewhere. A lot of communities aren't as attached to the environment as they are. Most importantly, a lot of other beach communities aren't as attached to that wave as they are. There are scarlet macaws and monkeys down there and other things to do, but the few businesses that are there basically live and die because of that wave.

Bystrom provided questionnaires asking residents what they felt were the three best attributes in their community. The overwhelming majority responded, "my neighbors," "my people," and "my respect for the natural beauty." Once they had communicated to Bystrom that they wanted to save Pavones from dirty tuna farms, balance tourism with development, conserve their values, and most importantly, retain the economic viability of their wave, he had the elements for a strong surf activism campaign. He had the community on record as stating that the wave was the single most important thing in Pavones from both an economic and a symbolic perspective. That would be critical information to getting Surfrider or another activist group to support Pavones's cause. However, Bystrom needed more ammunition. He wanted to prove that surfing was so important to tourism that there would be a serious financial cost to Costa Rica if it allowed a project like this to move forward. As in the case of the offshore drilling and open-pit mining projects, Bystrom hoped to expose the artificiality of the government's image of Costa Rica as an environmentally friendly country, given its approval of controversial projects that damage the environment.

"We had the lawsuit won, or at least it was decided that the project couldn't continue without a real current study that would guarantee where the metabolic waste would go, but it resurfaced when SETENA rejected the court's ruling, and it was obvious there was a government push for this to happen," Bystrom said. "The legal channels weren't working as we hoped, or as they should have, so there needed to be some outside influence exerted on the government to show that this is going to negatively affect the economy. We needed to send the message that if we screw up the environmental part, how it's not only going to affect nature and destroy water quality, but that the government is essentially destroying a town that relies on a wave. We felt that could be a powerful message."

According to Matt Warshaw's *History of Surfing*, the first recorded surfer in Costa Rica was a guy named Rusty from Gainesville, Florida, who surfed the Caribbean coast in 1968. Subsequently, the first article on surfing in Costa Rica was published in 1974, and then the first photographs of surfing were published in 1981, when Art Brewer and Bud Llammas were shot surfing in Pavones, soon to be followed by Rory Russell and Buttons Kaluhiokalani. In the ensuing two decades, Costa Rica experienced an explosion in surfing's influence. There are more than a one hundred surf shops spread over more than 767 miles of coastline (132 of which are on the Caribbean side, 635 on the Pacific). In 1974, there were an estimated twenty surfers in the entire country, nearly all of whom were foreigners. By 2002, the number of Tico surfers alone had grown from basically zero in the mid-1970s to more than five thousand. The number of foreign surfers surged dramatically during those three decades as well. A 2007 report published by Costa Rica's official tourism board, Instituto Costarricense de Turismo (ICT), stated that more than 220,000 visitors came to surf at Costa Rica's beaches, an increase of more than 100 percent since 2001, when the figure was about 100,000. In a country that enjoys more than two million visitors each year, roughly 11 percent of all visitors were coming for surf-related activities. The report also stated that foreign surf visitors generated $273 million for the country annually, staying an average of ten nights, with a daily cost of $119. Since then, the ICT has estimated that while the number of nights surfers stay has remained the same, their daily budgets have increased to almost $130, which means surf-related tourism contributed almost $300 million annually to the country's economy. After the turn of the century, a Costa Rica Surf Federation was created and a national surfing team was started.

Carlos Manuel Rodriguez, the former environmental minister who originally signed Granjas Atuneras's viability permit, is one of the country's original surfers. He met the Fowlies and surfed the wave in the late 1970s, when it sometimes took twelve hours to reach Pavones. He never heard of a gringo named Rusty being the first surfer; he said the first Tico surfer was a guy named Frank Mora. Although he acknowledges that surfing is a major part of the tourist economy, he remains skeptical of the numbers in the ICT's report.

"The issue is how do you define a surfer?" Rodriguez said.

For me a surfer is the person who carries his own board, not someone who rents a board and goes to surf schools or whatever. Are we calling them surfers? There is a difference between a surfer who comes to surf and the person who comes for the green experience, where surfing is part of that. Many people have land here and constantly come without their board, so how do you classify them? How do you calculate that? The truth is it's hard to know how many of these people there are. These people pay for the food, lodging, transportation. I know ICT doesn't have that specific information because I've gone to them and asked for it before.

Whether it's 20 percent or 15 percent or somewhere in between, surfing is a huge contributor to Costa Rica's tourism, which is now the country's third-largest economic sector behind coffee and agriculture exports. According to the ICT's figures, tourism brings in more money than fish exports. However, before the twenty-first-century boom began, Costa Rica was characterized as an undiscovered gem in the surfing fold.

In his surf memoir *In Search of Captain Zero*, which ends in Pavones, Allen Weisbecker writes:

Costa Rica's reputation as the ultimate surfers' paradise had no doubt had its basis in fact, for the proof is in the staying, and many had stayed. . . . The stories of other surfers who had gone before me were mostly paradisiacal. Costa Rica, they said, was a country of almost unlimited surf, with vast unexplored potential beckoning, like the blank regions of sea charts of yore. And although few of my wave-hungry fellows had tarried inland, there were also tales of still-unsullied cloud forests, outlandish endemic wildlife, and raging pristine rivers. . . . Surfing is the quintessential example here, for there are very few endeavors that so perfectly combined travel/exploration with a creatively satisfying relationship to the environment.

Weisbecker was no doubt describing the undeveloped environs of Pavones. He certainly wasn't referring to Jaco, the country's first mega-beach resort, which was well known by the late 1990s. About an hour and a half west of San José, Jaco has consistent, sizable beach-break waves. The first surf magazine was started there in 1997—there are now four in the country—as was the country's first surf camp—now there are over a hundred sprinkled along both coasts. Like Jaco, Tamarindo is another established beach town offering surf-related activities; unlike Pavones, both towns have a robust tourism industry in addition to surfing, and their surf industries differ from Pavones's as well. At the time the tuna farms were announced, Pavones had no official surf schools or surf shops; someone's garage served as a ding-repair shop. Most people who visited Pavones were serious surfers who brought their own gear. Of the more than three hundred available hotel beds in town, over 95 percent of them were rented to surfers, as Bystrom discovered during his research. If 95 percent of the people who stay at hotel rooms in Pavones were surfers, it's reasonable to conclude that 95 percent of all tourism-related business was also supported by surfers.

"Surf economics provides another tool to help protect surfing areas," wrote Chad Nelsen, Surfrider's environmental director.

The basic idea behind surfing economics is to raise awareness about the importance of surfing as a coastal recreation that should be considered when coastal management decisions are made. . . . The fact that we go the extra mile, so to speak, for a great surf session shows we value it more than a beachgoer who is less likely to be so selective and drive the extra distance. Surfers are also much more avid than other beachgoers, meaning that we tend to go to the beach more than regular beachgoers.

Pavones's surf-related business suffered a hit with the advancement of the Internet. Computer-generated swell forecasts on websites such as Magicseaweed.com and Surfline.com are becoming more accurate with each passing year, meaning that surfers aren't staying as long as they once were and therefore aren't spending the money they once did. Since Pavones needs a specific swell direction to start generating waves, surfers monitor swell forecasts before making their travel decisions. In Tamarindo or the Nicoya Peninsula or Jaco, there always seem to be waves. Surfers tend to hang out in those towns and support the local economy for longer durations. When the swell is predicted to increase in Pavones, they immediately drive there to experience one of the world's best waves, but when one of the world's best waves becomes a lake, they immediately leave. These swell forecasts break down swell directions and sizes to the hour. On big-swell days, there can easily be more than one hundred people bobbing on their boards at the point in the morning, like so many floating ants. If the swell is expected to subside in the afternoon, a caravan of cars parades out of town by sunset, and the restaurants, the hotels, and the water are all empty by nightfall.

"We've all noticed that surfers aren't staying as long as they used to," said one hotel owner. "This wave is so good that it used to be surfers were willing to hang out as long as possible waiting for the next swell. Now everyone knows when that next swell is coming, so there's either a mad rush or there's no business for anyone."

With market economics and computer forecast models already straining Pavones's surf-based economy, the government was naïve, if not obtuse, if it thought that an idea like a tuna farm project would be met with anything but skepticism and outright disdain.

In 1989, after allowing Dan Fowlie to absorb the cost of the construction of dirt and gravel roads in the Pavones area, the government announced it would finally pave the road to Pavones. There are even government-produced maps in San José that show paved roads in the area, an indication that somebody, somewhere, intended to follow through on the announcement. But, of course, there are no paved roads in Pavones.

In 2011, the telecommunications company Claro installed a tower in Pavones. When the company truck driver was returning to Conte, he drove over a bridge that collapsed. The municipality in Golfito estimated it would cost between two and three thousand dollars to repair the bridge. If Pavones could contribute $1,200 toward the cost, the regional government would cover the rest. Realizing that the town would starve financially if surfers couldn't reach it, Pavones immediately collected its portion of the payment and delivered it to Golfito. Three months later, the bridge hadn't been repaired. Everyone had anticipated a delay, though, so one morning, every man in town suspended his plans for the day and walked down to the river. In a matter of hours, they had moved boulders and chopped down trees and sawed logs and built a makeshift bridge to ensure surfers could access the surf break.

"If nobody can get here to surf that wave, nobody can make any money," said one hotel owner. "It was actually pretty inspiring to see that if the town puts its mind to something, it can get something done. But that usually happens when it concerns the wave. If there is no wave, there is no town."

During the process of repairing the bridge themselves, town residents began taking cobble from the Rio Claro and taking it to the bridge site. Within an hour, a huge mob had developed and was lambasting the workers because the wave is formed by the cobble that flows out of the river and deposits in the Golfo Dulce. With Pavones already hypersensitive about any change in the number of surfers who will visit town, as well as anything that could impact the wave, it is surprising and troubling that it took as long as it did for those opposed to the tuna farm to buttress their arguments with the surfer perspective, which proved to be so critical.

Nonetheless, the economic importance of surfing to Costa Rica was firmly established, and then reinforced by a 2011 report entitled "A Socioeconomic and Recreational Profile of Surfers in the United States." According to this report, the typical surfer at Trestles Beach in Southern

California was thirty-four years old, had a college education, if not a post-graduate degree, and was employed full-time, earning between fifty and seventy thousand dollars per year. In the United States, where the majority of Costa Rica's visitors originate, surfers made approximately one hundred beach visits annually and spent almost $70 per day on those visits. This data suggests that American surfers are educated and have the financial means to be selective when choosing an international beach to visit.

Bystrom and Pretoma used this information to suggest that if Pavones—and Costa Rica as a whole—was viewed as a place that polluted and didn't make surfing a priority, not only would surf-related income for the country be reduced in the short term, but tourism would also suffer in the long term. Bystrom's argument was that if word spread that surfers were shunning Costa Rica for environmental reasons, there be could a domino effect such that nonsurfers would also ignore Costa Rica. Bystrom reinforced these points with the potential impact of the tuna farms on Pavones's water quality and on its surfers. If contamination from the farm flowed into the gulf, nutrients would increase, and these, in turn, would create red tides and an abundance of dead fish that could attract more sharks. When it comes to sharks, many surfers joke that they would never surf if they actually saw the number of sharks underneath them in the lineup. But as for the contamination, it's an issue that doesn't resonate the same way with all surfers. Some believe dirty water will mean waves that are less crowded; some will surf good waves regardless.

"All surfers care about is getting waves," Sam George, former editor of *Surfer* magazine told the *Los Angeles Times* in 2001. "If their concern was clean water, nobody would surf Malibu."

One professional surfer thinks that view is rather short-sighted when it comes to foreign surf breaks like the one in Pavones. In Southern California and other industrialized shorelines, surfers have come to accept that dirty water is part of the deal. But when a surfer travels internationally, one benefit is finding a place devoid of the necessary evils of one's home break. In other words, it's a tougher sell to convince someone from Los Angeles who surfs in dirty water to visit Pavones and surf in tuna shit when there are clean-water surf options elsewhere. Kyle Thiermann, a

Santa Cruz–based professional surfer, has spent several years attacking banks for funding environmentally destructive projects such as coal power plants and pulp mills in Latin America.

"The fact that we have to surf in polluted water doesn't make it okay," Thiermann said.

> Staph infections, coughing and sneezing, getting ear infections, those aren't things you want to worry about. I don't think people want to travel to Costa Rica to surf in polluted water. They'll go somewhere else. We should be striving for something better, and that begins by us being critical of what is happening. I know companies that will set up shop by the ocean and don't give a fuck how clean their project is. They are setting up a pulp mill or a coal power plant to make money, and it's a flawed system because they are obligated to make money, which often means not caring about the environmental impact of how they make their money. A lot of it is because these companies won't get the backlash from small towns in Latin America. There aren't a lot of regulations down there. But, more importantly, a rural community likely won't say anything or stick up for themselves in these places because in a more impoverished place they are probably less focused on environmental issues and more focused on day-to-day survival. In Pavones, people aren't impoverished like other areas of Latin America, but most people aren't living as comfortably as Americans. They don't have the free time to engage in social change and so it can be easy for companies to slip in projects.

As Bystrom compiled evidence for the economic and environmental impact of the tuna farms in Pavones, emotions were rising along with the case. Leilani McGonagle, a talented young surfer and Pavones resident, wrote a letter to President Óscar Arias urging him to stop the tuna farms. According to Dan Fowlie, her family is living illegally on his land; both their personal residence and their hotel, the Pavones Riviera, the first Pavones hotel to offer air conditioning in its rooms, are on his property, he claims. Regardless, parents Sean and Jamie McGonagle are raising two surfers who are among the best in their age groups in Central America; both are also members of Costa Rica's national surf team.

One evening at sunset, Sean and Jamie, along with other spectators, watched their children from the concrete sea wall near the cantina. Noe, their son, took off from the point and darted along the face of the wave. Everyone admired his athletic prowess. One spectator said "Boy, he's getting tall Sean. I remember when you used to push him into waves." Sean's response: "They grow up fast, don't they?" Sean told me the tuna farms would have been more popular had they provided jobs for the community. "Nobody is getting rich in Pavones, but nobody is making any money if there isn't a wave. Once that became the message, the town couldn't support the tuna farms."

For all the practicality of Sean's response, it was his daughter's letter to President Óscar Arias that really encapsulated the town's feelings about the wave. Written on November 15, 2009, the eleven-year-old Leilani McGonagle's letter said:

The other day I went surfing here in Pavones. It was such a beautiful day. The water was clear and pretty. I saw a manta ray jumping, a pelican diving in for his breakfast, and a sea turtle floating by. When I went under the water, I could hear the whales singing. Have you ever heard whales? They sing the most beautiful songs! As I came up from under the water, I had a terrible thought. . . . Will there come a day when this Gulf that I love so much [will] be so contaminated from the tuna farms that the manta rays will no longer jump? Will there be a day that the pelicans no longer come here to fish for their breakfast? Will there be a day that the turtles no longer want to lay their eggs on our beaches? Will there be a day when the whales no longer want to come and sing their sweet songs?

I hope with all my heart that this day will never come! This is why I am writing you today. I am asking you to please, please help us to stop the tuna farms from coming here!!! Please use all your power as president to stop this project from contaminating our beautiful Golfo Dulce.

Thank you for your time,
Leilani McGonagle

There was another plea to President Arias, this one from Jonathan Haas, another Pavones resident; his was printed as a letter to the editor in the *Tico Times*:

There is a battle going on for the soul of Costa Rica, and it is taking place in the Golfo Dulce. Southern Zone locals, fishermen, surfers, environmentalists and those with tourism-related businesses are fighting efforts to put a tuna farm in some of the most pristine waters in the world. This issue has re-emerged and is close to final approval.

This is a classic example of a few powerful wealthy foreigners seeking private profits to the detriment of everyone. Granjas Atuneras S.A. is a Venezuelan and Spanish company looking to place between 10 and 100 cages measuring 50 meters in diameter and 20 meters in depth just outside of the mouth of the Golfo Dulce. The tuna would be corralled by helicopters, nets, dynamite and speedboats hundreds of miles out to sea and then dragged back to the Golfo Dulce to be placed in the cages.

The problems with this project are immense, beyond the deceptive approach, lack of transparency and accountability of its promoters, and include:

- The death and destruction of fish that don't survive the netting and 30-day towing process. Many dolphin, marlin, sailfish, tuna and other marine life will die in the process.
- A no-fishing zone will hurt local fishermen and negatively impact the community.
- The use of huge amounts of feed to fatten up the tuna so they can be sold and flown to Japan will cause many problems. Frozen sardines brought over from Peru can contaminate local waters with foreign elements introducing new viruses and unknown illness to the local ecosystem. This has been documented in Australia and the Mediterranean Sea.
- The cages will pose a serious risk to sea turtles, humpback whales, whale sharks and other marine life that passes through the mouth of the Golfo Dulce.

- Many tuna will die in captivity due to stress and weakened immune systems. These dead fish and feed debris will attract sharks and other unwanted predators in waters that are enjoyed by local surfers, divers and tourists.
- The concentrated fecal matter from the caged tuna will add another blow to the environmental balance of this fragile ecosystem. This may pose the biggest threat to the Golfo Dulce. Even the company admits an eight-year viability window before the waters are spent and it needs to move on. Those with personal experience from Maine to Panama to Australia can attest the environmental damage and degradation of local waters of these projects.
- This is an unnatural and destructive process that will add no local benefit. It will only add death and contamination to one of our last virgin waters. The only ones to benefit will be the closely held owners and their favored politicians.

President Óscar Arias, what type of legacy do you want to leave? Please help us save the Golfo Dulce and Costa Rica's reputation as a defender of natural splendor at a time when it is most under attack.

By 2011, Bystrom had collected enough information to make an official pitch to Surfrider, but there was a problem: Surfrider focuses on domestic battles or defers to its various chapters around the world for international cases. Costa Rica didn't have its own chapter. However, Surfrider recommended that Bystrom contact Save the Waves, another nonprofit activist group that focuses on protecting international surf spots. Based in Santa Cruz, Save the Waves has worked with dozens of surf communities around the world on threats ranging from pulp mills in South America to marina projects in Europe. While Save the Waves provides support for any endangered wave, its most powerful program is World Surfing Reserves, through which it chooses a few endangered surf spots each year from a list of nominees and then invests its full political and financial muscle in the cause. In 2008, Save the Waves helped fight a foreign company called Grupo Caribeño that submitted plans for a 398-slip marina that would cover five hectares of sea on Costa Rica's Caribbean coast. The marina would boost the local economy with more than two hundred jobs, according to the company, although there would be fewer after the two-year construction period was finished. Salsa Brava, a heavy reef barrel wave, was located in Puerto Viejo, less than a mile south of the proposed marina site. The marina would block any swell from the north and northeast directions, destroying Salsa Brava, as well as a beginner wave nearby. Developers didn't address the potential negative environmental and economic impact on the town, which subsists on surf tourism, and the $40 million project was suspended indefinitely.

"In that case, the wave would have been destroyed," said Carlos Manuel Rodriguez. "I'm not sure that was really the case with Pavones."

In 2009, at the International Surfing Association World Surfing Games held in Jaco, Bystrom presented his case about the endangered status of Pavones. The director of the Costa Rica Surf Federation named Pavones the country's official nominee for the World Surfing Reserves Program; Save the Waves accepted Pavones as a candidate. While Pavones did not become the focus case that year, the partnership led to additional media opportunities. Bystrom's "Save Pavones" campaign was mentioned in a *Surfer* magazine article, and an awareness advertisement was published in a catalog for Patagonia, a popular clothing company founded by surfer and climber Yvon Chouinard. As "Save Pavones" started going viral, surfers worldwide became angered that Costa Rica was not doing enough to protect Pavones. They took to Internet message boards where they criticized the country; in extreme cases, they even advocated a boycott of Costa Rica.

"I think the involvement of the international surfing community was critical to the campaign," Bystrom said. "That started from the grassroots level in Pavones with surf contests and getting local surfers on board, and then it kind of snowballed from there. We showed the international surf community that the government of Costa Rica is not protecting the environment but it is promoting that it is protecting the environment. It was an extra level on top of the legal and local levels that had been work-ing but not enough obviously. All of this pressure was being put on the country and essentially whistle-blowers saying, 'Hey, you're not practicing what you are preaching.' All of that helped tremendously."

While Carlos Manuel Rodriguez acknowledges that adding surfing to the opposition's argument was effective, he downplayed its overall significance.

"Surfing is very important, but I never saw them as well-organized to be a formal force of opposition," Rodriguez said. "This company, Granjas Atuneras, went through the rounds. They went through round one and round two with some minor, although increasing, opposition, but it was not the opposition that shut down the project. If the project went a third and fourth round, then I think the opposition would grow from environment groups, civil people, surfers, those kinds of people, and create something very strong, something very similar to what the mining company at Las Crucitas faced. But the reality is the opposition wasn't the deciding factor; money was the deciding factor."

Eduardo Velarde wasn't pleased that the domestic media onslaught had turned into international surf campaign. He found it unsavory to add an argument that was completely unrelated to the original ones set forth by Pretoma and Sagot when the project was introduced in 2004. While he felt that many of the opposition's complaints were not scientifically viable, the surfing argument was morally offensive to him. He felt the surfing crowd was simply piling it on, presenting nothing more than a last-ditch, opportunistic attempt at sabotaging a project that had just been reapproved by the government.

"I could have stayed in Pavones and made T-shirts and did all that stuff, but I didn't have the time," Velarde said. "I make money by working, not by accepting money from others and making up causes. My son said he likes to surf and that he'd go down there to help us, but I told him it's too dangerous and the reputation for violence in that area is too great."

Despite even the most outrageous imaginations out there, Velarde was sure there was nothing about his tuna farm that could affect a wave. Still, the damage had been done in the court of public opinion. The surf community's fervor led to the project being tarnished in international publications. Then, although SETENA had announced that the project could continue in 2009, Velarde received a call from Manuel de Iglesia, whose patience had run out. In a matter of fact tone, he told Velarde that he was no longer investing in the tuna farm project. As Velarde retells it,

> He was pissed long before the surf stuff. He asked me "Why do I have to go court? We haven't even started the business yet and I'm already in the Supreme Court?" He spent $250,000 to get the best people in the country to do the environmental study and the social study and pay me for two years, and I wasn't cheap. I felt bad for the guy that I was asking him to go to court and talk in front of judges. When we won in court, he was confident things would improve, but no investor likes a scandal even though it was all baloney. He saw all these things being written and published and said it wasn't worth it anymore. They are saying we're killing turtles, whales, sharks, and now surfers are saying we are ruining a wave. He knew it was all bullshit, but he already makes millions of dollars fishing tuna and said he didn't need this. Sometimes you have to cut your losses. All of a sudden the money was gone.

Velarde was devastated. Here he was in 2010, six years into this project, with all the permits for the world's first yellowfin tuna farm in hand, but no investor. SETENA granted him a year's extension to find another one.

"The economy was not doing well, and nobody would touch this project in Costa Rica with everything that had gone on. But I kept trying to find an investor, convinced I would find one, but I never did."

In early November of 2011, a Pavones resident sat in Álvaro Sagot's unassuming office in Palmares. As the resident conversed with him about possibly filing a lawsuit regarding a cell phone tower erected illegally near her property, Sagot's fax machine lit up and papers exited the spool. Sagot excused himself to check the contents of the fax. He scanned the first page and began to smile. It had been more than three years since his court date, and now the faxed document was stating that the court was requiring SETENA to produce not only the current study with special attention to the direction of the currents but also the interview notes from SETENA's visit to the Pavones area. If SETENA didn't produce these items by the end of the month for a project to which it had granted environmental viability permit, SETENA's leaders would face fines and jail time for unlawfully disregarding court orders.

Within a week of that fax, on November 9, 2011, SETENA officially announced it was canceling Granjas Atuneras's permit to construct a yellowfin tuna farm at the mouth of the Golfo Dulce and was no longer considering the project. After seven years, Pavones won, but it remained unclear what would happen to Dan Fowlie—and the town—in the future.

15   End of the Road

I alone cannot change the world, but I can cast a stone across the waters to create many ripples.
—Mother Teresa

On a stretch of ash-colored sand, beyond the tin roof of the fish house, lay a collection of fiberglass *pangas* (small boats) their bows perched on logs. Standing on the concrete platform, William Mata wore an unwrinkled red-collared shirt and sandals. Once he finished explaining the story of Pavones and Granjas Atuneras, he described how local fishermen banned commercial shrimp boats in the Golfo Dulce. According to him, big hearts and big minds, if rooted appropriately, tend to get things done in Costa Rica as much as big words and big education. He reiterated that nature doesn't respond to fancy degrees; it responds well to those who treat it well. William isn't like fishermen elsewhere in the world. He isn't equipped with stories of how many fish there once was. He's the first generation of fishermen in Pavones, and his approach is different from those used by fishermen who live in other places where there are long histories.

With the tuna farms less of a pressing concern, his next priority was getting rid of shrimp boats. William didn't have hard data to support his view, but he was convinced that he was spending more time on the water and that there were noticeably fewer shrimp than before the commercial shrimp boats arrived. Since commercial boats employ destructive fishing methods that result in considerable amounts of bycatch, their pursuit of shrimp was harming not only shrimp but other species that William and his buddies fish for. He was afraid if the trawlers continued to impact his marine occupation, he would need to find another one. And job prospects aren't great for middle-aged men with third-grade educations. Not wanting to jeopardize his future, he felt it was time to mount an organized effort.

While he helped to establish the Bahía Pavones Fishermen Association, William also encouraged the region's other fishermen to establish their own official associations. This effort allowed them to form an umbrella association that influenced rules and policies in the region. In 2009, six fishing associations representing Golfo Dulce communities created a Marine Area for Responsible Fishing, a zone that stretches from Punta Banco across the mouth of the Golfo Dulce and extends just north of Cabo Matapalo. The area prohibits shrimp trawling, and the only fishing gear allowed inside the gulf is hard lines, rods and reels, and traps.

William believed he had circumnavigated a corrupt system by establishing a marine-protected area that shrimp trawlers, under the direction of INCOPESCA, were compelled to honor. Within weeks, shrimp boats disappeared from the horizon. After the shrimp boats disappeared, William encouraged other associations not to catch shrimp until they were confident the population had rebounded. In time, the fishermen saw an increase in shrimp numbers. William's smile widened again when he told me how monumental a victory it was for a contingent of small, relatively weak, ill-equipped anglers. He admitted the confidence grew from the success the town experienced battling the government over the tuna farms.

"It was a very big accomplishment for us and we were very proud, but we need the area to be larger," said William. "We could make more money if we fished more, but then we might not have that many fish in the future for everyone, so what would be the point? We want to conserve what we have. We don't want people fishing here without the same ethic."

Randall Arauz, founder of Pretoma, said the expulsion of the shrimp trawlers from the Golfo Dulce didn't exactly unfold as William described. According to Arauz, wealthy sport fishermen in the region wanted to prohibit shrimp trawlers and had paid $1 million for the trawlers to disappear. Two months before the responsible fishing area was created, two prominent sport fishermen visited Arauz and suggested they work together on eliminating shrimp trawlers. He estimated it would take about $5 million to oust the shrimpers. He also suggested that an international campaign be started to conduct scientific studies and ensure that the marine-protected area would be created in such a way as to fit everyone's needs. Two months later, the responsible fishing area was created, although the sport fishermen had opted not to partner with Pretoma and instead decided to spend $1 million paying off the commercial shrimp fishermen, with a little leftover for the region's fishing associations.

"My problem with the fishing area in the Golfo Dulce is that it's not based on any science," Arauz said.

Getting rid of the shrimp trawlers happened because of a push from the sport-fishing industry, not William and his fishing buddies. The sport fishermen gave seventeen thousand dollars to each of the fifty-seven licenses operating down there. One guy had five licenses and got eighty thousand dollars, but none of his boats work and are just sitting there docked in Golfito. So they created this area by putting the money in the right corrupt officer's pockets. William doesn't realize they were paid off. The fishermen were promised eighty dollars a month for their associations and, in Pavones, a freezer if they stopped using gill nets. But that never happened, and they still use gill nets because there is no enforcement. It was all done the wrong way and without any science. I told William that if things are going to be done that way, with money and no science, then there is no room for Pretoma to work down there. If you work with the local fishermen and give them money to get things done, then your relationship is trashed because then they will always want money to get things done when science is what should determine what gets done. It's the same old story down there: the only way things get done in the Golfo Dulce is money. I don't do things that way, so I pulled out of there.

After more than a decade of protecting sea turtles at Punta Banco, Pretoma stopped funding the turtle nesting site in 2012. Before that, Pretoma had paid one resident to collect eggs and educate the community about the importance of protecting sea turtles; after Pretoma stopped funding the site, one well-informed resident said the group's former employee then became the area's most prolific poacher. When Eduardo Velarde learned that Pretoma stopped trying to protect sea turtles at Punta Banco, where the opposition had based its initial attempts to stop the tuna farm project in court, he shook his head in disgust.

"If turtles were that important, why did they leave them for the poachers? Yet my project was going to kill turtles. What a pity."

As much as William tried to expand its current boundaries, the marine-protected area he helped create didn't extend beyond Punta Banco where Eduardo proposed a site for his tuna farm. While there are five types of marine-protected areas in Costa Rica, the one selected by William—and approved by INCOPESCA—was a responsible fishing area, which still allows aquaculture. Thus, not only could aquaculture projects like tuna farms be allowed inside the Golfo Dulce, but nothing prohibits a tuna farm from being established outside the Golfo Dulce. William suggested an enlarged boundary to INCOPESCA, but his requests were ignored. Perhaps INCOPESCA had allowed the particular type of marine-protected area merely to appease William and other noncommercial fishermen. With shrimp yields dropping anyway, perhaps prohibiting trawlers within that zone was just a token gesture.

At the time of this writing, there is no aquaculture project in the Golfo Dulce, but that doesn't mean there won't be. Led by Peter Aspinall, the community is trying to reclassify William's responsible fishing area to allow sport fishing and traditional fishing but not aquaculture projects or commercial fishing. The area would also be extended beyond the mouth of the gulf, thus ensuring that a tuna farm could not be established there, though it could elsewhere in the country. But since mañana is the busiest day in Costa Rica, the reclassification has yet to be achieved, and as of early 2015, the area remains susceptible to future aquaculture projects. In the meantime, while Peter continues to welcome guests to his Tiskita Lodge, a jungle property that is considered one of country's gems, yellowfin tuna is worse off globally than when Velarde introduced the project in 2004.

In 2011, the International Union for the Conservation of Nature (IUCN) stated that five of the eight existing species of tuna, including yellowfin, are threatened or near threatened. When Velarde's project was first proposed, yellowfin didn't have that status, but with the highly coveted bluefin tuna becoming nearly extinct, the pursuit of other types of tuna has increased. Half of the non-bluefin commercial tuna stocks are now considered overfished and destined to meet the fate of the bluefin unless there are major changes in fishing practices, according to the International Seafood Sustainability Foundation. Velarde's investor, Manuel de Iglesia, and his company, Suevia, are still supplying Costa Rica's largest tuna cannery, Sardimar, with thousands of tons of tuna each year, but with the tuna clippers catching smaller tuna and spending more time at sea, all indicators point to a threatened yellowfin tuna population. Indeed, according to Velarde, de Iglesia said that he intended to continue fishing until there was nothing left to fish.

"They acted like this little town defeated this big company," Velarde said. "The town may have won, but let's look at who really lost. Commercial fishermen aren't going to stop catching tuna. This whole time we could have been investing in research to produce tuna from an egg, but they wanted their Tarzan jungle to stay pure. So, okay, Pavones stopped a tuna farm, but the species is still being depleted and we're no closer to reproducing tuna from an egg. So what did they really do to protect sea turtles and tuna? Nothing."

At the Achotines Lab in Panama, scientists have been studying the rearing of larval and early juvenile yellowfin tuna since 1996. The lab was the world's first to reproduce a live tuna from an egg. However, the lab's focus is on the behavioral aspects of the tuna at the early stages, not the reproduction of tuna to replace wild stocks. One of the complications of breeding tuna in captivity is diet. Tuna aren't used to eating dry food, which would be necessary for their survival in the early stages while in captivity. More challenging, however, is that young tuna are voracious eaters. When surrounded by other tuna, they cannibalize each other to sate their enormous appetites, thereby sabotaging efforts to reproduce tuna. Regardless, because the Achotines Lab works with yellowfin tuna eggs, Velarde pegged the lab as the perfect place to invest his company's research and development budget.

"Millions of dollars are invested in this lab but not to reproduce," Velarde said.

> This was the lab we wanted to work with because, right now, this lab is funded by people with fishing interests, not aquaculture interests. The people who fund the lab want to know about the fish for fishing purposes. They want to know what the fish eat, shit, and dream so they can be better fishermen. The lab has eggs and they are producing the eggs. They could do it in large quantity, but their purpose isn't for that. Our tuna farm project was going to invest so they could start doing it in large quantities for aquaculture purposes so I could help save the species.

When Arauz heard Velarde's claim that he was going to work with the lab in Panama to reproduce eggs in captivity for large-scale commercial aquaculture, he said: "We will have that discussion when the technology is there. When he proposed the project, and even right now, it's not." Aquaculture companies, though, are investing in breeding tuna from an egg.

Spain-based Ricardo Fuentes and Sons, which nearly partnered with Manuel de Iglesia to establish a yellowfin tuna farm in Panama before de Iglesia hired Velarde in Costa Rica, has been investing in the reproduction of bluefin tuna in captivity. In 2009, oceanographers hired by the company obtained 150 million bluefin eggs, three million of which the company attempted to hatch. But one biologist familiar with the project told *Time* magazine that "maybe 50 will survive to the weight of one gram, or about 50 days old. We're still a long way off." While his conclusion was identical to that of the lead scientist at Achotines, a Panamanian company named Global Royal Fish announced in 2010 that it had been able to feed a dry diet to juvenile yellowfin tuna that had been spawned from eggs in captivity. It was a breakthrough moment, with the next step being transferring the juvenile tuna into cages at sea to continue feeding them. The race continues, but it's unclear who will cross the finish line first: the person who perfects the technology to breed tuna in captivity from egg to adult or the fisherman who catches the last tuna in the ocean and eliminates the species.

Velarde continues to work on his snapper farm along Costa Rica's central coast. He and his son successfully rear snapper in captivity from eggs to commercially viable adults. His business operates a few miles out in the open water, near national parks and residential areas. He lives in a comfortable place in the upscale suburb of Escazú between San José and the Pacific coast, still determined to follow his childhood hero, Jacques Cousteau.

"This project is environmentally challenging because Quepos [a town near the popular Manuel Antonio National Park along the central Pacific coast] is a highly commercialized area with people living there, but I didn't hear a peep from the NGOs or Pretoma on this project. Funny."

Knowing there is a global hunt for yellowfin tuna to provide sashimi and sushi for consumers, I felt guilty for not feeling guilty about catching a yellowfin tuna one morning when out fishing with William Mata. We were within eyesight of Velarde's now defunct tuna farm project, and a solitary tree hovered over the misting, wild coastline. The water was calm; swells arrived, but nothing our fifteen-foot *panga* couldn't handle. Two fishing poles were jammed into what looked like drink holders on either side of the fiberglass boat. About two hours into a trip meant primarily to spot turtles at sea (of which we saw one), both poles snapped simultaneously. William's eyes, dark like coffee beans, widened as he barked for me to grab one of the poles. It took more than a minute to reel in my catch. Before I could see my hooked tuna spinning below the boat, William reeled his in, yanked it on board, and gently dislodged the hook from its mouth. His tender touch was a sign of appreciation and respect for the fish. As my tuna rose to the surface, it glowed white in the blue ocean chop and continued to fight. It was a strong sucker, and bigger than any fish I'd ever caught, which isn't saying much. As it twisted and curled, flashing above the surface, William yanked it into the boat. Again, he delicately dislodged the hook and tossed both dying tuna into an ice-filled cooler.

It may seem rather hypocritical to object to fattening juvenile tuna on a tuna farm and harvesting them before they have a chance to reproduce, and then to reel in two juveniles. Mine was a strong little guy, perhaps fifteen pounds and eighteen inches long, or about the size that Velarde would cage and fatten, but this tuna and William Mata's were pole caught, which is one of the least environmentally harmful fishing methods there is. I felt no remorse as the tuna flapped inside the cooler and gasped for their last breaths. He would sell these fish and they would feed his family. And when he offered one of the fish to me back at the fish house, free of charge, I felt grateful that he would sacrifice a meal for his family so I could enjoy my catch. In the boat, he had noticed my appreciation of the muscular fish. I inspected both for several minutes as their bodies were covered in melting ice pellets and blood. I told William they were beautiful, even in death, and he agreed. It's impossible for those who fish from helicopters and satellites and drag hundred-yard-long nets to have the same appreciation. For these people, fishing is a business, and tuna are a link in the chain. There is no reason for them to think otherwise. At the end of that chain, do people know about the various fishing methods and the differences between them? Do those who eat tuna even care how the fish was caught or where it was caught? For them, does the end justify the means? When I bit into the tuna that night at my hostel in Pavones, so fleshy and tasty, I suspected most people know when the fish on their plate tastes great, and that's about it. But for every action there is a reaction.

Pavones is a surf town at the end of the road, and tuna is just one resource. As the global population increases, however, we're all becoming neighbors. The way people live in the United States affects people in Pavones. It may not have always been that way, but it is now. Ignoring that reality doesn't change it; ignorance is no longer a credible defense for irresponsible action. The hunt for global resources, whether tuna or coffee, is as interconnected as a wave. A wave that starts at the tip of Chile and travels thousands of miles, from cold waters into tropical waters, passing through the gills of sharks and whales and tuna and over a cobblestone point break and crashing into Pavones—this process brings smiles and income to people. Nature has provided for humans to take and enjoy, but we've now exhausted its capability by taking more than it can give.

"Sustainable" is a term that floats around environmental circles, but it has been repeated so often that its meaning has become diminished to the point where some think it means nothing. Yvon Chounaird, founder of the Patagonia clothing company, said in the surf and climbing documentary *180 Degrees South* that "it's a bogus term, it doesn't mean anything." But according to a 1987 article published by the United Nations entitled "Our Common Future," it does: "Sustainable development is development that meets the needs of the present without compromising the ability of future generations to meet their own needs."

If Pavones had been wrong about Velarde's tuna farm, the fish would still swim, the wave would still break, and the town would still survive off surfing. That it's a surf town at the end of the road in Costa Rica means little when we all live in the same neighborhood. If Granjas Atuneras was wrong about its farm's potential impact on water quality, the effect on sea turtles and existing fish species, the fish *might* still swim, the turtles *might* still nest there, and the town's surf-reliant economy *might* continue supporting a few thousand denizens at the end of the road in Costa Rica. But if the town was wrong about the farm's potential impact and those complaints ultimately resulted in the project not being completed, things would go on as they always have: the fish will still swim, the sea turtles will still nest, and the town's surf-reliant economy will continue supporting its citizens. One possibility deals with chance, the other with certainty, and gambling with science and people's livelihoods isn't the best recipe in environmental battles. Ticos and gringos, fishermen and businessmen, everyone banded together and fought for a common cause, which means a lot to a town whose reputation has been stained by violence and infighting. Even if Pavones was scientifically wrong about a tuna farm's potential impact, as the former environmental minister who surfs Pavones believes it was, any town should rebel against perceived government corruption and company lies. Autonomy and empowerment, to me, are righteous in a shrinking and interconnected world. A town that's been exploited since its inception finally had a voice in shaping its future.

Since the tuna farm battle ended, Pavones was recognized by the Municipality of Golfito as an organized town that has a vote in municipality matters. It's still a jungle town connected to the outside world by a muddy road, and the tallest things around are the trees, but now it has a local business association hoping to attract a pharmacy and a medical clinic. There is a plan to build a high school to reduce the dropout rate; there is even a police presence and a governing town council with Gerardo Mendoza, the son of one of Dan Fowlie's closest allies, elected as its president. Pavones may have been saved from the tuna farms, but the man who helped save the town is waiting for the gavel to be dropped on his own life.

Back in Cabo San Lucas, a seventy-nine-year-old Dan Fowlie sat on a chair on the concrete patio of his crumbling brick casita. He spent most of the morning watching old video footage of his reign in Pavones. The brick casita was his caretaker's unit back when the money flowed like the Ganges River after a monsoon, but now it's pretty much all he has left. One of his ex-wives lives nearby in his former home, the result of divorce proceedings; Al Nelson's abode is just beyond a ridge in the desert. The view through a corridor of overgrown baby palms leads to the sapphire blue of the Pacific. In clear sight, gray whales dance along the horizon. Dan knocked back beers and stared at the cactus-studded landscape, his mind fixated on a jungle town at the end of the road in Costa Rica. He may have helped save Pavones from the tuna farms, but as the sun sets on his life, that's not enough. He remains in dogged pursuit of his land in Pavones because, well, it's all he has left.

His family is fractured. His son Gus, who served a lesser sentence for his role in the family drug ring, is married, lives Southern California, and has estranged himself from his father and his brother; Dan's other son, Dan Junior, clings to the hope that his father can reclaim his land as it seems Dan Junior can't provide for himself; Dan's daughter died in a vehicle accident; and Dan isn't close with any of his ex-wives. The self-proclaimed King of Pavones is determined to recapture the past, which I suppose is common for most men when life's curtain is almost pulled shut.

Earlier that day, Dan cited extended family members who lived past 110 years of age, and he sees no reason in his mind why he won't live just as long. He discussed the securing of a loan with a Mexican bank, which would allow him to install a water and sewer system in Pavones, as well as start construction of a resort near Pilon, north of Pavones. He has detailed renderings of the proposed resort, which he drew himself, and they include plans for an eighteen-hole golf course and living quarters for Tico employees. The resort would be built on a five-hundred-acre patch of waterfront jungle he calls "Langostino," which is one of the original properties he purchased in the 1970s. It remains the only property he's won in court since his battle to reclaim his land began. (His lawyer has submitted more than sixty cases to the court system on his behalf.) There are currently more than fifty squatters living on his Langostino property, but he can't evict them—and has no interest in doing so—until he can reenter the country. What's the point of evicting them? If he isn't present to defend the land, they'd just return, he contends. He is also convinced that when he does return to Costa Rica and evict them, the squatters will gladly allow this to happen because, as a consolation, he will offer them jobs and provide dormitory-style living.

"At this point I hope he doesn't come back because the squatters, the *precaristas*, will just shoot him," said one hotel owner who didn't want to be identified.

In November of 2013, Dan said, Costa Rica granted him permission to reenter into the country, but, he added, "It was the rainy season. Why do I want to go there when it's raining every day? I'll wait until the weather improves and then go down there." After being prohibited from entering the country for almost a decade, it seemed far-fetched that rain falling in a rain forest would cause him to delay traveling there. (If he ever makes it down there again, he will see that his beloved Esquina del Mar, one of the most unique bars in the world, was burned by arsonists in November of 2011.) By 2015, following several dry seasons, he still hadn't reclaimed his land.

Perhaps he's delaying his return because he might have to face the realization that his land is all gone. Or is it? Al Nelson, whom Dan accuses of illegally selling his land while he was in prison, contends that Dan is delusional and doesn't believe that Al owns some of the property— property that Dan had authorized Al to purchase when Dan was fighting extradition in a Mexican prison.

"I still own his land down there, it's all his, it's just in my name," Al said. "He can have it back anytime."

Not exactly. One sunny day in Baja, Dan broke his silence with Al. The two crossed paths on the beach, and Dan, according to Al, struck up a conversation with him for the first time in years. It was a breakthrough moment, and Dan offered an olive branch to his childhood buddy. Dan said he would pay Al thirty thousand dollars for each year he was in prison ($540,000 for eighteen years) to compensate him for his efforts to keep most of his land away from squatters and others. Humoring him, Al said, "Let's make it an even five hundred thousand dollars."

"The only problem is he is broke and doesn't have any money," Al said.

He hangs out in that dirty garage and draws all these renderings of a resort and calls banks and tells me how this loan or that loan is coming through, but it never happens. Meanwhile, I'm going to have control of several million dollars' worth of his property all because he couldn't hold up his end of the agreement, and I'm just going to end up giving it away. We're both going to die soon and this land he's wanted back forever, he could've had it the entire time. I don't want it.

When I asked Dan about this so-called arrangement, he said, "Al acquired that property illegally. He is in there to jimmy up and make it hard for me to get it back. He told me, 'I know I don't have this property, just give me five hundred thousand dollars.' It's an extortion thing. He is trying to con me out of five hundred thousand dollars. He's already sold pieces of my land down there worth hundreds of thousands of dollars, and he still wants more. I want to build a jail down there. And when he gets down there, he will be in there."

One morning in Cabo, Al and I met for breakfast. He brought with him a folder that contained information about various properties in Pavones and their current ownership structure. According to the documents, about one thousand acres are owned by four corporations; each has a name and a list of board members. The board members transferred the land into Al's name shortly after Dan's release from prison. Following up on Al's story, I verified that the properties are registered in the National Registry of Costa Rica. As screwy as Costa Rica can be, the fact is that the national registry doesn't allow more than one owner of an individual parcel. Whatever Dan thinks happened to those thousand acres while he was in prison, they are now owned by a group of Al Nelson–controlled corporations. Dan could reclaim ownership of land that is worth several million dollars tomorrow if he paid Al the five hundred thousand dollars.

Yet, time passes on. Al is in his mid-seventies, sipping a variety of alcoholic beverages from his abode overlooking the Pacific. He remains friendly with Dan, and the two are on speaking terms. Surf writer Allan Weisbecker, who wrote about Pavones and Dan in one of his books, was shocked to hear about a rekindling of Dan and Al's friendship:

"You coulda knocked me over with a feather hearing that Dan and Al are getting along well. Are you sure?"

If Al knows that Dan is broke and doesn't have the credit history to secure a loan for five hundred thousand dollars, why doesn't he sell some of the land so Dan can acquire the funds necessary to pay him off? Upon investigating the titles in the national registry, I discovered that the land has numerous liens and complaints, which were levied by Dan and his lawyer. Without a clear title, Al can't ever sell the land—at least not without some additional legal maneuvering. And if Al can never sell the land, Dan can never have any money, let alone ever see the rest of his land again. Dan, who is reluctant to accept Al's story because it contradicts his own, won't even entertain the idea of removing the complaints because then "if he is telling the truth, he'd sell that land and I'd never see a penny."

Dan was slightly annoyed when he learned that I was documenting Al's side of the story, but he understood why I would publish it and never discussed it further. Meanwhile, Al told me never to contact him again once he learned I was printing Dan's side of the story (we haven't corresponded since). After several unsuccessful attempts to connect with Dan prior to the completion of this manuscript in order to get an update on the status of his land dispute and reentry into Costa Rica, I assume there has been no change and he still resides in his crumbling brick casita outside Cabo San Lucas, Mexico.

In an almost eulogistic tone, Al's final comments about the King of Pavones were:

"Dan's his own worst enemy. His ego and mind are what doomed him before. And now he is going to die broke and crazy and alone with his ideas, all because he can't let go of the past. Dan continues to live in his own personal universe and I don't honestly believe he will ever be able to pay me. He just turned eighty and appears to be dead broke."

BIBLIOGRAPHY

Blachman, Morris J., William M. Leogrande, and Kenneth Sharpe. *Confronting Revolution: Security through Diplomacy in Central America*. New York: Pantheon, 1986.

Bunck, Julie Marie, and Michael Ross Fowler. *Bribes, Bullets, and Intimidation: Drug Trafficking and the Law in Central America*. University Park: Pennsylvania State University Press, 2012.

Clover, Charles. *The End of the Line*. New York: New Press, 2006.

Corson, Trevor. *The Story of Sushi: An Unlikely Saga of Raw Fish and Rice*. New York: Harper Perennial, 2008.

Dedina, Serge. *Wild Sea: Eco-Wars and Surf Stories from the Coast of the Californias*. Tucson: University of Arizona Press, 2011.

Earle, Sylvia A. *The World Is Blue: How Our Fate and the Ocean's Are One*. Washington DC: National Geographic Society, 2009.

Ellis, Richard. *Tuna: A Love Story*. New York: Alfred A. Knopf, 2008.

Engel, J. Ronald, and Joan Gibb Engel, eds. *Ethics of Environment and Development: Global Challenge, International Response*. Tucson: University of Arizona Press, 1990.

Greenberg, Paul. *Four Fish: The Future of the Last Wild Food*. New York: Penguin, 2010.

Heller, Peter. *Kook: What Surfing Taught Me about Love, Life, and Catching the Perfect Wave*. New York: Free Press, 2010.

Hemingway, Ernest. *The Old Man and the Sea*. New York: Charles Scribner's Sons, 1952.

Issenberg, Sasha. *The Sushi Economy: Globalization and the Making of a Modern Delicacy*. New York: Gotham, 2008.

Jones, Chester Lloyd. *Costa Rica and Civilization in the Caribbean.* New York: Russell & Russell, 1935.

Langewiesche, William. *The Outlaw Sea: A World of Freedom, Chaos, and Crime.* New York: North Point Press, 2004.

Molyneaux, Paul. *Swimming in Circles: Aquaculture and the End of Wild Oceans.* New York: Thunder's Mouth Press, 2007.

Moore, Michael Scott. *Sweetness and Blood: How Surfing Spread from Hawaii and California to the Rest of the World, with Some Unexpected Results.* New York: Rodale, 2010.

Paik, Koohan, and Jerry Mander. *The SuperFerry Chronicles.* Kihei HI: Koa, 2009.

Perez-Brignoli, Hector. *A Brief History of Central America.* Translated by Ricardo B. Sawrey and Susana Stettri de Sawrey. Berkeley: University of California Press, 1989.

Schell, Gregory, Greg Weaver, and Spyder Wills. *Chasing the Lotus.* DVD. Directed by Gregory Schell. Schell Bell Productions, 2006.

Warshaw, Matt. *The Encyclopedia of Surfing.* Boston: Harcourt Press, 2003.

———. *The History of Surfing.* San Francisco: Chronicle, 2010.

Weisbecker, Allan C. *Can't You Get Along with Anyone?* Bournemouth, Dorset, UK: Humdrumming, 2006.

———. *In Search of Captain Zero: A Surfer's Road Trip beyond the End of the Road.* New York: Jeremy P. Tarcher/Putnam, 2001.

Zimmerman, Michael E., J. Baird Callicott, John Clark, Karen J. Warren, and Irene J. Klaver. *Environmental Philosophy: From Animal Rights to Radical Ecology.* Englewood Cliffs NJ: Prentice Hall, 1993.